St Antony's Series
General Editor: **Paul Betts**, Professor of Modern European History, European Studies Centre, St Antony's College, Oxford and Othon Anastasakis, Research Fellow of St Anthony's College, Oxford and Director of South East European Studies at Oxford.

Recent titles include:

Jochen Prantl (*editor*)
EFFECTIVE MULTILATERALISM
Through the Looking Glass of East Asia

James Densley
HOW GANGS WORK
An Ethnography of Youth Violence

Ilsen About, James Brown, Gayle Lonergan, Jane Caplan and Edward Higgs (*editors*)
IDENTIFICATION AND REGISTRATION PRACTICES IN TRANSNATIONAL PERSPECTIVE
People, Papers and Practices

Daniel Altschuler and Javier Corrales
THE PROMISE OF PARTICIPATION
Participatory Governance, Citizen Engagement and Democracy in Guatemala and Honduras in the 2000s

Nayef R.F. Al-Rodhan
META-GEOPOLITICS OF OUTER SPACE
An Analysis of Space Power, Security and Governance

Carla L. Thorson
POLITICS, JUDICIAL REVIEW AND THE RUSSIAN CONTITUTIONAL COURT

Daisuke Ikemoto
EUROPEAN MONETARY INTEGRATION 1970–79
British and French Experiences

Nayef R.F. Al-Rodhan
THE POLITICS OF EMERGING STRATEGIC TECHNOLOGIES
Implications for Geopolitics, Human Enhancement and Human Destiny

Dimitar Bechev
CONSTRUCTING SOUTH EAST EUROPE
The Politics of Balkan Regional Cooperation

Julie M. Newton and William J. Tompson (*editors*)
INSTITUTIONS, IDEAS AND LEADERSHIP IN RUSSIAN POLITICS

Celia Kerslake , Kerem Öktem, and Philip Robins (*editors*)
TURKEY'S ENGAGEMENT WITH MODERNITY
Conflict and Change in the Twentieth Century

Paradorn Rangsimaporn
RUSSIA AS AN ASPIRING GREAT POWER IN EAST ASIA
Perceptions and Policies from Yeltsin to Putin

Motti Golani
THE END OF THE BRITISH MANDATE FOR PALESTINE, 194
The Diary of Sir Henry Gurney

Demetra Tzanaki
WOMEN AND NATIONALISM IN THE MAKING OF MODERN GREECE
The Founding of the Kingdom to the Greco-Turkish War

Simone Bunse
SMALL STATES AND EU GOVERNANCE
Leadership through the Council Presidency

Judith Marquand
DEVELOPMENT AID IN RUSSIA
Lessons from Siberia

Li-Chen Sim
THE RISE AND FALL OF PRIVATIZATION IN THE RUSSIAN OIL INDUSTRY

Stefania Bernini
FAMILY LIFE AND INDIVIDUAL WELFARE IN POSTWAR EUROPE
Britain and Italy Compared

Tomila V. Lankina, Anneke Hudalla and Helmut Wollman
local governance in central and eastern europe
Comparing Performance in the Czech Republic, Hungary, Poland and Russia

Cathy Gormley-Heenan
political leadership and the northern ireland peace process
Role, Capacity and Effect

Lori Plotkin Boghardt
kuwait amid war, peace and revolution

Paul Chaisty
Legislative Politics and Economic Power in Russia

Valpy FitzGerald, Frances Stewart and Rajesh Venugopal (*editors*)
globalization, violent conflict and self-determination

Miwao Matsumoto
technology gatekeepers for war and peace
The British Ship Revolution and Japanese Industrialization

Håkan Thörn
Anti-Apartheid and the Emergence of a Global Civil Society

Lotte Hughes
Moving the Maasai
A Colonial Misadventure

Fiona Macaulay
Gender Politics in Brazil and Chile
The Role of Parties in National and Local Policymaking

Stephen Whitefield (*editor*)
POLITICAL CULTURE AND POST-COMMUNISM

José Esteban Castro
water, power and citizenship
Social Struggle in the Basin of Mexico

Valpy FitzGerald and Rosemary Thorp (*editors*)
economic doctrines in latin america
Origins, Embedding and Evolution

Victoria D. Alexander and Marilyn Rueschemeyer
art and the state
The Visual Arts in Comparative Perspective

Ailish Johnson
european welfare states and supranational governance of social polic

Archie Brown (*editor*)
the demise of marxism-leninism in russia

Thomas Boghardt
spies of the kaiser
German Covert Operations in Great Britain during the First World War Era

Ulf Schmidt
justice at nuremberg
Leo Alexander and the Nazi Doctors' Trial

Steve Tsang (*editor*)
PEACE AND SECURITY ACROSS THE TAIWAN STRAIT

James Milner
REFUGEES, THE STATE AND THE POLITICS OF ASYLUM IN AFRICA

Stephen Fortescue (*editor*)
RUSSIAN POLITICS FROM LENIN TO PUTIN

---

**St Antony's Series**
Series Standing Order ISBN 978–0–333–71109–5 (hardback)
978–0–333–80341–7 (paperback)
(*outside North America only*)

You can receive future titles in this series as they are published by placing a standing order. Please contact your bookseller or, in case of difficulty, write to us at the address below with your name and address, the title of the series and the ISBNs quoted above.

Customer Services Department, Macmillan Distribution Ltd, Houndmills, Basingstoke, Hampshire RG21 6XS, England

# Constitutionalism and the Politics of Accommodation in Multinational Democracies

Edited by

Jaime Lluch
*Fellow, Democracy, Citizenship, and Constitutionalism Program,*
*University of Pennsylvania, USA*
*Professor of Political Science, University of Puerto Rico, USA*

*In Association with St Antony's College, Oxford*

Editorial matter, selection and introduction © Jaime Lluch 2014
Remaining chapters © Respective authors 2014
Softcover reprint of the hardcover 1st edition 2014 978-1-137-28898-1

All rights reserved. No reproduction, copy or transmission of this publication may be made without written permission.

No portion of this publication may be reproduced, copied or transmitted save with written permission or in accordance with the provisions of the Copyright, Designs and Patents Act 1988, or under the terms of any licence permitting limited copying issued by the Copyright Licensing Agency, Saffron House, 6–10 Kirby Street, London EC1N 8TS.

Any person who does any unauthorized act in relation to this publication may be liable to criminal prosecution and civil claims for damages.

The authors have asserted their rights to be identified as the authors of this work in accordance with the Copyright, Designs and Patents Act 1988.

First published 2014 by
PALGRAVE MACMILLAN

Palgrave Macmillan in the UK is an imprint of Macmillan Publishers Limited, registered in England, company number 785998, of Houndmills, Basingstoke, Hampshire RG21 6XS.

Palgrave Macmillan in the US is a division of St Martin's Press LLC, 175 Fifth Avenue, New York, NY 10010.

Palgrave Macmillan is the global academic imprint of the above companies and has companies and representatives throughout the world.

Palgrave® and Macmillan® are registered trademarks in the United States, the United Kingdom, Europe and other countries.

ISBN 978-1-349-45003-9        ISBN 978-1-137-28899-8 (eBook)
DOI 10.1057/9781137288998

This book is printed on paper suitable for recycling and made from fully managed and sustained forest sources. Logging, pulping and manufacturing processes are expected to conform to the environmental regulations of the country of origin.

A catalogue record for this book is available from the British Library.

Library of Congress Cataloging-in-Publication Data
Constitutionalism and the politics of accommodation in multinational democracies / edited by Jaime Lluch, University of Pennsylvania, USA.
   pages cm. — (St. Anthony's series)

1.  Multinational states—Case studies.   2.  Democracy—Case studies.
3.  Federal government—Case studies.   4.  Separatist movements—
Case studies.   I.  Lluch, Jaime, author, editor of contribution.
JC311.C6448 2014
320.4′049—dc23                                                          2014022094

Typeset by MPS Limited, Chennai, India.

# Contents

| | |
|---|---|
| *List of Figure and Tables* | vii |
| *Preface* | viii |
| *Acknowledgments* | xi |
| *List of Contributors* | xii |

Introduction: The Multiple Dimensions of the Politics of Accommodation in Multinational Democracies  1
*Jaime Lluch*

### Part I  Constitutionalism and the Accommodation of National Diversity

1 Varieties of Territorial Pluralism: Prospects for the Constitutional and Political Accommodation of Puerto Rico in the USA  21
*Jaime Lluch*

2 (Mis)recognition in Catalunya and Quebec: The Politics of Judicial Containment  46
*Elisenda Casanas Adam and François Rocher*

3 The Limits of Constitutionalism: Politics, Economics, and Secessionism in Catalonia (2006–2013)  70
*Hèctor López Bofill*

### Part II  The Multiple Dimensions of the Politics of Accommodation in Multinational Polities

4 The Accommodation of Island Autonomies in Multinational States  87
*Eve Hepburn*

5 From Autonomism to Independentism: The Growth of Secessionism in Catalonia (2010–2013)  108
*Jordi Argelaguet*

6 The Multilevel Politics of Accommodation and the Non-Constitutional Moment: Lessons from Corsica  132
*André Fazi*

## Part III  Constitutionalism and the Practice of Autonomism, Federalism, and Devolution

7  Flexible Accommodation: Another Case of British Exceptionalism?  159
*Stephen Tierney*

8  Italy: Autonomism, Decentralization, Federalism, or What Else?  180
*Francesco Palermo and Alice Valdesalici*

9  Autonomous Areas as a Constitutional Feature in the People's Republic of China and Finland  200
*Markku Suksi*

*Index*  223

# List of Figure and Tables

## Figure

9.1  Various autonomy positions                                              219

## Tables

5.1  Constitutional preferences of the relationships between
     Catalonia and Spain according to Centre d'Estudis
     d'Opinió surveys (2006–2013)                                            111
5.2  Subjective national identity in Catalonia (1979–2013)                   113
5.3  Evolution of the options about Catalan independence                     120
5.4  Socio-political variables and the referendum on
     independence (1)                                                        121
5.5  Socio-political variables and the referendum on
     independence (2)                                                        123
5.6  Socio-political variables and the referendum on
     independence (3)                                                        125
6.1  Nationalist parties and elections in Corsica (1982–2012)                141
6.2  Political equilibrium in Corsica: regional elections
     (1982–2010)                                                             142
6.3  Principal state policy periods and the politics of
     accommodation in Corsica                                                145

# Preface

This volume had its genesis in a two-day conference I organized on 16–17 June 2011 at the European Studies Centre, St Antony's College, University of Oxford, while I was the Santander Fellow in Iberian and European Studies. The conference was co-sponsored by the Centre for International Studies of the Department of Politics and International Relations at Oxford, thanks to the support of Professor Kalypso Nicolaïdis.

The conference was on the "Politics of Accommodation in Multinational Democracies." We had the good fortune of having Brendan O'Leary of the University of Pennsylvania as keynote speaker, speaking on power-sharing systems. The participants in the conference included Francesco Palermo, Stephen Tierney, François Rocher, Elisenda Casanas Adam, André Fazi, Montserrat Guibernau, Xavier Arbós, José María Sauca, Enric Martínez, Héctor Luis Acevedo, and Gwendolyn Sasse.

The conference aimed to be interdisciplinary, bringing together comparative politics and comparative constitutional law. The following were the core questions that guided all the participants at the St Antony's College 2011 conference, and the chapters in this volume echo these themes as well:

1. How can we build a fruitful and genuine interdisciplinary dialogue between comparative politics and comparative constitutional law to address the politics of accommodation?
2. How can we unpack the notion of "accommodation?" What are its component parts? Can we measure it, or develop clear criteria for assessing when "accommodation" has been successful?
3. What is the role of constitutionalism in facilitating "accommodation?"
4. If constitutions can constitute the very demos by projecting a vision of the nature of the political community that governs itself under the constitutional regime, how can we devise a constitutional regime that is plural, tolerant, and inclusive?
5. What is the role of political culture in facilitating "accommodation?" Can the traditions and ideologies that have influenced a country's political culture – with respect to the tolerance for cultural, ethnic, racial, national, and cultural diversity – influence the

degree to which it may be able to accommodate substate national societies?
6. Related to the issue of political culture, how can we "federalize society?" How can we make citizens, political parties, civic associations, and political institutions in a plurinational state more open to the values of a plural, inclusive, and open federalism?
7. In the case of formerly unitary states that are in a process of federalizing their model of state (e.g., Spain or Italy), how can their societies be correspondingly "federalized?"
8. Does our common understanding regarding the unitary and unidimensional nature of citizenship, which has been uniform in state-building processes, represent a form of constitutional self-understanding that needs to be reformulated, in order to devise novel institutional forms of accommodation?
9. How does accommodation as a constitutional strategy vary in states that practice territorial pluralism (Canada, Spain, etc.) and states that use a hybrid strategy of liberal integrationism and multicultural accommodation (the USA), and those states that practice republican integrationism (France, Turkey, etc.)?
10. How can a culture of dialogue and mutual accommodation be constructed between state (majority nation) nationalism and substate (minority nation) nationalism?
11. Can the central state accommodate new proposals for more autonomism, or greater self-government as a constituent unit of a federation?
12. How can we encourage forms of substate nationalism that are open to working with the central state and finding formulas for accommodation?
13. What are the varieties of independentist parties in substate national movements and what do they really seek? Similarly, what are the varieties of autonomist and federalist parties?
14. Do substate national movements respond in a mechanistic and deterministic way to economic and material conditions, or do they also follow a "political logic" that does not always exhibit instrumental rationality?

. Whether or not they originated as contributions made at the conference, all the chapters are new and written specifically for this book. Given that the 2011 conference was organized while I was the Santander Fellow at St Antony's, it had a strong emphasis on the conundrums facing contemporary Spain as it tries to accommodate its internal national diversity. In this volume, however, while a number of chapters do address the current dilemmas facing Spain, and especially Catalonia in its relation with the central state, the rest of the chapters address the dynamics of the constitutional and political accommodation of national pluralism in Canada, the United Kingdom, France, and the USA, and include analyses of China (Hong Kong and Macau), Finland (Åland Islands), Puerto Rico, Valle d'Aosta, South Tyrol, and Corsica.

*Jaime Lluch*

# Acknowledgments

I would like to thank Brendan O'Leary and Rogers M. Smith for all their unswerving support in the last few years. Since 2012, the intellectual environment at the Program on Democracy, Citizenship, and Constitutionalism at the University of Pennsylvania has stimulated my interdisciplinary research agenda.

I was the Santander Fellow in Iberian and European Studies at St Antony's College (University of Oxford) during 2010–2011, and I would like to thank Kalypso Nicolaïdis and Jane Caplan for their support and encouragement during that period. I would also like to thank Othon Anastasakis. I was able to organize a major conference at St Antony's College during 16–17 June 2011 on "The Politics of Accommodation in Multinational Democracies." The idea for this book, and many of the chapters herein, originated in that conference.

I would also like to thank the Collegio Carlo Alberto in Turin, Italy, where I was a postdoctoral scholar at URGE (2009–2010), and also a Visiting Fellow in Italian Studies, during 2011–2012. Also, thanks to the staff of the *Centro Studi sul Federalismo* at Collegio Carlo Alberto.

If, in spite of all this generous help I received, this work still contains deficiencies, these are due to my own errors and omissions.

*Jaime Lluch*

# List of Contributors

**Elisenda Casanas Adam** is Lecturer in Public Law and Human Rights, School of Law, University of Edinburgh, UK.

**Jordi Argelaguet** is Professor of Politics, Universitat Autònoma de Barcelona, Spain, and Director of the Centre d'Estudis d'Opinió, Generalitat de Catalunya, Spain.

**Hèctor López Bofill** is Professor of Constitutional Law at Universitat Pompeu Fabra, Barcelona, Spain.

**André Fazi** is Professor of Politics, Université de Corte, Corsica, France.

**Eve Hepburn** is Senior Lecturer in the Department of Politics, University of Edinburgh, UK.

**Jaime Lluch** is Fellow of the Penn Program on Democracy, Citizenship, and Constitutionalism at the University of Pennsylvania, and Professor of Political Science at the University of Puerto Rico.

**Francesco Palermo** is Director, Institute for Studies on Federalism and Regionalism, EURAC, Bolzano/Bozen, Italy, and Professor of Law, University of Verona, Italy.

**François Rocher** is Professor of Politics at the University of Ottawa.

**Markku Suksi** is Professor of Law, Department of Law, Åbo Akademi University, Finland.

**Stephen Tierney** is Professor of Constitutional Theory, School of Law, University of Edinburgh, UK.

**Alice Valdesalici** is Researcher at the Institute for Studies on Federalism and Regionalism, EURAC, Bolzano/Bozen, Italy.

# Introduction: The Multiple Dimensions of the Politics of Accommodation in Multinational Democracies

*Jaime Lluch*

## What is accommodation? Constitutional strategies of accommodation in multinational democracies

The chapters in this volume are motivated by the observation that the "nation-state" is often a misnomer, given that "stateless nations are the overwhelming majority of nations and only a small number of states represented in the UN are technically nation-states" (Linz et al., 2011; Nimni, 2011: 55). One estimate is that "fewer than twenty UN member states are ethnically homogeneous in the sense that cultural minorities account for less than 5 percent of the population" (Nimni, 2011: 55). At present, new possibilities may be opening up for institutional accommodation given that in contemporary plurinational democracies a transformation may be taking place in the relation between territorial spaces, national identities, and political institutions (Keating, 2001: 2; Nimni, 2011: 56).

While independence-seeking nationalism remains a vital force in societies such as Quebec, the Basque Country, Scotland, Northern Ireland, and more recently in Catalonia, substate autonomists and federalists play a prominent role as well, and they seek an autonomous special status, or greater power as a constituent unit of a fully formed federation. In plurinational democracies, the challenge posed by substate national societies to the central state has been often formulated in three varieties of substate nationalism: independentist, autonomist, and pro-federation nationalisms (Lluch, 2010, 2012a, 2012b, 2014). This book shows how the implementation of constitutional strategies of accommodation has led to the rethinking and reformulation of creative models of accommodation within existing states, although with varying degrees of success.

Most of the cases covered by the contributors in this volume are less deeply divided cases of national diversity, located in multinational polities. While ethnic conflict doubtlessly remains an important source of violence in the 21st century, not every conflict has regional or global repercussions, "nor are there, in fact, that many ethnic conflicts" (Cordell and Wolff, 2011: 3).[1] Furthermore, while cases such as Kashmir, Sri Lanka, Northern Ireland, Kosovo, and Cyprus involve ethnic conflict, other cases such as Canada, Estonia, Belgium, and France are about identities and conflicting interest structures, "yet their manifestations are less violent and are better described in terms of tensions than conflict" (Cordell and Wolff, 2011: 3). Thus, in less deeply divided states with national and ethnic diversity such as Canada, Belgium, Italy, and the UK, ethnonational violence is less endemic, and these are states where one can more easily deploy constitutional and political strategies for the accommodation of national diversity. In an increasing number of multinational democracies, substate nations are seeking to exercise self-determination "without constituting separate states, using instead mechanisms of devolution or national accommodation" (Nimni, 2011: 57). As Arend Lijphart wrote in his first major book, entitled *The Politics of Accommodation*, the politics of accommodation in states with significant diversity involves the "settlement of divisive issues and conflicts" where there is often minimal consensus, but where there is a "widely shared attitude that the existing system ought to be maintained and not be allowed to disintegrate" (Lijphart, 1968: 103).

In this book, we address some of the varieties of territorial pluralism used by multinational states to accommodate national diversity. Two fundamental families of constitutional strategies are available to democratic states in managing national and ethnic diversity. One alternative is integration: "Integrationists primarily seek the equality of individual citizens before the law and within public institutions. With the sole exception of the state's citizenship they are against the public institutional recognition of group identities, but they accept collective diversity in private realms" (McGarry et al., 2008: 41). The other constitutional strategy is accommodation, which "promotes dual or multiple identities, and its proponents advocate equality with institutional respect for differences" (McGarry et al., 2008: 41). The most important difference with "integrationists, which unites all accommodationists, is the public and private recognition of substate ethnic, linguistic, religious, or national group categories. Accommodationists stress the need to address the needs and aspirations of such communities rather than primarily the needs and aspirations of the nation ... coterminous with the state" (McGarry et al., 2008: 69). The institutional repertoire of accommodationists includes the recognition of several peoples or nationalities in a plurinational state, more than one official (public) language, state and regional bills of rights with an emphasis on both individual and group rights, a decentralized territorial division of powers, and power-sharing arrangements (McGarry et al., 2008: 71).

The accommodationist family of state approaches to diversity has four varieties: centripetalism, multiculturalism, consociationalism, and territorial pluralism (McGarry et al., 2008). Both centripetalism and consociationalism offer prescriptions that address the dilemmas of deeply divided societies, often with endemic levels of violence, but in this book our main interest will be the promises and failures of territorial pluralism as a strategy of accommodation.

The chapters in this volume present a nuanced analysis of a wide variety of cases that cover the spectrum of constitutional strategies of accommodation used by states such as Canada, Spain, the United Kingdom, France, and the USA, ranging from republican or liberal integrationism and multiculturalism, to territorial pluralism. Moreover, in addition to the well-known cases of Canada-Quebec, Spain-Catalonia, UK-Scotland, this book includes analyses of China (Hong Kong and Macau), Finland (Åland Islands), Puerto Rico, Valle d'Aosta, South Tyrol, and Corsica.

## Bridging comparative constitutional law and comparative politics

Constitutionalism has traditionally been the primary mechanism for facilitating the mutual accommodation of substate and state national societies in plurinational states (Tierney, 2004: 17). However, as recently noted, in multinational democracies (which are a subset of the genus of "divided societies"), if we are to address the complexities of constitutional mutual accommodation, "*comparative constitutional law* must expand its intellectual agenda to encompass issues that have hitherto been the exclusive domain of *comparative politics* in order to be of relevance" (Choudhry, 2008: 13 emphasis added). In addressing the politics of accommodation and constitutionalism in multinational democracies, therefore, "there is a need to bridge comparative politics and comparative constitutional law through a genuinely interdisciplinary conversation" (Choudhry, 2008). Indeed, "[t]he work of constitutional law and comparative constitutional law cannot carry forward in intellectual isolation from the work of other disciplines of political science, sociology"

(Jackson and Tushnet, 2002). Studying constitutionalism and politics in such settings calls for disciplinary syncretism. Comparativists who try to bridge two disciplines are required to "speak in the 'familiar and recognizable vocabularies' of more than one disciplinary community," and this may well seem like a daunting task, but it is bound to yield substantial cumulative knowledge (Adams and Bomhoff, 2012: 13).

As Sujit Choudhry has noted, a "legal approach to the accommodation of minority nationalism has both its strengths and weaknesses" (Choudhry, 2008: 172). He further states that "we face genuine difficulty in constituting and regulating moments of constitutive constitutional politics, because at those moments, the very concept of political community those rules reflect is placed in contention by the minority nation" (Choudhry, 2008: 172). Therefore, Choudhry concludes, it is at this point that "we come up against the limitations inherent in constitutionalism itself, at least with regard to its ability to accommodate minority nationalism."

Another of these challenges is directed toward a narrow form of legal formalism that pervades much of contemporary constitutional scholarship: mainstream theorists are asked to re-imagine the very concept of the plurinational constitutional state. "In methodological terms, this challenge critiques the artificial distinction between the legal and the political: constitutional formalism, it is argued, is itself conditioned by, and dependent upon, politically-informed assumptions about reality which may themselves by false. As Resina reminds us, 'constitutionalism, no less than nationalism, is a functional myth'" (Tierney, 2007: 237). Thus, there is a need for a more historically or sociologically contextualized account of constitution-making. It follows that "if the plurinational constitution is to be legitimate in the eyes of all of the state's constituent demoi, elite state actors must be prepared to embrace the idea of the constitution as a living, reflexive instrument. This requires lawyers to broaden their methods and engage with historical and sociological arguments as useful tools in the task of constitutional interpretation" (Tierney, 2007: 237).

## Constitutionalism, comparative law, and comparative politics

This book adopts a syncretistic approach to the multiple dimensions of the politics of accommodation, which opens up new intellectual vistas, and makes us appreciate the contribution that political science perspectives can make to law, and how law and jurisprudence can enrich the study of politics.

Constitutionalism "is an ideal that may be more or less approximated by different types of constitutions and that is built on certain prescriptions and certain proscriptions" (Dorsen et al., 2010: 36; Holmes, 2012: 190). Conceptualized as a normative theory, constitutionalism has been often understood as a set of legal and political instruments limiting power (Walker, 1993: 93; Sajó, 1999: xiv). Thus, constitutionalism has been seen as a political theory that was developed as part of a liberal political philosophy, which has been mainly concerned with the norms that modern constitutions should embody, placing limits on power and specifying the procedures for wielding such power (Loughlin, 2010: 55). Yet, constitutionalism is no longer seen solely as a normative political theory that expresses its conviction about the importance of a limited, accountable state. Martin Loughlin asserts that it can also be seen "as a meta-theory which establishes the authoritative standards of legitimacy for the exercise of public power wherever it is located" (Loughlin, 2010: 61). Thus, it is possible to conceptualize it in two alternative ways: "as a repository of the notions of the common good prevalent in a certain community and as an instrument for organizing power in pursuit of that common good," which can create a "deliberative framework in which competing notions of the common good can be made compatible or arbitrated in a manner acceptable to all" (Poiares Maduro, 2005: 333).

This conceptualization of constitutionalism allows us to understand how in multilevel and multinational polities, a "distinctive discourse of constitutionalism beyond the state has emerged which argues, with varying emphases, that non-state forms of political authority should also be characterized as sites of constitutionalism" (Anderson, 2012: 360). The rise of multilevel governance, and the challenge to the more unitary conceptualization of constitutionalism within the state, has given rise to a new constitutional vocabulary in the academy, as theorists routinely use the terms "plurinational" or "postnational" constitutionalism, etc. (Walker, 2008: 521; Anderson, 2012: 360). The notion of "plurinational constitutionalism" has been characterized as part of a "conceptual leap [of] audacious proportions" in constitutional theory (Anderson, 2012: 360).

This book argues that to understand how constitutionalism is a critical dimension of the politics of accommodation in multinational polities, one must transgress disciplinary boundaries. Many legal scholars "believe that law has its own internal logic and legal scholarship has its own highly valued research activity, which usually has little to do with causal explanation ... Legal scholarship often follows the rules of persuasion and advocacy, not the rules of inference" (Meuwese and

Versteeg, 2010: 233). Yet, there are a number of reasons for broadening our disciplinary horizons. First, the work of many comparative constitutional law scholars is suffused with causal claims, and to assess these, one must use the methods of comparative politics (Meuwese and Versteeg, 2012: 233–234). Second, as we have argued above, the field faces new questions and challenges – such as the ones posed by the politics of accommodation – and for these, the traditional comparative law methodology will prove inadequate.

Comparative law from a quotidian perspective is the practice of looking at foreign legal systems in order to answer one or more of a range of questions about law (Adams and Bomhoff, 2012: 7). It generally engages with "the foreign," as comparative politics does. What the best method is for addressing a subject is largely a function of the nature of the questions addressed. In terms of methodological choices, there are basically two major tendencies in contemporary scholarship: those that exemplify a "turn towards jurisprudence" and those that turn instead to the social sciences, with a third camp trying to bridge the gap between these two approaches. The first tendency embodies the "internal perspective" for comparison, trying to develop an understanding of foreign legal systems "on their own terms." After all, and quite understandably, comparative lawyers are *juristes d'abord* aiming to make a juridical contribution to comparative questions. The second tendency urges comparative legal scholarship to borrow some of its methods from the social sciences, including both qualitative and quantitative approaches (Adams and Bomhoff, 2012: 4). Solid qualitative or quantitative empirical evidence may help to produce better scholarship, when compared to the traditional "intuitions and hunches of law professors" (Adams and Bomhoff, 2012: 11). The tension between these two tendencies is evident in many of the chapters in this book. While some of the chapters below seek principally to make a juridical contribution, as all legal scholarship does, others seek to incorporate in some way methods, literatures, questions, and authorities that are borrowed from the social sciences while also making a juridical contribution.

**Disaggregating accommodation: the multiple dimensions of the politics of accommodation**

There are two senses in which constitutionalism is a critical dimension of the politics of accommodation in multinational polities. First, constitutions tend to constitute the very demos that governs itself under and through the constitutional regime (Tierney, 2008). Constitutions can constitute a demos by projecting a given vision of political community with the aim of altering the very self-understanding of citizens, often encapsulated in "constitutional moments." A constitutional moment is a higher order constitutional event, which impacts the relationship between the central state – largely controlled by the majority nation – and the minority nation embedded within the same state. It is of a higher order than ordinary legislative activity (Ackerman, 1991; Lluch, 2010). Such "constitutional moments" are relatively rare, and they represent a critical event that crystallizes the nature of the relationship between the central state and the embedded minority nations. These critical constitutional transformative events include: the adoption of a new constitution, the adoption or proposal of significant constitutional amendments, the adoption or proposal of a new organic statute for the government of the embedded minority nation, etc. Second, constitutions "enable decision making by creating the institutions of government [such as the kind of federal system it creates], by allocating powers to them, by setting out rules of procedure to enable these institutions to make decisions, and by defining how these institutions interact" (Choudhry, 2008: 5).

However, this book shows that constitutionalism is not the only essential dimension of the politics of accommodation in multinational democracies. The notion of accommodation in plurinational polities (Taylor, 1994) needs to be unpacked and disaggregated and all of its multiple dimensions need to be analyzed, integrating comparative politics and comparative constitutional law into the analysis. The book explores three fundamental dimensions of the politics of accommodation: constitutionalism, political culture, and nationalism. The chapters in this volume recognize the multidimensionality of the politics of accommodation, and several chapters explore the interaction between some of these dimensions.

Institutions structure political interactions and in this way affect political outcomes. Institutional choices can shape people's ideas, attitudes, and even preferences. The political structures created by constitutions and by constitutional moments shape the goals political actors pursue and the way they structure power relations among them, and the possibilities for the evolution of political systems (Thelen and Steinmo, 1992: 2). Important dissimilarities exist in constitutional structure, which provide for variation in degrees of self-government and autonomy, symmetries and asymmetries, institutional opportunity structures, forms of representation in the central state, and in recognition of plurinationality.

The second critical dimension of the politics of accommodation is political culture, which has been defined by Sidney Verba as "the system of empirical beliefs, expressive symbols, and values which defines the situation in which political action takes place" (Almond and Verba, 1963; Kincaid, 1982: 5). Culture is of course a foundational concept for social science, and as an abstract generalizing concept includes "symbols, ideas, beliefs, norms, customs, and knowledge" (Sabetti, 2007: 342).

The traditions and ideologies that have influenced a country's political culture – with respect to the tolerance for cultural, ethnic, racial, national, and linguistic diversity – will influence the degree to which it may be able to accommodate substate national societies. Societies approach the problem of ethnic and national diversity "equipped with a cultural repertoire that tends to vary along sociodemographic, political, and national lines. This cultural repertoire includes, among other things, knowledge, habitus, stories, memories, and worldviews, upon which people draw more or less consciously when framing objects and problems" (Díez Medrano, 2003: 6). Culture orders political priorities, that is, "it defines the symbolic and material objects people consider valuable and worth fighting over, the contexts in which such disputes occur, the rules (both formal and informal) by which politics takes place and who participates in it. In doing so, culture defines interests and how they are to be pursued" (Ross, 1997: 46). Culture "does these things by organizing meanings and meaning-making, defining social and political identity, structuring collective actions, and imposing a normative order on politics and social life" (Ross, 2009: 134). Culture forms identity groups, and specifies expectations regarding patterns of association within and between them (Ross, 2009:140).

In federal political systems that are multinational polities, in particular, social forces are important influences. "The essence of federalism 'lies not in the institutional or constitutional structure but in the attitudes of society'" (Kincaid and Cole, 2010: 53). Carl J. Friedrich urged us "to pay increasing attention to ... the social substructure of federal orders" (Kincaid and Cole, 2010: 53). As Daniel Elazar noted, "the maintenance of federalism involves 'thinking federal,' that is, being oriented toward the ideals and norms of ... constitutionalism, and power sharing" (Kincaid and Cole, 2010: 53).

The third critical dimension of the politics of accommodation is the mutual interaction between the nationalisms of majority nations and minority nations coexisting within the same state. In the minority–majority dynamics that one observes in multinational democracies, the national society that constitutes a majority tends to control the central state. The nationalism and the nationalist ideologies of the national society that is a majority within the state will influence the degree to which the state may be able to accommodate substate national societies. State nationalism can also exacerbate substate nationalism and vice versa. By nationalist ideology, I mean a "particular body of arguments and ideas about what defines the nation – its members, its core values and goals, the territory it ought to occupy, and its relations to other nations. A nationalist ideology is an effort to give specific content and political direction to a group's consciousness of difference from other nations and their beliefs" (Citrin et al., 1994; Gagnon, 2003: 295).

Theories of nationalism have tended to overemphasize structure over agency (Beissinger, 2002: 451). This perspective is unsatisfying. First, it relies on a deterministic view of causation, which even in the natural sciences is no longer the reigning paradigm (Lluch, 2014). It misses the element of contingency in political life, and the interdependency of human actions within and across spatial contexts (Lluch, 2014). "The interdependence of human activity across time and space presents a problem for deterministic, linear, or atemporal explanations of political and social phenomena" (Beissinger, 2002: 453). The approach taken here will underscore the role of agency in nationalism, focusing on how constitutionalism and substate and state nationalisms interact with each other, and some of the chapters below discuss this mutual and non-deterministic interaction (Lluch, 2014). Part of the strength of nationalism is that it is grounded in the mechanics of everyday life (Billig, 1995: 6), which explains the extraordinary capacity it has to reproduce itself. Given that "most people expect that their life chances and those of their offspring are shaped in critical respects by the configuration of the state's territorial boundedness, its membership, and its rules of cultural intercourse" (Beissinger, 2002: 19), the dynamics of state and substate nationalisms in multinational democracies represent a critical variable.

As I have noted previously, central state constitutional moments can be interpreted by minority nationalists in multinational democracies as an instance of majority nation nationalism. "Such constitutional moments impact the intersubjective relations of reciprocity between minority nationalists and majority nation nationalism. Statewide solidarity and unity may be promoted by a culture of reciprocity and accommodation between sub-state nationalists and the majority nation. Thus, intersubjective relations of reciprocity between sub-state nationalists and majority nation nationalism are essential for understanding the 'trigger' event that serves as the immediate catalyst" (Lluch, 2010: 354) for the growth of substate secessionist nationalism. Indeed, the perspective offered in this book underscores "the dynamic and fluid nature of nationalism, and its contingent and non-deterministic nature" (Lluch, 2010: 356). In sum, Nationalism follows a political logic and it is embedded in intersubjective relations of reciprocity (Lluch, 2010: 356).

## Disaggregating accommodation: the chapters ahead

The chapters in the book are divided into three parts. The first one presents chapters that take up the challenge to explore the relation between constitutionalism and politics, in cases where a constitutional strategy of territorial pluralism has been used to accommodate national diversity. The authors in this part make explicit use of interdisciplinary approaches, and some of them are constitutional law scholars while others are political scientists, and some are both. The second part is composed of chapters written by political scientists, but who explore the multiple dimensions of the politics of accommodation, and who blend into their analyses some consideration of constitutional issues. The third part explores the nexus between constitutionalism and the actual practice of autonomism, federalism, regionalism, and devolution in several regions of the world. The authors in this last part are constitutional law scholars, but they integrate into their work some of the concerns, questions, methods, literatures, or authorities of comparative politics.

The first part is on "Constitutionalism and the Accommodation of National Diversity." The chapter by Jaime Lluch is a thorough examination of the constitutional and political conundrum facing both Puerto Rico and the USA. The question in this chapter is whether the USA could accommodate a genuine substate national society like Puerto Rico in a non-subordinate relationship, either in a non-subordinate special status autonomy arrangement, or as a constituent unit of the US federation, under a form of asymmetric federalism. Among the varieties of territorial pluralism available, there is the present "unincorporated territory" autonomy, a non-subordinate form of autonomism that we can label "Enhanced Commonwealth," and becoming a unit of the federation. Lluch weaves into his analysis both constitutional law analysis and comparative politics perspectives. He analyzes three fundamental dimensions of the politics of accommodation in the case of the United States and its political dilemma regarding Puerto Rico: the limits fixed by the US Constitution and the US model of federalism, the political culture of the USA with respect to the tolerance of national pluralism, and how national identity, language, and nationalism in the USA affect the likelihood that Puerto Rico could be accommodated within the USA. Lluch's chapter is a good exemplar of the disciplinary syncretism this book seeks to promote.

The joint chapter by François Rocher and Elisenda Casañas Adam also exemplifies the disciplinary cohabitation this book embodies. Their chapter compares two cases of plurinationalism in Canada and Spain that have figured prominently in the literature. Quebec has of course been a longtime prominent case of territorial pluralism and the constitutional battles of the 1990s still resonate today, and it is still a province with very active independentist and federalist parties. Since 2006, the autonomous community of Catalonia has undergone a dramatic political transformation, and it has rapidly transitioned from a pro-autonomism or pro-federation orientation to a pro-sovereignty one. They analyze the interaction between constitutional law and politics in Canada and Spain by examining in depth the recent Spanish Constitutional Court decision of June 2010, regarding the constitutionality of the Catalan Statute of Autonomy of 2006, and the Canadian Supreme Court's decision on the Quebec secession reference of 1998. These constitutional court decisions have served to specify the contours of the varieties of territorial pluralism implemented in Canada and Spain to accommodate Quebec and Catalonia. Rocher and Casañas Adam seek to make a juridical contribution in the sense that their chapter is a very nuanced and juridically solid analysis of these decisions, but they also seek to show the interaction between constitutional law and politics, and they weave into their analysis some of the methodological concerns of comparative politics. They are very methodologically conscious about the similarities and differences between their cases, about unit of analysis issues, and about establishing causation. The evidence they provide and the literature they cite bring together constitutional law and comparative politics. Moreover, they show the multidimensionality of the politics of accommodation, showing that constitutionalism interacts with nationalism, and vice versa, and that any account that seeks to explain developments in Canada and Spain must indeed disaggregate the notion of accommodation. Their thesis, which they label "the politics of judicial containment," is a compelling contribution to the study of constitutional politics.

The chapter by Hèctor López Bofill complements the previous one because it also analyzes recent developments in Spain and Catalonia, with some additional insights. In addition to examining the effect of Spanish constitutionalism on substate nationalist politics, it assesses the impact of the failure of the fiscal agreement with Spain during 2010–2012 in the context of the on-going and deep economic crisis, and the impact of a number of court rulings on issues of language and culture. It also examines the current constitutional and political stalemate by examining the Spanish constitutional framework regarding the right to hold a referendum on independence (the "right to decide"), and discusses alternatives for transcending the Spanish constitutional framework. López Bofill is a professor of constitutional law and also a public intellectual with a presence in the media. He concludes that stressing the effects of Spanish constitutionalism on the internal dynamics of nationalist politics in Catalonia can help to explain these recent developments, but it also has its limits.

The second part is on the "Multiple Dimensions of the Politics of Accommodation in Multinational Polities." The chapter by Eve Hepburn examines the politics of accommodation in island regions forming part of multinational states (such as Italy, Canada, and Finland). She examines island regions with three different institutional configurations: a federacy (the Åland Islands in Finland), a devolved autonomous region (Sardinia in Italy), and a constituent unit of a federation (Prince Edward Island in Canada). The chapter begins with a review of island autonomy and accommodation, and then undertakes a case-study analysis using the conceptual and theoretical framework of the volume, exploring three dimensions of accommodation: (1) constitutionalism and the constitutional constraints on accommodation; (2) nationalism and political mobilization, that is, the success of statewide parties in propagating a statewide nationalism and integration of island politics compared with the demands of substate nationalist movements; and (3) specific state strategies of accommodation. Hepburn's chapter dovetails very well with the general arguments of the book: while writing from a political science perspective, she examines the constitutional structures that frame each of her cases, and indeed one of her conclusions is that a key factor explaining whether accommodation will work is whether the constitutional structures of the central state are flexible and open enough to allow for revision and modification. Moreover, she disassembles the notion of accommodation, and looks at statewide and substate nationalism, constitutionalism, and specific state accommodation strategies.

The chapter by Jordi Argelaguet contributes a wealth of public opinion data to explain the rise of a pro-sovereignty orientation in the national movement of Catalonia, while at the same time showing how Spanish constitutionalism and decisions by the Constitutional Court of

Spain have played a major role in stimulating secessionist nationalism. Argelaguet is the director of the Center for the Study of Public Opinion of the Catalan government, and thus is well positioned to contribute up-to-date data on the rapidly evolving political situation there. In a very clear and crisp style, he traces the most recent developments in Spain, especially since 2010, and situates the Spanish Constitutional Court decision of 28 June 2010 as the catalyst for the shift in public opinion in favor of sovereignty, although he also notes the subsequent role of economic factors such as the fiscal deficit and the ongoing economic debacle, and the role played by subsequent Court decisions regarding the linguistic immersion policies in Catalonian schools. Argelaguet writes from his perspective as a political scientist mindful of the questions, issues, and methods that comparativists are using to address the politics of accommodation and nationalism, yet he shows remarkable sensitivity to the nuances of Spanish constitutionalism and the specificities of key Constitutional Court decisions. As of this writing, the Catalan government is going full steam ahead with its plans for holding a referendum on independence in the Fall of 2014, while the Spanish government asserts that even the planning of such a referendum is illegal, and thus the analysis by Argelaguet is very timely and will generate interest.

The chapter by André Fazi seeks to integrate the case of Corsica (France) into the scholarly debates on the politics of accommodation. As Fazi writes, the case of France – the epitome of a unitary state with a long tradition of republican integrationism – has too often been overlooked. He seeks to examine the analytical framework relating to the politics of accommodation through the case of Corsica. Corsican nationalism involves clandestine organizations that have perpetuated thousands of attacks, but whose violence is less radical than what we have seen in Euskadi or Northern Ireland. In addition, there are no political parties in Corsica dedicated to the defence of the continental French. Also, while nationalist parties have obtained over 35% of the vote, they have never managed to win major public posts. Significantly, Fazi underscores the fact that one of the most important features of the France–Corsica relationship is that Corsica has never had a "constitutional moment." Thus, it has been impossible to make the constitutional exceptions that would have allowed, for example, compulsory education in the Corsican language, etc. Fazi contributes a more global framework for analysis, favoring comparative analysis, and "exploiting the nexus between political science and constitutional law." For Fazi, accommodation is indeed a multidimensional concept, and an excessive emphasis on constitutionalism can become a "prejudicial bias." He writes that the non-constitutional moment in Corsica may yet be due to the political balance of power between nationalists and non-nationalists, which is not sufficient to justify "exceptions to constitutional principles because the political cost of such exceptions would be high in a country where unitary ideology remains strong."

The third part is on "Constitutionalism and the Practice of Autonomism, Federalism, and Devolution." The chapter by Stephen Tierney examines the case of British constitutionalism and its "flexible accommodation" model. With the referendum on independence in Scotland scheduled to be held on 18 September 2014, his contribution has become all the more relevant and topical. He begins by questioning the adequacy of the language of accommodation, when seen as states managing minorities, because it does not adequately portray the constitutional challenge posed by stateless nations. The latter contest the idea that the state "represents a discrete category of nation which embraces the entire polity, an idea that is so embedded in political theory that the state is often presented as somehow neutral with regard to nationality." For him, the challenge in multinational democracies is not so much about the politics of difference, but rather about the politics of similarity. The peculiarities of British constitutionalism resulted in an inchoate and untidy process of devolution to the substate nations of the UK, but it was precisely the flexibility of British constitutionalism that brought devolution so quickly and with such varied and asymmetrical arrangements for Scotland, Northern Ireland, and Wales. It was due to an "unwritten constitution that devolution was effected in such an ad hoc way." Britain's approach has been exceptional from a constitutional law standpoint, but as Tierney points out, it has also been exceptional from a political science perspective. The political culture of Britain is remarkably flexible in the sense that it readily recognizes that the British state is a union of nations. Many see the UK as a series of unions, and the notion of the UK as a "union state" has been predominant. Thus, the "symbols and motifs of the state" (such as flags, royal family paraphernalia) also denote this union nature, shaping the political culture of the state. Tierney's chapter seeks to make a juridical contribution to comparative questions, but he is also interested in adopting some of the questions and concerns of comparative politics, as he weaves into his account an analysis of British political culture and British identity and nationalism.

The joint chapter by Francesco Palermo and Alice Valdesalici addresses recent developments in the process of federalizing Italy, which in 2001 championed the most significant "federalizing" constitutional reform of the western world in the last decade or so. Italy is a state with a high degree of diversity, and the 1948 constitution instituted an innovative experiment with regionalization. As a matter of constitutional law, the system has been characterized by an asymmetrical design creating five special or autonomous regions (including significant national minorities in Aosta Valley and Trentino-South Tyrol) and 15 ordinary regions. Their chapter seeks to account for the difficult administrative implementation of the constitutional reforms of 1999 and 2001, and the perception that the federalizing process has come to a standstill, bringing about a counter-wave of centralization. The chapter analyzes the trajectory of fiscal federalism in Italy, and how this issue has recently monopolized every aspect of the federalizing process. Besides constitutionalism, the authors discuss other factors that are hampering a complete transition of the country into a fully fledged federal system, including the party system and the organization of the civil service. The authors seamlessly weave into their argument methods and issues of constitutional law with methods and concerns derived from a comparative politics perspective. One of their most important conclusions is that the absence of a shared culture of federalism and the absence of any real understanding of the theory and practice of federalism among the main political actors is one of the principal obstacles on the road to federalizing Italy. In view of the absence of a sound federal political culture, the authors argue that the Constitutional Court has become the main actor in Italian federalism during the last three decades and is bound to continue as such for the coming decades.

The chapter by Markku Suksi is a methodologically sophisticated comparison of the long-standing autonomy arrangement of the Åland Islands in Finland with the more recent territorial autonomy arrangements for Hong Kong and Macau vis-à-vis China, born out of international treaties with the UK and Portugal, respectively. Unitary states such as China and Finland are less monolithic in their constitutional design than expected. The chapter considers the issue of whether, given that the Chinese commitment to Hong Kong and Macau is temporal, extending until 2047 and 2049 respectively, the method of incorporating provisions concerning the Åland Islands in Finland's Constitution could be useful for renewing the autonomous status of Hong Kong and Macau in the Chinese constitutional firmament, after the treaty commitments expire in the 2040s. En route to resolving that issue, the chapter presents an illuminating analysis of how the international commitments by Finland and China indicated how these would be implemented in their state legal orders, presents a comparative analysis of how autonomy arrangements can be legally entrenched, and discusses the distribution of powers accorded to these substate entities. Regarding the latter, Suksi sees Hong Kong and Macau as typical territorial autonomies, and the Åland Islands as a modified territorial autonomy. This chapter is also equidistant between constitutional law and comparative politics in its disciplinary approach, and is perhaps the best exemplar in the volume combining a juridically and constitutionally sophisticated analysis with serious attention to methodological issues in comparative politics. Specifically, Suksi is very attentive to the logic of comparison in the three regions and two states he discusses, unit of analysis issues, and the effect of institutions (constitutionalism) on the sorts of autonomy arrangements that can be visualized, and places his entire analysis in a broad comparative perspective, as can be gleaned from his discussion about the two dimensions of autonomy arrangements: the normative level dimension, and the dimension of the powers accorded to the substate entities.

## Note

1. According to Fearon and Laitin, in view of the world's considerable ethnic and national diversity, the cases of ethnonational violence are actually not as numerous as one might expect (Fearon and Laitin 1996).

## References

Ackerman, Bruce. *We the People* (Cambridge: Harvard University Press, 1991).
Adams, Maurice and Jacco Bomhoff. "Comparing Law: Practice and Theory" in Maurice Adams and Jacco Bomhoff (eds), *Practice and Theory in Comparative Law* (Cambridge University Press, 2012).
Almond, Gabriel and Sidney Verba. *The Civic Culture* (Princeton: Princeton University Press, 1963).
Anderson, Gavin. "Beyond 'Constitutionalism Beyond the State,'" *Journal of Law and Society*, Vol. 39, No. 3 (September 2012), pp. 359–383.
Beissinger, Mark. *Nationalist Mobilization and the Collapse of the Soviet State* (Cambridge: Cambridge University Press, 2002).
Billig, Michael. *Banal Nationalism* (London: Sage, 1995).
Choudhry, Sujit. "Bridging Comparative Politics and Comparative Constitutional Law: Constitutional Design in Divided Societies," in Sujit Choudhry (ed.), *Constitutional Design for Divided Societies: Integration or Accommodation?* (Oxford: Oxford University Press, 2008).
Citrin, Jack and Ernst Haas, "Is American Nationalism Changing? Implications for Foreign Policy," *International Studies Quarterly*, Vol. 38, No. 1 (March, 1994), pp. 1–31.

Cordell, Karl and Stefan Wolff (eds), *Routledge Handbook of Ethnic Conflict* (London: Routledge, 2011).
Díez-Medrano, Juan. *Framing Europe: Attitudes to European Integration in Germany, Spain, and the United Kingdom* (Princeton: Princeton University Press, 2003).
Dorsen, Norman, Michel Rosenfeld, András Sajó, and Susanne Baer, *Comparative Constitutionalism: Cases and Materials*, Second Edition (St Paul, Minnesota: West Publishers, 2010).
Fearon, James D. and David Laitin, "Explaining Interethnic Cooperation," *American Political Science Review*, Vol. 90, No. 4 (1996), pp. 715–735.
Gagnon, Alain. "Undermining Federalism and Feeding Minority Nationalism: The Impact of Majority Nationalism in Canada," in Alain Gagnon, Montserrat Guibernau, and François Rocher (eds), *The Conditions of Diversity in Multinational Democracies* (Montreal: Institute for Research on Public Policy, 2003).
Holmes, Stephen. "Constitutions and Constitutionalism," in Michel Rosenfeld and András Sajó (eds), *The Oxford Handbook of Comparative Constitutional Law* (Oxford University Press, 2012).
Jackson, Vicki C. and Mark Tushnet, *Defining the Field of Comparative Constitutional Law* (Westport: Praeger, 2002).
Keating, Michael. *Plurinational Democracy* (Oxford: Oxford University Press, 2001).
Kincaid, John (ed.) *Political Culture, Public Policy and the American States* (Philadelphia: ISHI, 1982).
Kincaid, John and Richard Cole. "Citizen Attitudes toward Issues of Federalism in Canada, Mexico and the United States," *Publius: the Journal of Federalism*, Vol. 14, No. 1 (2010), pp. 53–75.
Lijphart, Arend. *The Politics of Accommodation: Pluralism and Democracy in the Netherlands* (University of California Press, 1968).
Linz, Juan, Alfred Stepan, and Yogendra Yadav. *Crafting State Nations: India and other Multinational Democracies* (Baltimore: Johns Hopkins University Press, 2011).
Lluch, Jaime. "How Nationalism Evolves: Explaining the Establishment of New Varieties of Nationalism within the National Movements of Quebec and Catalonia," *Nationalities Papers: The Journal of Nationalism and Ethnicity*, Vol. 38, No. 3 (2010), pp. 337–359.
—— (2012a), "Autonomism and Federalism," *Publius: the Journal of Federalism*, Vol. 42, No. 1 (Winter 2012), pp. 134–161.
—— (2012b) "The Internal Variation in Substate National Movements and the Moral Polity of the Nationalist," *European Political Science Review*, Vol. 4, No. 3 (2012), pp. 433–459.
—— (forthcoming). *Visions of Sovereignty: Nationalism and Accommodation in Multinational Democracies* (Philadelphia: University of Pennsylvania Press, 2014).
Loughlin, Martin. "What is Constitutionalism?" in Petra Dobner and Martin Loughlin (eds), *The Twilight of Constitutionalism?* (Oxford: Oxford University Press, 2010).
Meuwese, Anne and Mila Versteeg. "Quantitative Methods for Comparative Constitutional Law," in Petra Dobner and Martin Loughlin (eds), *The Twilight of Constitutionalism?* (Oxford: Oxford University Press, 2010).
McGarry, John, Brendan O'Leary, and Richard Simeon. "Integration or Accommodation? The Enduring Debate in Conflict Regulation," in Sujit

Choudhry (ed.), *Constitutional Design for Divided Societies: Integration or Accommodation?* (Oxford: Oxford University Press, 2008).

Nimni, Ephraim. "Stateless Nations in a World of Nation-States," in Karl Cordell and Stefan Wolff (eds), *Routledge Handbook of Ethnic Conflict* (London: Routledge, 2011).

Poiares Maduro, Miguel. "The Importance of Being Called a Constitution: Constitutional Authority and the Authority of Constitutionalism," *International Journal of Constitutional Law*, Vol. 3, No. 2–3 (May 2005), pp. 332–356.

Ross, Marc Howard. "Culture and Identity in Comparative Political Analysis," in Mark I. Lichbach and Alan Zuckerman (eds), *Comparative Politics: Rationality, Culture, and Structure* (Cambridge: Cambridge University Press, 1997).

———. "Culture in Comparative Political Analysis," in Mark I. Lichbach and Alan Zuckerman (eds), *Comparative Politics: Rationality, Culture, and Structure*, Second Edition (Cambridge: Cambridge University Press, 2009).

Sabetti, Filippo. "Democracy and Civil Culture," in Carles Boix and Susan C. Stokes (eds), *The Oxford Handbook of Comparative Politics* (Oxford: Oxford University Press, 2007).

Sajó, András. *Limiting Government: An Introduction to Constitutionalism* (Budapest: Central European University Press, 1999).

Taylor, Charles. "The Politics of Recognition," in Amy Gutman (ed.), *Multiculturalism: Examining the Politics of Recognition* (Princeton: Princeton University Press, 1994).

Thelen, Kathleen and Sven Steinmo. "Historical Institutionalism in Comparative Politics," in Sven Steinmo, Kathleen Thelen, Frank Longstreth (eds), *Structuring Politics: Historical Institutionalism in Comparative Analysis* (Cambridge: Cambridge University Press 1992).

Tierney, Stephen. *Constitutional Law and National Pluralism* (Oxford: Oxford University Press, 2004).

———. "Giving with one hand: Scottish devolution within a Unitary State," in Sujit Choudhry (ed.), *Constitutional Design for Divided Societies: Integration or Accommodation?* (Oxford: Oxford University Press, 2008), pp. 141–172.

———. "We the Peoples: Constituent Power and Constitutionalism in Plurinational States," in Neil Walker and Martin Loughlin (eds), *The Paradox of Constitutionalism* (Oxford: Oxford University Press, 2007), pp. 229–247.

Walker, Graham. "The Constitutional Good: Constitutionalism's Equivocal Moral Imperative," in *Polity*, Vol. XXVI, No. 1 (Fall 1993), pp. 123–138.

Walker, Neil. "Taking Constitutionalism Beyond the State," *Political Studies*, Vol. 56, No. 21 (2008), pp. 519–543.

# Part I
# Constitutionalism and the Accommodation of National Diversity

# 1
# Varieties of Territorial Pluralism: Prospects for the Constitutional and Political Accommodation of Puerto Rico in the USA

*Jaime Lluch*

### The demos problem in multinational democracies

In contemporary multinational states, the dominant constitutional and political view in substate national societies[1] (such as Scotland, Quebec, the Basque Country, Catalonia, Northern Ireland, and South Tyrol) challenges contemporary assumptions about the nation-state, namely, the "monistic demos" thesis. The traditional assumptions of contemporary republican theory are disputed in these substate national societies: the notion of a "monistic conception of the nation as the embodiment of a unified demos" is rejected (Tierney 2007: 232; Walker 2008: 521).

Thus, substate political actors present "particular challenges to constitutional form which do not generally arise in uninational states" (Tierney 2007: 236). Their voices often seek "a reconfiguration of the internal constitution of the host state in full recognition of the national pluralism of the state in question" (Tierney 2007: 230). They often demand a "rethinking of orthodox state-centered assumptions concerning both the nature of the *demos* and the empirical and normative dimensions of constituted authority within plurinational states" (Tierney 2007: 231).

In this chapter, I examine the case of Puerto Rico ("PR"), an unincorporated territory of the USA, and I do so by analyzing it in relation to the rich contemporary literature on the political and constitutional accommodation of national diversity in multinational democracies. There are a number of minority nations in the USA, including North American Indians, Puerto Rico (PR), etc. This chapter seeks to explore the issue of whether the United States can accommodate such substate national societies. Although Puerto Ricans on the island represent a relatively small and geographically isolated population, and have been marginal to the self-identity of the people of the USA, they are perhaps the best example of a stateless nation in the USA. The overwhelming number of people in PR are natives of the island, have Spanish as their native language, a long history that is separate and distinct from that of the USA, a flourishing "national" culture and civil society, and autonomous local political institutions that they fully control, i.e., a degree of local self-government.

Most analysts tend to think of the USA as a polyethnic nation-state, rather than a multinational state, in part because stateless nations within it are a relatively small proportion of the population, geographically isolated, and living under subordinate political arrangements. Yet, Puerto Ricans in Puerto Rico – a part of the USA since 1898 – have a genuinely distinct societal culture. Their homeland was incorporated into the USA by conquest and colonization. At the time of their incorporation, the people of PR "constituted an ongoing societal culture, separated from the anglophone culture. They did not have to re-create their culture in a new land, since their language and historical narratives were already embodied in a full set of social practices and institutions, encompassing all aspects of social life."[2] In the case of PR, the USA has followed a quite different strategy from the one used in the case of voluntary (and involuntary) immigrants. PR has been accorded a special status and it is in control of substate governmental institutions within its territorial boundaries.

## Puerto Rico as a distinct substate *demos*

Assertions of nationality "are a particular type of demand, requiring specific forms of recognition and accommodation" (Keating 2001: 2). Unlike other forms of identity politics (such as multiculturalism or feminism), "nationality claims have a special status, carrying with them a more or less explicit assertion of the right to self-determination" (Keating 2001: 3). Thus, "national pluralism ... represents a different order of diversity from that of cultural pluralism" (Tierney 2007: 232).

A study of PR's societal culture and symbols of "national" identity found that the most consistently cited element of the Puerto Rican sense of identity was the Spanish language. Another commonly cited element that respondents felt defined PR and set it apart was the island's history.[3] Most respondents in the study also seemed to possess a strong consciousness of being a distinct society, having a "clear sense of PR as having a defined culture, distinguishable from others by specific traits." Respondents remarked, for example, that "being Puerto Rican is feeling an identification with a nationality that excludes other nationalities," and "[we have] a history that defines us as a group separated from the others," and "We Puerto Ricans are a distinct culture that is well defined."[4]

"Puerto Ricans of all persuasions are principally cultural nationalists. The overwhelming majority consider themselves Puerto Ricans first and Americans second."[5] In fact, "a 1996 poll showed that only 25% of all the people of PR consider the U.S. to be their nation. For the other 75%, their nation is PR."[6] Many in PR seem to want to continue in a relation with the US, but also want to preserve and protect their distinctive societal culture.

Congressional attention on the political status options of Puerto Rico has been concentrated in recent years in the periods from 1989–90 period and 1997–98. During 1989–90, three versions of a bill were filed in the US Senate (S.710–S. 712) by Senator Bennett Johnston, chairman of the Committee on Energy and Natural Resources (in charge of PR affairs), which called for a plebiscite sponsored by Congress on the three status formulas, as defined by each party and revised by Congress, the preferred status to become law without further action. The bill eventually died in Committee in 1991.[7] A similar process was repeated in the period from 1997–98 when "A Bill to Provide a Process Leading to Full Self Government for Puerto Rico" (H.R. 856) was narrowly passed by the US House of Representatives, but was ultimately defeated in the US Senate. The hearings that were conducted during these two attempts to provide for a Congressionally-sponsored mechanism for resolving PR's political dilemma elicited compelling testimony on the nature of PR's distinct societal culture, among other matters.

For example, the President of the Ateneo Puertorriqueño, the oldest cultural institution in PR, stated that: "[W]e Puerto Ricans are a nation, independent from the political acceptance that this word also has. Although lacking in sovereignty, PR is a nation inhabited by Puerto Ricans with a history and culture that is common and of its own, with a common native language, Spanish; with a way of being, a particular mentality and folklore, with its own customs and traditions ... with its own artistic, musical and literary expression, in existence even before the United States invasion."[8] The President of the pro-independence party put it this way in hearings held on 19 March 1997 in Washington, DC: "PR is a distinct, mature, Spanish-speaking, Latin American Caribbean nation ... For a nation such as PR, statehood would be a dilution, if not an abdication, of our right to govern ourselves as Puerto Ricans ... The problem of PR ... is not a problem of disenfranchisement of a minority or an issue of civil rights, as some people believe. It is not a problem of individual rights. It is a problem of national rights, of the inalienable rights of a nation, of a people, to govern themselves."[9]

Thus, Puerto Rico's situation as an island people exhibiting the contours of nationhood is radically different from that of other regions that were incorporated into the US nation-state, such as Arizona's borderlands, where the majority was able to impose its own classifications of ethnicity and race on the newly incorporated peoples (Meeks 2007: 4). Arizona's borderlands were incorporated into the US, while "defining the cultural and racial boundaries of full citizenship" (Meeks 2007: 10). To understand Puerto Rico, by contrast, it is better to use the language of accommodation and recognition in plurinational polities.

## An "unincorporated territory" within the US federal political system

In PR, two axes exist in its political party system: one on national identity and about the constitutional relationship between the substate unit and the central state, and the other on political economy. As in many other stateless nations throughout the world, the former predominates over the latter.

People of all political persuasions, moreover, find the current political arrangement inadequate. As US Senator Ron Wyden declared recently: "the current relationship undermines the United States' moral standing in the world. For a nation founded on the principles of democracy and the consent of the governed, how much longer can America allow a condition to persist in which nearly four million U.S. citizens do not have a vote in the government that makes the national laws which affect their daily lives?"[10]

PR is an unincorporated territory of the US (Rivera Ramos 2001) and it is subject to the plenary powers of the US Congress under the Territory Clause of the US Constitution (Aleinikoff 2002: 76). Article IV, Section 3 of the latter gives Congress the "Power to dispose of and make all needful Rules and Regulations respecting the Territory or other Property belonging to the United States." It gives Congress "general and plenary" power with respect to federal territory (Lawson & Sloane 2009), which relates specifically to "full and complete legislative authority over the people of the Territories and all the departments of the territorial governments."[11] "Case law from more than a century ago gives Congress freedom to legislate for at least some territories in a fashion that would violate the Constitution in other contexts" (Lawson & Sloane 2009: 1146). A series of decisions by the Supreme Court, dating from the period 1901–22 and known as the Insular Cases, created the category of "unincorporated territories" and it held that the inhabitants of these areas only enjoyed the protection of those provisions of the Constitution deemed as "fundamental" by the Court, in the absence of Congressional action making other provisions applicable.[12] The Insular Cases are still good law, although no contemporary scholar, of any methodological or political inclination, defends them (Lawson & Sloane 2009: 1146).[13]

The political status quo in PR is known as the Estado Libre Asociado (ELA) (literally, "free associated state"). With it, the USA has sought to accommodate PR's distinctive societal culture, but in an inferior and subordinate relationship. The ELA was established in 1952, artfully translated into English as "Commonwealth." Public Law 600 was passed by the US Congress in 1950 and it aimed to provide a regime of limited self-government for the people of PR. After approval by the people in a referendum, Congress ratified the local Constitution, and the newly baptized ELA came into effect on 25 July 1952 (Ramírez Lavandero 1988).

Watts's typology of federal systems is highly regarded (Watts 2008: 8), and if we accept that "federal political systems" is a broad genus encompassing a whole spectrum of specific non-unitary forms; i.e., species ranging from "quasi-federations," "federations," and "confederations," and beyond. Following Watts, if we see the USA as a federal political system composed of 50 constituent units of the core federation, one federal district, two federacies, three associated states, three unincorporated territories, Native American domestic dependent nations, etc. (Watts 2008: 12), then it is clear that PR is part of this broad federal political system that we call the USA, although it is not part of the federation, nor is it seen as part of the "nation."

As in PR, substate national movements in multinational polities tend to bifurcate or, at times, trifurcate, into two or three basic political orientations: independence, autonomy, and, oftentimes, pro-federation orientations (Lluch 2010, 2012; forthcoming). Adherence to the movement that wants PR to become a constituent unit of the US federation has grown from 12.9% of the electorate in 1952 to 49.9% in the general elections of 1990, and 52.84% in the 2008 election. Support for independence has declined from 19% of the electorate in 1952 to 3.1% in 1960, 6.4% in 1976, and 3–5% in recent elections. Support for the status quo (the autonomy that we call the ELA), has declined from 67% in 1952 to 45.3% in 1976, and 41.26% in the 2008 election.[14] Puerto Ricans have an inalienable right to independence, and independence is one of its clear alternatives for a better future. For the foreseeable future, however, in light of the current weakness of the pro-independence forces in PR, the island is bound to continue being a part of the US federal political system, and thus its two possible constitutional futures are autonomism or federalism. The question in this chapter is whether the USA could accommodate a genuine substate national society like PR in a non-colonial relationship, either in a non-colonial special status autonomy arrangement, or as a constituent unit of the US federation, under a form of asymmetric federalism (Aleinikoff 2002: 94).

## Varieties of territorial pluralism: autonomism and federalism in multinational democracies

As explained in the Introduction to this volume, the accommodationist family of state approaches to diversity has four varieties: centripetalism, multiculturalism, consociationalism, and territorial pluralism. Both centripetalism and consociationalism offer prescriptions that address the dilemmas of deeply divided societies, often with endemic levels of violence. They are inapplicable to Puerto Rico. The USA in part utilizes a strategy of multicultural accommodation, which at times seems to be liberal integrationism in disguise, to manage its ethnic diversity (McGarry et al. 2008: 57). Yet, in the case of Puerto Rico, it has implemented a strategy of territorial pluralism, but with an inadequate special status arrangement.

What sort of autonomy is PR? Building on previous scholarship (Benedikter 2009; Lluch 2011; Suksi 2011), and given space constraints, I present a short characterization of it. Autonomism does not seek independence – at least for the medium to short term – but seeks to promote the self-government, self-administration, and cultural identity of a territorial unit populated by a society with national characteristics (Henders 2010), and it can also be distinguished from models of federation (Weller & Nobbs 2010; Lluch 2011; Gagnon & Keating 2012).

In many multinational democracies, models of federation are the preferred form of territorial pluralism for the accommodation of national diversity (Elazar 1987; Burgess & Gagnon 1993; McRoberts 1997; Gibbins et al. 1998; Kymlicka 1998; Hechter 2000; Stepan 2001; Keating 2004; Griffiths et al. 2005; Karmis & Norman 2005; Norman 2006; Gagnon & Iacovino 2007; Watts 2008). Yet, there are autonomist national parties in substate nation-states that reject a model of federation as an appropriate institutional design to address their needs (Lluch 2011). Instead, some advocate autonomy as the ideal institutional design to accommodate them. This is the case in PR: it is one of the world's premier instances of "territorial autonomy," as opposed to national cultural autonomy (Burnett & Marshall 2001; Rivera Ramos 2001; Nimni 2009).

PR is neither a "federacy" as defined in the literature (O'Leary 2005; Rezvani 2007; Linz & Stepan 2011; Suksi 2011), nor a "free-associated" state.[15] Among the wide variety of actually existing autonomies in federal political systems, it is a non-federal territorial autonomy. There are four ways in which its autonomy is non-federalist. First, in autonomies such as PR the formal distribution of legislative and executive authority between the two levels of government is not constitutionally entrenched (Lluch 2011). Second, autonomies such as PR are non-federalist because they are constitutionally subordinate to the center. The "shared rule" component between the central state and the autonomous unit is weak or practically non-existent. Third, autonomies such as PR are non-federalist if their influence over the policy-making institutions of the center is weak or negligible (Lluch 2011). Fourth, autonomies are also non-federalist if the two orders of government that have been set up are so unequal that the element of "self rule" in the relationship gives the autonomy a special status arrangement that is not part of the core institutional apparatus of the central state (Lluch 2011).

In a recent referendum held on 7 November 2012, 54% of the voters expressed their dissatisfaction with the present territorial arrangement. "There is no disputing that a majority of the voters in Puerto Rico – 54 percent – have clearly expressed their opposition to continuing the current territorial status."[16] In the US federal political system (as defined by Watts 2008), therefore, there are at least *two varieties of territorial pluralism* that could be implemented to accommodate PR: either through a non-colonial model of autonomism,[17] or a form of asymmetric federalism as a constituent unit of the federation.

## Disaggregating accommodation and territorial pluralism in the United States

### Constitutionalism and "Enhanced Commonwealth"

What are the constitutionally sound forms of territorial pluralism (autonomism or federalism) that could accommodate PR? Let us first consider whether US constitutionalism could accommodate PR under a form of autonomism that is non-subordinate and non-colonial. I rely on the analyses found in two Reports by the President's Task Force on Puerto Rico's Status (of 2005 and 2011). I find that the analysis in the 2005 Report is more authoritative and scholarly, but will also make reference to the 2011 one.

It would seem that the US Constitution allows unambiguously for three options: independence, becoming a unit of the federation, or the current "unincorporated territory" status. However, autonomists in PR[18] have for decades put forward proposals for greater autonomy (R.L. Nieves 2009) that have been labeled as "culminated or enhanced ELA," or "New ELA or Commonwealth." Are "New ELA or Commonwealth" proposals feasible under the US Constitution? The White House Task Force of 2005 has signaled that some of these proposals for more autonomy would not be constitutionally feasible, largely relying on a Memorandum of Law by the Office of Legislative Affairs of the US Department of Justice (DOJ), dated 18 January 2001.

The DOJ recognizes that the creation of the ELA from 1948–52 did not take PR outside the ambit of the Territory Clause (President's Task Force 2005: Appendix E). Thus, "Congress [pursuant to the Territory Clause] ... may treat Puerto Rico differently from States so long as there is a rational basis for its actions" (*Harris v. Rosario*, 446 U.S. 651 [1980]). See also *Califano v. Torres*, 435 U.S. 1, 3 n. 4 (1978) (*per curiam*) ("Congress has the power to treat Puerto Rico differently..."). "The Department of Justice has long taken the same view, and the weight of appellate case law provides further support for it" (President's Task Force 2005: Appendix E, at 6).

Under "New Commonwealth," the island would "become an autonomous, non-territorial [and non-colonial], non-State entity in permanent union with the United States under a covenant that could not be altered without the 'mutual consent' of Puerto Rico and the federal Government" (President's Task Force 2005: 6). The US Constitution:

> does not allow for such an arrangement. For entities under the sovereignty of the United States, the only constitutional options are to be a State or territory. As the U.S. Supreme Court stated in 1879, "All territory within the jurisdiction of the United States not included in any State must necessarily be governed by or under the authority of Congress." *First Nat. Bank v. Yankton County*, 101 U.S. 129, 133 (1879). (President's Task Force 2005: 6)

Furthermore,

> it is a general rule that one legislature cannot bind a subsequent one ... Thus, one Congress cannot irrevocably legislate with regard to a territory ... and, therefore, cannot restrict a future Congress from revising a delegation to a territory of powers of self-government ... It

therefore is not possible, absent a constitutional amendment, to bind future Congresses to any particular arrangement for Puerto Rico as a Commonwealth. (President's Task Force 2005: 6)

As the DOJ argues, "as a matter of domestic constitutional law, the United States cannot irrevocably surrender an essential attribute of its sovereignty. *See United States v. Winstar Corp.*, 518 U.S. 839, 888 (1996) (the United States "may not contract away 'an essential attribute of its sovereignty...'") Thus, to the extent a covenant to which the United States is party stands on no stronger footing than an Act of Congress, it is, for purposes of federal constitutional law, subject to unilateral alteration or revocation by subsequent Acts of Congress. *Marbury v. Madison*, 5 U.S. (1 Cranch) 137, 177 (1803); *Fletcher v. Peck*, 10 U.S. (6 Cranch) 87, 135 (1810). Thus, any New Commonwealth proposal with a mutual consent provision would be constitutionally unenforceable (President's Task Force 2005: Appendix E, at 8).

Regarding the continuity of US citizenship under any New Commonwealth proposal, the DOJ argues that if the citizenship provision is accompanied by a mutual consent provision, this would not be constitutionally sound. Putting aside that stipulation,

we think Congress could also change that rule and provide that, in the future, birth in Puerto Rico shall no longer be a basis for United States citizenship. We are unaware of any case addressing the power of Congress to withhold prospectively non-Fourteenth Amendment citizenship from those born in an area subject to United States sovereignty, when persons previously born in that area received statutory citizenship by birthright, and we think it is unclear how a court would resolve that issue. (President's Task Force 2005: Appendix E, at 10–11)

Regarding whether, under a New Commonwealth proposal, PR could enter into commercial and tax agreements with other countries, etc., the Treaty Clause and the Compact Clause in the Constitution vest the foreign relations power of the US (including the treaty-making power), in the federal government. *Curtiss-Wright Export Corp.*, 299 U.S. at 304, 318 (1936). It is unclear whether the Treaty Clause or the Compact Clause apply to PR, insofar as it is not a "State" (President's Task Force 2005: Appendix E, at 12).

The President's Task Force Report of 2011 was more generous with Commonwealth supporters, but it nevertheless maintained a concern with the issue of which status options are "constitutionally sound" and reaffirmed that at least "one aspect of some proposals for enhanced Commonwealth remains constitutionally problematic," referring to the mutual consent provision discussed above (President's Task Force 2011: 26).

## Constitutionalism, federalism, and Puerto Rico

Now, let us consider whether US constitutionalism could accommodate PR as a constituent unit of the federation. Federations can be multinational or mononational. In the former, the boundaries of the internal units are usually sculpted so that at least some of them are controlled by stateless nations. "In addition, more than one nationality may be explicitly recognized as co-founders ... of the federation ... (as in Belgium, Canada, etc.)" (McGarry & O'Leary 2007: 181). On the other hand, the USA is the paradigmatic example of a "national federation," and its model has been emulated by other states, such as Mexico, Argentina, Venezuela, Germany, and Austria. National federations "may be nationally homogeneous (or predominantly so), or they are organized, often consciously, so as not to recognize more than one official nationality ... The official goal behind national federation is nation building, the elimination of internal national (and perhaps also ethnic) differences" (McGarry & O'Leary 2007: 182).

In the US federation, its citizens equate "national" with their "federal government." They believe that "federation is antithetical to nation building if it is multinational, multiethnic, or 'ethnofederal'" (McGarry & O'Leary 2007: 186). As the USA expanded from its original 13 colonies, "it was decided that no territory would receive statehood unless minorities were outnumbered by ... WASPs" (McGarry & O'Leary 2007: 186). By contrast, multinational federalists in states such as Canada and India support federation "to unite people who seek the advantages of membership of a common political unit, but differ markedly in descent, language, and culture" (McGarry & O'Leary 2007: 189). For them, a proper interpretation of liberalism requires respect and protection for the culture of individuals who belong to distinctive demoi.

Linz and Stepan have argued that US-style federalism is inappropriate to deal with national diversity in multinational societies. US federalism is highly symmetrical. "Whether a constitution is symmetrical or asymmetrical has important consequences for what can be done, or especially what cannot be done, to manage politics in a polity with multinational dimensions" (Linz & Stepan 2011: 260). Of the 11 states that have been continuous federal democracies since 1988, Linz and Stepan "note that all of the polities that have a territorially based multinational dimension to their societies are asymmetrical" (Linz & Stepan 2011: 263). The US style of federalism makes it impossible to utilize "asymmetrical" federal formulas. The kinds of asymmetrical arrangements we have seen in Canada, Belgium, Spain, etc. would be unconstitutional in the USA (Linz & Stepan 2011: 264). Moreover, US-style presidentialism, contrary to parliamentarism, makes it impossible for a territorially based, minority-nationalist party to be part of the ruling majority at the center, given that presidentialism is an "indivisible good." It is thus impossible to have the kinds of moderating incentives on state and substate nationalisms that one can have in parliamentary systems (Linz & Stepan 2011: 265).

In the USA, the 13 original colonies "considered themselves free and independent states which took over, separately and together, the attributes of sovereignty."[19] None of the framers in the Philadelphia Convention of 1787 went there determined to create a federal system. "Some went to try to secure a stronger center of power in the United States to serve pressing public needs; others went determined to protect the states against that very centralization."[20] We can only be sure that the framers of the Constitution regarded federalism as one of several mechanisms to limit the power of government in the USA. Therefore, any attempt to argue for a particular relation between the national government and the states – "in particular for a precise division of powers between them – must fall flat for lack of constitutional corroboration."[21]

Still, "it is possible to say something about what the states can do. In general, they can exercise all those powers which have not been removed from their jurisdiction by prohibition or by federal preemption, constitutional or otherwise."[22] Moreover, the states have the power to handle their own internal organization, structure, and procedures. "Although the Congress was able to prescribe limitations and/or restrictions on territories before they were admitted to statehood, once they came into the Union, states were free to draw up their own constitutions and frame their governments as they wished and to alter them as it suited them later on."[23] In fact, the Constitutional Convention of 1787 paid little attention to diversities of race and ethnicity because it was creating a union of preexisting states, and the states controlled these matters.[24]

At least one scholar, Paul Gewirtz of Yale Law School, has argued that in the case of PR, there is no constitutional obstacle to continuing English and Spanish as co-official languages. "The Constitution does not establish a language policy for the United States but rather leaves the States and localities free to accommodate the use of languages other than English .... [It] would be audacious to suggest that the Federal Constitution precludes an official role for the Spanish language in the State of Puerto Rico."[25] Moreover, Gewirtz argues that there are serious constitutional obstacles to Congressional restrictions on the use of Spanish in PR. First, *Coyle v. Smith*, 221 U.S. 559 (1911), held that Congress may not impose any conditions on a newly admitted State "which would not be valid and effectual if the subject of congressional legislation after admission", 221 U.S. at 573. Federal language restrictions, however, are likely to infringe a range of constitutional rights of states and their citizens. *Coyle* stands for the principle that a new State stands on "equal footing with the original States in all respects whatsoever", 221 U.S. at 567.

Second, the 10th Amendment stands for the principle that the States as well as the nation are sovereign entities in the US polity. In addition, although the "Supreme Court in recent years has been sharply divided on the extent to which the Constitution establishes judicially-enforceable state sovereignty limits on Congress' power, there remain certain bedrock rights that States retain to determine their basic structures and processes."[26] Third, the "equal footing" doctrine would also prevent Congress from singling out the State of PR for language restrictions. This doctrine requires that new states be admitted with "parity as respects political standing and sovereignty," *United States v. Texas*, 339 U.S. 707, 717 (1949). It requires equal treatment regarding "political rights and sovereignty." Any attempt to restrict the leeway of a state regarding language clearly concerns "political rights and sovereignty" 339 U.S. at 344. Thus, despite the fact that the USA has become increasingly centralized,[27] Gewirtz argues that as far as the substantive principles of federalism are concerned, the State of PR would not face constitutional obstacles in having the Spanish language share official status with English.

However, with respect to the actual historical practice in the USA, the concrete record is less encouraging. In 1787, the USA exhibited a great deal of religious and racial diversity, and a considerable degree of ethnic diversity. There were Anglo-Americans (including Scots, Welsh, and Scotch-Irish), Negro slaves, Dutch, German, Jews, French, Irish, and many more. "We can detect, if not nations in the America of 1787, quasi-nations. But nowhere was a concentration or a quasi-nation within a state of the U.S. so great that it could raise the fear, in the minds of the Founding Fathers or their successors, that parts of the union would break away or demand greater autonomy because of a distinctive religious, racial, or ethnic group concentration."[28] Therefore, "the careful delineation of the powers and roles of the states in the Constitution had no bearing on the question of the autonomy of religious, racial, or ethnic groups."[29] Thus, "[i]n the absence of ethnic and racial concentrations dominating one or more states ... it became difficult for most groups to envisage claims to national rights – for example, the right to use their language in a state's government, or to establish institutions reflecting their distinctive ethnic culture, or to secede."[30] Nathan Glazer cites four important exceptions to "this general picture of the establishment of ethnic groups through immigration, broadly distributed throughout the U.S., and without opportunity to claim national rights on the grounds of settlement before the establishment of the authority of the U.S."[31] These are: the Spanish-speaking population of the Southwest, black slaves concentrated in the Southern states, the Native Americans, and PR. "If Puerto Rico were to become a state it would break the general pattern. This would have to be a Spanish-speaking state. It would be inhabited almost entirely by a single ethnic group. There would be little likelihood once it became a state that its dominant population would be diluted much by migrants from other parts of the U.S. ..."[32]

Thus, in view of this historic evolution of ethnic relations and territory in the USA, federalism there has aimed to "consolidate, then expand, a new country and to protect the equal rights of individuals within a common national community, not to recognize the rights of national minorities to self-government."[33] Moreover, in the USA, "decisions about state borders, or about when to admit territories or states, have been explicitly made with the aim of ensuring that there will be an anglophone majority. States in the American South-West and Hawaii [and Alaska] were only offered statehood when the national minorities residing in those areas were outnumbered by settlers and immigrants."[34] Ultimately, Paul Gewirtz's analysis of the substantive principles of federalism concluded that the State of PR could have Spanish as co-official language. Moreover, he defended the historical record with respect to language restrictions in the cases of Louisiana and New Mexico.[35] However, other distinguished scholars have offered a less optimistic view of the historical record. Trías Monge wrote that when Louisiana was admitted as the 18th state in 1812, the enabling act required that judicial and legislative proceedings be conducted in English. In the case of New Mexico and Arizona, Congress went further and insisted that school instruction be conducted in English. Oklahoma was admitted to statehood in 1906, but with the condition that instruction in the public schools "shall always be conducted in English."[36]

## Political culture in the USA and national pluralism

Political culture has been defined by Sidney Verba as "the system of empirical beliefs, expressive symbols, and values which defines the situation in which political action takes place."[37] Although framed within the limitations of modernization theory (Goldfarb 2012: 22), Almond and Verba's definition remains a classic: "the term political culture ... refers to the specifically political orientations – attitudes toward the political system and its various parts, and attitudes toward the role of the self in the system" (Almond & Verba 1963: 13). The traditions and ideologies that have influenced a country's political culture – with respect to the tolerance for cultural, ethnic, national, and linguistic diversity – may influence the degree to which a state may be able to accommodate national pluralism. With respect to the USA, we should underscore the fact that US politics is "best seen as expressing the interaction of multiple political traditions, including liberalism, republicanism, and ascriptive forms of Americanism, which have collectively comprised American political culture, without any constituting it as a whole."[38] In opposition to the Tocquevillian-Hartzian thesis of Lockean liberalism's hegemonic role in US political culture, the "multiple traditions thesis holds that Americans share a common culture but one more complexly and multiply constituted than is usually acknowledged ... [The thesis] holds that the definitive feature of American political culture has not been its liberal, republican, or 'ascriptive Americanist' elements but, rather this more complex pattern of apparently inconsistent combinations of traditions, accompanied by recurring conflicts."[39] It follows that purely liberal and republican conceptions of civic identity are often unsatisfying to many in the USA. It has also been typical, and not unusual, for US institutions to embody strikingly opposed principles. In addition, when older types of ascriptive inequalities have been rejected as illiberal, typically, new forms of hierarchical subordination have been adopted. One instance of the contradictory combination of traditions that has characterized US political culture – which is pertinent for our purposes – is the special status developed for Puerto Ricans between 1898 and 1917, and thereafter. The syncretism of their political and civil status "did not fully satisfy either those who believed that all U.S. citizens should have equal rights or those who thought that inferior races should be denied citizenship."[40] The multiple-traditions thesis highlights the fact that nativist and racist ideologies have not just been occasional occurrences in US politics. Building on, but going beyond John Higham's work, the thesis sees "American nativism as a species of modern nationalism."[41] Higham writes that "the concept that the United States belongs in some special sense to the Anglo-Saxon 'race' offered an interpretation of the source of national greatness. The idea crystallized in the early 19th century as a way of defining nationality in a positive sense ... [Thus, in fact] Anglo-Saxonism gave only the slightest inkling of its nativistic potentialities until the late 19th century."[42] By the 1890s, nativists "repeatedly championed the values of nationalism in a very conscious explicit way ....They pleaded for a reawakened sense of nationality. Sometimes in place of any specific accusation against the newcomers, they argued simply that a great nation requires a homogeneous people."[43] In the USA, minorities that have tried to maintain their sense of worth as a distinct people and as a culture have not been accepted as equals by the larger society. As Kenneth Karst puts it, "the history of discrimination by culturally dominant Americans against people they see as cultural outsiders provides one cautionary tale after another."[44] If, according to the multiple traditions thesis, nativist, xenophobic, and racist ideologies – such as those explored by Higham – have been an important tradition in US political culture, it would seem that such ideologies are also bound to influence political development in the USA, and, in particular, the degree to which the USA is prepared to accommodate a stateless nation with a distinctive societal culture. These elements in the political culture of the USA have not facilitated the equal and fair treatment of ethnic and racial minorities. Thus, it would be even more difficult to convince the mainstream population to accept a minority that has nation-like characteristics, with a distinctive language and societal culture, the symbols of nationhood, and a clearly bounded territory, in particular if it were to seek accommodation within the USA as a unit of the federation.

Furthermore, in federations such as the USA, the public attitudes that help to create and maintain a federal polity are very important. Thus, a "federal political culture" must be shared widely by the citizens of a federal polity. As Elazar has noted, "there is no federal system that is commonly viewed as successful ... whose people do not think federal, that does not have a federal political culture and a strong will to use federal principles and arrangements" (cited in Kincaid & Cole 2010: 67). Also, a federal society is "'a means to accommodate diversity as a legitimate element in the polity,' and 'uniformity is antithetical to federalism'" (cited in Kincaid & Cole 2010: 67). The USA, despite a tendency to centralization in recent decades, continues to have a robust federal political culture when compared to other federations such as Canada and Mexico. More than half of respondents in a study of the US federal political culture indicated they "did not believe that a homogeneous country is preferable to a heterogeneous country," in a study comparing Canada, Mexico, and the USA (Kincaid & Cole 2010: 68). Furthermore, when a question was posed about whether "a country in which everyone speaks the same language is preferable," 14.1% of the US respondents answered "strongly agree," 24.6% indicated "somewhat agree," 22% said "somewhat disagree," 34.4% answered "strongly disagree," and 4.8% answered "don't know." On this score, the robustness of the federal political culture in the USA is a positive element that may facilitate the accommodation of PR within the US federal political system.

## National Identity, language, and nationalism in the United States

"The mechanisms for the promotion, reproduction, and expression of majority nationalism in Western states are diverse. Nevertheless, it is possible to distinguish broad categories: educations systems ... political practices, traditions, and institutions; and the use of myths and symbols" (Gagnon et al. 2011: 11). Majority nationalism (or state nationalism) is rooted in history and in the state-building processes in the Americas and in Europe in the 18th and 19th centuries. It expresses itself in the contemporary period through active nation building ... as in more routine expressions of national identity," often through the creation of symbols and narratives (Gagnon et al. 2011: 11). In the USA, as in other multicultural societies, one racial, linguistic, and ethnic group "constitutes the nation's ethnic core because of its historical role in creating the state, its numerical preponderance, or its political and cultural dominance. In the USA, of course, whites of European ancestry have traditionally represented that ethnic core. For this group, nation and ethnic group may be perceptually fused ..." (Citrin & Sears 2009: 167). This is the *Staatsvolk* of the United States (McGarry & O'Leary 2007: 197).[45] This ethnic core of the US polity is also the prime social locus for majority nation nationalism.

Measuring and evaluating the content of national identities through surveys is challenging, given that the meaning of such identities may itself be contested. Nevertheless, surveys are a common method, but may be used in conjunction with other methods, such as analyzing "the statements of political leaders, founding documents, laws, literature, and the impressions of commentators such as de Tocqueville ..." (Citrin & Sears 2009: 154). There is a rich empirical literature on US national identity, which has multiplied in recent years. One study of identity choice found that "80 percent of respondents in the pooled 1994, 1995, and 1997 surveys chose the 'just an American' identity over the 'mainly ethnic' responses. In the public as a whole, then, American national identity rather than membership in an ethnic subgroup is the dominant choice for self-categorization" (Citrin & Sears 2009: 156). With respect to patriotism in the USA, or the emotional attachment to the nation:

> the evidence of pervasive patriotism and emotional attachment to symbols of nationhood is overwhelming. In the 2002 American National Election Study, 91 percent of the sample said their love for the United States was either "extremely" or "very strong", and a slightly lower proportion, 85 percent, said they felt extremely or very proud when they saw the American flag. (Citrin & Sears 2009: 156; See also Huddy & Khatib 2007)

"'Ethnocultural' conceptions of U.S. identity are associated with nativism and ethnic prejudice, as well as a more general preference for cultural homogeneity rather than diversity" (Citrin et al. 2012: 471). A recent expression of an ethnocultural national identity in the USA may be the rise of the Official English movement. This controversial movement proposes a view about the normative content of US national identity; i.e., the criteria that define membership in the nation. It is about how much diversity the USA can tolerate, and about whether cultural pluralism should extend to language.[46] By April 1998, half of the states belonging to the Union had enacted Official English statutes or amendments to their Constitutions. With the Official English movement, language in the United States has become a paramount symbol of integral, ethnically tinted nationalism.[47] According to a recent study, 97% of respondents stated that speaking English was a very important trait in US national identity (Citrin & Wright 2009). Another study concluded that speaking English was widely seen as a constitutive norm of US national identity, with 71% of respondents stating that English was a "very important" component of US identity (Schildkraut 2007: 603). The combination of ethnic heterogeneity and linguistic homogeneity distinguishes the US experience with diversity and identity (Citrin et al. 2007: 35). Indeed, "knowing English is a powerful symbol of 'true' Americanism among most social and political groups" (Citrin et al. 1994: 19). Following Samuel Huntington, some have reified US culture as "English-speaking, Anglo, and Protestant" (Fraga & Segura 2006: 285).

These conceptions of US nationhood would clearly be recalcitrant to accommodating PR's societal culture. At the hearings before the US Senate Committee on Energy and Natural Resources in 1989 regarding Senate Bills 710–12 – providing for a Congress-sponsored plebiscite in PR – the US English representative testified that "the Federal Government in PR functions in English and it will continue to function in English. Therefore, any discussion of statehood must include a recognition that English is essential."[48]

## Conclusion: varieties of territorial pluralism

We have argued that territorial pluralism would be the most appropriate constitutional strategy of accommodation in the case of PR, within the US federal political system. Among the varieties of territorial pluralism available, there is the present "unincorporated territory" autonomy, a non-subordinate form of autonomism that we can label "Enhanced Commonwealth," and becoming a state of the federation. It would seem, however, that the US Constitution allows unambiguously for three options: independence,[49] becoming a unit of the federation, or the current "unincorporated territory" status. According to the DOJ, most "Enhanced Commonwealth" proposals are not constitutionally viable, and, in addition, many in PR find the current "unincorporated territory" status unsatisfactory (including many autonomists).

With respect to whether PR could be accommodated as a constituent unit of the federation, the social diversity thesis of state politics in the USA argues that the ethnic/racial composition of the states has a major impact on state politics and policies.[50] Mixtures or cleavages of various minority and/or racial/ethnic groups within a state – the types and levels of social diversity or complexity – are critical in understanding the politics and policies in the states."[51] States fall into three groups, relative to their racial/ethnic patterns: homogeneous, heterogeneous, or bifurcated. Homogenous states have populations that are primarily white or Anglo; i.e. of northern and western European descent. They also have very small minority (black and Latino) populations and relatively few white ethnics. If PR were to become a state, it would be the first Latin American homogeneous state, and with a distinct sense of collective self-identity as a nation. This chapter has provided an answer to the question of whether the USA could accommodate such a state. Senate Bill 710, considered in Congress in 1989, provided for the following in its definition of statehood: "The Commonwealth of Puerto Rico would be assured of its reserved state right under the Constitution to continue to maintain both Spanish and English as its official languages, as well as its right to preserve and enhance its particular cultural characteristics."[52] The Bill died in Committee in 1991. "Seven Republicans and three Democrats voted against the bill because of objections to statehood."[53] Clearly, economic considerations may have also weighed on these Congresspersons' minds, but, in general, it is also true that some "oppose offering statehood to PR precisely on the grounds that it will never have an Anglophone majority."[54]

Thus, the representatives of the people of the USA in Congress – in their pronouncements from 1989–90 and from 1997–98 regarding the political status options of PR – have been doubtful about whether the USA can accommodate PR as a state, in a non-subordinate relationship with the federal government. Stateless nations, such as the Catalans and the Quebecois, typically seek to promote and preserve their language and culture (in all its manifestations) and may seek to challenge centralized federal systems by demanding broad powers in the areas of communications, social services, regional development, and immigration. Ultimately, they seek formal recognition from the central state of their special status as a distinct society. There is no precedent in the USA for this kind of recognition of a state's special status, and the doubtfulness expressed by many Congresspersons in recent years seems to echo this historical fact. Our analysis of the USA above has, on balance, yielded a conclusion that coincides with many Congresspersons' assessment. The nativist, racist, and xenophobic elements of political culture in the USA do not facilitate the recognition of stateless nations. Similarly, neither do the predominant conceptions of national identity in the USA. Importantly, neither does the US model of federalism and its paradigmatic status as the quintessential "national federation." On the other hand, the fact that the USA has a robust federal political culture and that there is a secure and clear *Staatsvolk* may offer some encouragement to PR's federalists and mainstream autonomists (see Endnote 45). Yet, on balance, one would have to conclude that PR is unlikely to be accommodated as a substate national society within the USA's federal political system in a non-subordinate relationship.

## Notes

1. "Substate national societies" are historically settled, territorially concentrated peoples, with distinctive socio-linguistic traits whose territory has become incorporated into a larger state, and which have developed national consciousness. The incorporation of such societies has in some cases been through imperial domination and colonization, military conquest, or the cession of the territory by an imperial metropolis, but in some cases reflect a voluntary pact of association. These are also known as "stateless nations," "internal nations," "minority nations," or "national minorities." Such groups include the Quebecois and Puerto Ricans (in Puerto Rico) in the Americas, and the Flemish, Catalans, and Basques in Europe.
2. (Kymlicka 1995: 79).
3. Ibid.: 82–4.

40  *Jaime Lluch*

4. Ibid.: 96–7.
5. (Trías Monge 1997: 183).
6. Ibid.: 184–85.
7. Trías Monge 1997: 134.
8. Hearings 9 March 1990, 876–77.
9. Hearings 19 March 1997, 55.
10. Statement of Senator Ron Wyden, Energy and Natural Resources Committee SD-366, U.S. Senate, 1 August 2013.
11. *Nat'l Bank v. County of Yankton*, 101 U.S. 129, 133 (1880).
12. *Balzac v. Porto Rico*, 258 U.S. 298, 312–13 (1922).
13. See *Boumediene v. Bush*, 128 S. Ct. at 2255 (2008) ("century old doctrine [of the Insular Cases] informs our analysis in the present matter").
14. (Cabranes 1978: 80).
15. As has been inaccurately reported in some sources ( Benedikter 2007; Keating 2009; Lawson & Sloane 2009).
16. Statement of Senator Ron Wyden, Energy and Natural Resources Committee SD-366, U.S. Senate, 1 August 2013.
17. Also referred to as a form of autonomism that is not subject to the Territory Clause, and, hence "non-territorial."
18. Some of them are members of the Partido Popular Democrático.
19. (Wildavsky 1998: 88).
20. (Leach 1970: 5).
21. Ibid.: 9.
22. Ibid.: 39.
23. Ibid.: 40.
24. (Glazer 1989: 61).
25. Hearings June 1, 2, 1989: 340–41.
26. Hearings June 1, 2, 1989: 343.
27. (Martin Lipset 1990: 198).
28. (Glazer 1989: 63).
29. Ibid.
30. (Glazer 1977: 73).
31. Ibid.
32. Ibid.: 76.
33. (Kymlicka 1998: 137).
34. (Kymlicka 1995: 112).
35. (Hearings 1989: 347).
36. (Trías Monge 1997: 185).
37. (Kincaid 1982: 5).
38. (Smith 1993: 550).
39. Ibid.: 558.
40. Ibid.: 560.
41. Ibid.: 555.
42. (Higham 1994: 9).
43. Ibid.: 74–5.
44. (Karst 1989: 99).
45. Note that O'Leary argues that a *Staatsvolk*, with a clear demographic majority, may feel secure in its status and thus make concessions in a multinational federation (McGarry & O'Leary 2007: 198). Given the solid majority

that the core ethnic group in the US represents, this may increase the chances of accommodating PR. However, there is now the Hispanic demographic challenge to the US *Staatsvolk*, and its true repercussions remain to be seen (Citrin et al. 2007: 35).
46. (Crawford 1992: 87).
47. (Reiterer 1998: 107–8).
48. Hearings 11,13,14 July 1989: 366.
49. Or a genuine free-association status.
50. (Hero 1998: 3).
51. Ibid.: 6.
52. (Hearings 1–2 June 1989: 9). From the Puerto Ricans' perspective, even if PR were a state with two official languages, one additional concern would be how to avoid *diglossia*. Sociolinguists use this term to refer to a non-symmetric bilingual condition, where matters of importance are the reserve of the "high" language, while matters of affection, or private affairs, are discussed in a "low" language. With the passage of time and further assimilation, diglossia could become the norm, and eventually English-language hegemony could be established in PR. See (Laitin 1989: 309).
53. (Trias Monge 1997: 134).
54. (Kymlicka 1995: 112; Glazer 1977: 76).

# References

Agranoff, Robert and Ramos, J. (1997). "Toward Federal Democracy in Spain: An Examination of Intergovernmental Relations", *Publius* Vol. 7 (Fall ), pp. 23–45.
Aleinikoff, Alexander. (2002). *Semblances of Sovereignty: The Constitution, the State, and American Citizenship* (Cambridge: Harvard University Press).
Benedikter, Thomas. (2007). *The World's Working Regional Autonomies: An Introduction and Comparative Analysis* (New Delhi: New York: Anthem Press).
Boucher, Marc. (1997). "The Struggle to Save Canada: A Quebec Perspective", *Orbis* Vol. 41 (Summer), pp. 56–89.
Bru de Sala and Tusell. (eds) (1998). *Espana-Catalunya: Un Dialogo con Futuro* (Barcelona: Planeta).
Burnett, Christina Duffy and Burke Marshall. (eds) (2001). *Puerto Rico, American Expansion, and the Constitution* (Durham: Duke University Press).
Cabranes, Jose. (1978–79). "Puerto Rico Out of the Colonial Closet", *Foreign Policy* Vol. 33 (Winter), pp. 90–112.
Carr, Raymond. (1984). *Puerto Rico: A Colonial Experiment* (New York: Vintage).
Chambers, Simone. (1998). "Contract or Conversation: Theoretical Lessons from the Canadian Constitutional Crisis", *Politics and Society* Vol. 26 (March), pp. 111–130.
Citrin, Jack, Ernst B. Haas, Christopher Muste, Beth Reingold. (March 1994). "Is American Nationalism Changing? Implications for Foreign Policy," *International Studies Quarterly* Vol. 38, No. 1, pp. 1–31.
Citrin, Jack, Amy Lerman, Michael Murakami, and Kathryn Pearson. (2007). "Testing Huntington: Is Hispanic Immigration a Threat to American Identity?" *Perspectives on Politics* Vol. 5, No. 1, pp. 230–245.
Citrin, Jack and David O. Sears. (2009). "Balancing National and Ethnic Identities: The Psychology of E Pluribus Unum," in R. Abdelal, Y.M. Herrera,

A.I. Johnston, and R. McDermott (eds), *Measuring Identity: A Guide for Social Scientists* (Cambridge University Press).

Citrin, Jack, Matthew Wright. (2009). "Defining the Circle of We: American Identity and Immigration Policy," *The Forum* Vol. 7, No. 3, Article 6, pp. 23–45.

Citrin, Jack, Matthew Wright, and Jonathan Wand. (2012). "Affirmative Measures of American National Identity: Implications for the Civic-Ethnic Distinction," *Political Psychology* Vol. 33, No. 4.

Crawford, James (ed.). (1992). *Language Loyalties* (Chicago: University of Chicago Press).

Fraga, Luis and Gary M. Segura. (July 2006). "Culture Clash? Contesting Notions of American Identity and the Effects of Latin American Immigration," *Perspectives on Politics* Vol. 4, No. 2, pp. 34–70.

Gagnon, Alain, Andre Lecours, Genevieve Nootens (eds). (2011). *Contemporary Majority Nationalism* (Montreal: McGill-Queen's University Press).

Glazer, Nathan. (1977). "Federalism and Ethnicity: The Experience of the U.S.", *Publius* Vol. 7 (Fall), pp. 112–145.

Glazer, Nathan. (1989). "The Constitution and American Diversity" in R. Goldwin (ed.), *Forging Unity Out of Diversity* (Washington, DC: American Enterprise Institute).

Goldfarb, Jeffrey. (2012). *Reinventing Political Culture: The Power of Culture Versus the Culture of Power* (Cambridge: Polity Press), pp. 67–82.

Greenfeld, Liah. (1997). "The Origins and Nature of American Nationalism in Comparative Perspective," in K. Krakau(ed.), *The American Nation-National Identity-Nationalism* (Munster: Lit Verlag).

Gibernau, Montserrat. (1997). "Nations without States: Catalonia", in M. Guibernau and J. Rex. (eds), *The Ethnicity Reader* (London: Routledge). pp. 67–82.

Handler, Richard. (1988). *Nationalism and the Politics of Culture in Quebec* (Madison: The University of Wisconsin Press).

Hearings, Committee on Interior and Insular Affairs, House of Representatives, 28 June 1990 (Washington, DC: U.S. Government Printing Office).

Hearings, Committee on Interior and Insular Affairs, House of Representatives, 9 March 1990 (Washington, DC: U.S. Government Printing Office).

Hearings, Committee on Energy and Natural Resources, US Senate, 11, 13, 14 July 1990 (Washington, DC: U.S. Government Printing Office).

Hearings, Committee on Energy and Natural Resources, US Senate, 1, 2 June 1989 (Washington, DC: U.S. Government Printing Office).

Hearings, Committee on Energy and Natural Resources, US Senate (testimony of Paul Gewirtz) 1, 2 June 1989 (Washington, DC: U.S. Government Printing Office).

Hearings, Committee on Resources, House of Representatives, 19 March 1997 (Washington, DC: U.S. Government Printing Office).

Hero, Rodney. (1998). *Faces of Inequality: Social Diversity in American Politics* (Oxford: Oxford University Press).

Higham, John. (1994). *Strangers in the Land: Patterns of American Nativisms, 1860–1920* (Rutgers: Rutgers University Press).

Hollinger, David. (1995). *Postethnic America: Beyond Multiculturalism* (New York: Basic Books).

Huddy, Leonie, Nadia Khatib. (January 2007). "American Patriotism, National Identity, and Political Involvement," *American Journal of Political Science* Vol. 51, No. 1, pp. 63–77.

Karst, Kenneth. (1989). *Belonging to America: Equal Citizenship and the Constitution* (New Haven: Yale University Press).
Keating, Michael. (2001). *Plurinational Democracy* (Oxford: Oxford University Press).
Kincaid, John (ed.). (1982). *Political Culture, Public Policy and the American States* (Philadelphia: ISHI).
Kincaid, John and Richard Cole. (2010). "Citizen Attitudes toward Issues of Federalism in Canada, Mexico and the United States," *Publius: the Journal of Federalism* Vol. 14, No. 1, pp. 53–75.
Kymlicka, Will. (1995). *Multicultural Citizenship* (Oxford: Oxford University Press).
Kymlicka, Will. (1998a). *Finding Our Way* (Oxford: Oxford University Press).
Kymlicka, Will. (1998b). "American Multiculturalism in the International Arena" *Dissent* Vol. 45 (Fall).
Laitin, David. (April 1989). "Linguistic Revival: Politics and Culture in Catalonia", *Comparative Studies in Society and History* Vol. 31, No. 2, pp. 297–317.
Lawson, Gary and Robert Sloane. (2009). "The Constitutionality of Decolonization by Associated Statehood: Puerto Rico's Legal Status Reconsidered," *Boston College Law Review* Vol. 50, pp. 201–237.
Leach, Richard. (1970). *American Federalism* (New York: Norton).
Levine, Marc. (1990). *The Reconquest of Montreal: Language Policy and Social Change in a Bilingual City* (Philadelphia: Temple University Press).
Lind, Michael. (1995). "Are We a Nation?", *Dissent* Vol. 42 (Summer), pp. 134–156.
Lind, Michael. (1995–96). "Prescriptions for a New National Democracy", *Political Science Quarterly* Vol. 110, No. 4, pp. 238–267.
Linteau, Paul Andre (ed.). (1991). *Quebec Since 1930* (Toronto: James Lorimer & Co).
Linz, Juan, Alfred Stepan, and Yogendra Yadav. (2011). *Crafting State Nations: India and other Multinational Democracies* (Baltimore: Johns Hopkins University Press).
Lluch, Jaime. (2010). "How Nationalism Evolves: Explaining the Establishment of New Varieties of Nationalism within the National Movements of Quebec and Catalonia", *Nationalities Papers: The Journal of Nationalism and Ethnicity* Vol. 38, No. 3, pp. 245–276.
Lluch, Jaime. (2012a). "Autonomism and Federalism", *Publius: the Journal of Federalism* Vol. 42, No. 1, Winter, pp. 334–365.
Lluch, Jaime. (2012b). "The Internal Variation in Substate National Movements and the Moral Polity of the Nationalist," *European Political Science Review* Vol. 4, No. 3, pp. 178–201.
Lluch, Jaime. (forthcoming). *Visions of Sovereignty: Nationalism and Accommodation in Multinational Democracies* (Philadelphia: University of Pennsylvania Press).
McGarry, John and Brendan O'Leary. (2007). "Federation and Managing Nations", in Michael Burgess and John Pinder (eds), *Multinational Federations* (London: Routledge).
McGarry, John, Brendan O'Leary, and Richard Simeon. (2008). "Integration or Accommodation? The enduring debate in conflict regulation," in Sujit Choudhry (ed.), *Constitutional Design for Divided Societies: Integration or Accommodation?* (Oxford: Oxford University Press).
McGilp, Ian. (1992). *The Distinct Society Clause and the Charter of Rights and Freedoms* (Ontario: Background Studies of the York University Constitutional Reform Project No. 2).

Martin Lipset, Seymour. (1996). *American Exceptionalism: A Double Edged Sword* (New York: Norton).
Martin Lipset, Seymour. (1990). *Continental Divide* (New York: Routledge).
Meeks, Eric. (2007). *Border Citizens: the Making of Indians, Mexicans, and Anglos in Arizona* (University of Texas Press).
Morris, Nancy. (1995). *Puerto Rico: Culture, Politics, and Identity* (Westport: Praeger).
Meeks, Wayne. (2007). *Border Citizens: The Making of Indians, Mexicans, and Anglos in Arizona* (University of Texas Press Press)
Nieves, Ramón Luis. (2009). *El ELA que Queremos: Preguntas y Respuestas sobre el Desarrollo del Estado Libre Asociado* (San Juan: Ediciones Puerto).
Nimni, Ephraim. (2011). "Stateless Nations in a World of Nation-States," in Karl Cordell and Stefan Wolff (eds), *Routledge Handbook of Ethnic Conflict* (London: Routledge).
O'Leary, Brendan, John McGarry, and Khalid Salih. (eds) (2005). *The Future of Kurdistan in Iraq* (Philadelphia: University of Pennsylvania Press).
(2005). *President's Task Force on Puerto Rico* (Washington DC: US Government Printing Office).
(2011). *President's Task Force on Puerto Rico*. (Washington DC: US Government Printing Office).
Ramírez Lavandero, Marcos. (1988). *Documents on the Constitutional Relationship of Puerto Rico and the United States* 3rd ed. (Washington, DC: Puerto Rico Federal Affairs Administration).
Reiterer, Albert. (1998). "Neonativism as Linguistic Nationalism", *Canadian Review of Studies in Nationalism* Vol. XXV, pp. 45–89.
Rezvani, David. (2007). "The Basis of Puerto Rico's Constitutional Status: Colony, Compact, or 'Federacy'?" *Political Science Quarterly* Vol. 122, No. 1, pp. 115–140, Spring.
Rivera Ramos, Efrén. (2001). *The Legal Construction of Identity* (Washington DC: APA Press)
Schildkraut, Deborah J. (August 2007). "Defining American Identity in the Twenty-First Century: How 'There' is There?" *The Journal of Politics* Vol. 69, No. 3, pp. 597–615.
Schlesinger, Arthur. (1992). *The Disuniting of America* (New York: Norton).
Shabad and Gunther. (July 1982). "Language, Nationalism, and Political Conflict in Spain", *Comparative Politics* Vol 19, No. 2, July 1982, pp. 134–178.
Smith, Rogers M. (June 1988). "The 'American Creed' and American Identity: The Limits of Liberal Citizenship in the U.S." *Western Political Quarterly* Vol. 41, No. 2, pp. 89–123.
Smith, Rogers M. (September 1993). "Beyond Tocqueville, Myrdal ,and Hartz: The Multiple Traditions in America", *American Political Science Review* Vol. 87, No. 3, pp. 234–269.
Suksi, Markku. (2012). "On the Relationship between Autonomy and Federalism in the Sub-State Space", in Gagnon and M. Keating (eds), *Autonomy: Imagining Democratic Alternatives in Complex Settings*. (Basingstoke: Palgrave Macmillan).
Takaki, Ronald. (November 1993). "Multiculturalism: Battleground or Meeting Ground", *Annals AAPSS* Vol. 530, pp. 56–90.
Tierney, Stephen. (2004). *Constitutional Law and National Pluralism* (Oxford: Oxford University Press).

Tierney, Stephen. (2007). "We the Peoples: Constituent Power and Constitutionalism in Plurinational States," in Neil Walker and Martin Loughlin (eds), *The Paradox of Constitutionalism*. (Oxford: Oxford University Press), pp. 229–247.

Tierney, Stephen. (2008). "Giving with one hand: Scottish devolution within a Unitary State," in Sujit Choudhry (ed.), *Constitutional Design for Divided Societies: Integration or Accommodation?*. (Oxford: Oxford University Press), pp. 141–172.

Trias Monge, Jose. (1997). *Puerto Rico: The Trials of the Oldest Colony in the World* (New Haven: Yale University Press).

Tusell, Javier. (1999). *Espana: Una Angustia Nacional* (Madrid: ESPASA).

Walker, Neil. (2008). "Taking Constitutionalism Beyond the State," *Political Studies* Vol. 56, pp. 519–543.

Watts, Ronald. (2008). *Comparing Federal Systems* 3rd ed. (Montréal: McGill-Queen's University Press).

Weller, Marc and Katherine Nobbs. (2010). *Asymmetric Autonomy and the Settlement of Ethnic Conflicts* (Philadelphia: University of Pennsylvania Press).

Wildavsky, Aaron. (1998). *Federalism and Political Culture* (New Brunswick, NJ: Transaction).

# 2
## (Mis)recognition in Catalunya and Quebec: The Politics of Judicial Containment

*Elisenda Casanas Adam and François Rocher*

The issue of recognition of diversity in multinational states means that, in certain exceptional circumstances, political debates are transported into the judicial arena. The courts are thus required to define and circumscribe the political developments that are most able to maintain political stability while containing, to a certain extent, pressures from minority nations. In doing so, not only do they contribute to refocusing the debate on the conditions of acceptability of the claims of these minorities, but they also present, in a generally coherent way, the manner in which the majority group perceives itself. The recent Spanish Constitutional Court decision of June 2010, regarding the constitutionality of the Catalan Statute of Autonomy of 2006, has generated a serious crisis in the constitutional accommodation of Catalunya within Spain. The impact of this decision and the debates that have followed echo the significance of and discussion surrounding the Canadian Supreme Court's decision on the Quebec secession reference in 1998, highlighting again the fundamental role of the Supreme/Constitutional Courts in the accommodation of national minorities in multinational polities.

In both the Spanish and Canadian decisions, the Supreme/Constitutional Court had to arbitrate between the contested interpretation of aspects of the constitutional framework which directly affected the position of Catalunya and Quebec within the wider state, and the content of the decisions, although adopted from a position of apparent neutrality, ultimately favored the state (majority nation) nationalism to the detriment of that of the substate (minority nationalism). Starting from some brief theoretical considerations, this chapter carries out a comparative analysis of these decisions, focusing on their background and political context; the approach adopted by the court and their content; and their consequences in both the legal and political spheres. Its aims therefore to gain a better understanding of both decisions and also to contribute to the general reflection on these issues.

In accordance with the framework laid out in the Introduction to this volume, we examine the interaction between constitutional law and substate and state nationalist politics in Canada (Quebec) and Spain (Catalunya). We are interested in constitutional law and the state strategies of accommodation it creates, but also in the interaction between minority and majority nationalisms in multinational democracies. Both Lopez Bofill and Argelaguet in this volume also examine recent developments in Catalunya, but our chapter is more explicitly comparative in its scope.

## Some theoretical considerations

Sometimes, political debates shift into the legal arena. Courts are then called on to resolve disputes which are, as a result, presented in a more formal, acceptable (and accepted) rhetoric, bringing in different and in appearance more reasonable actors (judges, lawyers, experts and witnesses), and decided on the basis of a strict interpretation of the law. In other words, the judicialization of a political conflict has the effect of depoliticizing it. This chapter seeks to challenge this statement. We believe that the different conceptions of the state and of the global political community, such as those present in a plurinational setting, have an impact on the way the constitution is interpreted. Obviously courts that are called on to resolve political disputes in the final instance (for example, the Spanish Constitutional Court and the Canadian Supreme Court) rarely decide on conflicts which challenge the symbolic, political and institutional foundations of the overall political community. But then from time to time they have to decide on matters which touch directly on the relations of power between the national majority and the minority nations. It is important therefore to distinguish between the types of decisions adopted by these courts. Indeed, a degree of conflict between both levels of government on the interpretation of the constitution is inherent to a federal/plurinational system, and one of the roles of the constitutional/supreme court in these systems is precisely to mediate between them. It is through the on-going resolution of what can be described as low-profile political conflicts (for example, on a specific competence heading) that a court can establish a balanced and systematic case law. However, when a court is presented with a conflict in which one of the parties challenges the constitutional framework itself, the court is forced to look outside its own previous case law to come up with a decision. Because of this, the decision is less predictable (the court has a wider margin), but the constitutional interpretations and expectations of the different parties are also more polarized.

In such cases where there is a challenge to the constitutional framework, the interpretation of the decisions adopted by courts must take into consideration the convergence of three elements. First, constitutional norms cannot be disassociated from social and political norms, because they themselves are the object of symbolic and institutional battles. In this respect, courts must guarantee the continuity of the political community as it is established in the constitution. Second, within this dynamic of continuity, courts must take into account the fact that their decisions will be read, interpreted and discussed by different audiences, located at the same time within the majority and minority nations. There is therefore a connection between political factors and legal decisions that rests on the necessary correlation between the expectations, ideas, and claims formulated in the political sphere and the judicial product emanating from the decisions of the courts. Third, courts are particularly sensitive to the reception of their decisions, both with regard to the effect that they may have on the political stability of the system, and to maintaining their own legitimacy as a neutral and non-political institution.

Taking these three factors into consideration allows us to understand decisions that touch directly on the interpretation of the constitution from the point of view of the function carried out by law, of the logic that presides over the elaboration of constitutional norms, and of their reception. Furthermore, within the dynamics of the relations between the majority and national minorities, decisions adopted by the courts that touch directly on the development of the political institutions that reflect this particular diversity must at the same time ensure the stability of the political system and not alter the dominance exercised by the majority over the national minorities, while ensuring that the latter will accept the choices imposed by the court.

It is thus important to remember here that constitutions respond to relatively uniform processes that reflect the need of all societies to give themselves a formal framework within which to operate. In this sense, Chris Thornhill highlights that "Constitutions perform functions of abstraction, generalization, depoliticization and positivization for the political power of a modern society" (2010: 52). By doing this, norms formulated through legal codes, the implicit or explicit definition of the legal community, and the institutional modes of operation that are established in these texts are not defined in an abstract manner, outside the political relations, but rather reflect the configuration of the power relations that have given rise to such institutional arrangements and the normative basis on which they rest. The transformation of this configuration gives rise, periodically, to more or less substantive (re)interpretations or amendments of the constitution.

Nonetheless, the legal field allows for the establishment of a certain distance between protagonists in a conflict by removing it from the strictly political space and, in doing so, reinforcing the autonomy of the judiciary (Bourdieu 1977, 2012: 14). The objective is to subject the conflict to a mediation, to an interpretation of the written norm and non-written conventions, even if it means that the mediators, namely the judges, develop or invent new interpretations of these norms in order to rationalize the conditions that must be followed and accepted to guarantee the stability and the renewal of the legal system (Ocqueteau & Soubiran-Paillet, 1996).

A second element must also be taken into consideration. If the legal field, and in particular the courts, allows for the depoliticization of conflicts by referring them to an abstract norm, judicial decisions must nonetheless be located within a historically foreseeable interpretative framework. While sometimes showing evidence of a great deal of creativity and inventiveness in their reasoning and in their references to previous decisions and their (re)interpretation of legal norms, judges ensure that their decisions respond at the same time to legal criteria and to social and political expectations. This, therefore, means that their decisions are subject to a double test. In the first instance, it would have to satisfy other actors in the legal field (other judges, the courts, the legislature, the administration, legal experts, academics and writers of legal doctrine). In the second instance, and more globally, it would also have to be seen as acceptable by the general public (parties, the media and the citizens in general) (Lajoie 1997: 54–55). Hence, social and political actors also share their views on the reasonableness, acceptability and fairness of the decision (Perelman 1978: 421). In the judicial decisions where a national minority is challenging some fundamental element of the constitutional framework, the court becomes the focus of enhanced legal scrutiny, and also receives wider public and media attention. It is in these cases that there is a much higher pressure on the court to resolve the issue in such a way as to guarantee social and political stability and to maintain its own legitimacy.

Courts are therefore sensitive to the expectations expressed by their different target audiences and their decisions take them first and foremost into consideration, together with the normative and factual context within which the conflict is located. In a political community characterized by the existence of a national majority and minority nations, we must then multiply these audiences, as the general expectations of those in the different groups can vary substantively. In claims which involve the institutional accommodation of national pluralism within the political system, the representatives of the national minorities will seek to obtain not only a symbolic recognition, but also the confirmation of their control over their policies or institutions without them being subordinated to, or undermined by, the central power. This allows us to better circumscribe the reasons invoked by the judges to support their decisions and the arguments put forward to persuade the different audiences. This approach allows for the integration of the purely legal aspects of judgments (the internal coherence in the light of existing doctrine) with the constraints resulting from the social and political norms that guarantee the credibility and legitimacy of the decision (Lajoie 1997: 134–36). The rational formalism of law, combined with the connection between the decision and the values, expectations, and interests of the different audiences, enjoys the symbolic efficiency of law and ensures its respect precisely because it is imposed as the determinant of "legality" (and, by opposition, of illegality) (Bourdieu 1986: 8–9).

In sum, the legitimacy of courts in such cases derives from a series of factors: the capacity to respond adequately (or to be perceived as an adequate response – which is not exactly the same thing), with the appearance of neutrality, to the immediate problems in the eyes of all audiences (Gibson 1998; Knopff et al. 2009; Radmilovic 2010: 846–47; Brouillet & Tanguay 2011: 136–40). If, occasionally, their decision cannot satisfy the majority, it is important that it can seem acceptable to the national minorities for the courts to be perceived as legitimate. In other words, minorities must be able to believe that their expectations and concerns are taken into account by the judicial system.

It is in this way that judicial decisions on the constitution, while having an important impact on the functioning of political institutions and, in particular, on the configuration of the political relations between the national majority and minorities, face a double challenge. On the one hand, they have to ensure the stability and continuity of the political system, while favoring its transformation so as to reflect the new equilibrium in the power relations between the groups. In this respect, they accommodate ideological and institutional mutations resulting from the reinterpretation of the constitution, but ensuring that these same mutations are respectful of the expectations and the norms of the majority group. These limits take the form of conditions to be respected (institutional constraints) and fix the contours of the rhetoric to be used (ideological constraints). These practical and ideological constraints are defined and imposed by the dominant group, constraints that we can refer to as conditional tolerance or as "politics of judicial containment," to the extent that they respond to the expectations of this audience which is particularly sensitive to maintaining its privileged position within the political community. On the other hand, the legitimacy of these constraints and limits imposed by the courts depends on their acceptance by the largest number possible within the different target audiences, including those of minority nations. It is in the light of these multiple factors that we will now move on to analyze the Spanish Constitutional Court's decision on the Catalan Statute of Autonomy (2010) and the Canadian Supreme Court's decision on the Quebec Secession reference (1998).

## The Spanish Constitutional Court's decision on the Catalan Statute of Autonomy

The coincidence in time of a left-wing coalition in government in Catalonia (PSC-ERC-ICV), favorable to increasing and improving the quality of its self-government, with Jose Zapatero's socialist party, more accommodating to nationalist demands, winning the Spanish general elections in 2004, led to the start of a process of reform of the 1979 Catalan Statute of Autonomy. The aims of this reform were, first, a maximum expansion of the self-government of Catalonia within the possibilities allowed by the constitutional framework, while at the same time resolving some of the deficiencies of the system, due to the lack of minimum consensus for an overall top-down constitutional reform. Some of the novelties included were the detailed delimitation of the competence categories and fields assumed by Catalonia, its representation in certain state bodies and institutions and in EU decision making, new provisions on its financing system and the judicial branch, and a new Charter of Rights. Second, the reforms also had the aim of securing a better recognition of the history and identity of Catalonia as a minority nation within the constitutional framework. Novelties from this perspective included references to Catalonia "a nation," to its "historical rights" and to its "national symbols," among others. The Catalan initiative was then followed by a wave of other Autonomous Communities not wanting to be left behind, and was described as a "second constitutive moment" for the Spanish "State of the Autonomies" (Estado de las Autonomias).

In accordance with the procedure for reform established in the Statute, the proposal was initially discussed and drafted in the Catalan Parliament. While it started with the participation of all the political parties with representation in Catalonia, the Partido Popular (PP) voted against the final draft, which was agreed on by 120 votes in favor and their 15 against (20 September 2005), considering it to be an "undercover reform of the Constitution." The draft proposal was then sent to the Spanish Parliament, where it required the support of both chambers (Congress and Senate) and an absolute majority in a final vote on the whole text in the Congress. A commission with equal members of the Catalan Parliament and the Congress negotiated an agreement on the new reforms, with one of the most contentious issues being the reference to Catalonia as a "nation" in the new text. The final revision as agreed included the reference in the preamble, stating that "In reflection of the feelings and wishes of the citizens of Catalonia, the Parliament of Catalonia has defined Catalonia as a nation by an ample majority." With this and other substantial amendments, the statute was enacted as state Organic Act (Ley Organica) with the support of all parties except again the PP, here the main opposition party at state level, and ERC, which abstained, arguing that the original Catalan proposal had been cut back too far. It was then submitted to referendum in Catalonia, with the ironic situation of only two parties campaigning for the "no" vote (PP and ERC) for completely opposing reasons. Notwithstanding this opposition, the new Statute was endorsed by the people of Catalonia (73.9 % of votes in favor and a participation of 49.4 %), and it entered into force on 18 June 2006.

As has been seen above, the PP had opposed the new Statute since the initial proposal left the Catalan Parliament and, once in force, they challenged it before the Spanish Constitutional Court for being in violation of the Constitution.[1] This challenge was particularly significant as, coming from one of the two main state-wide parties which represented a substantive majority of Spanish citizens. Two additional aspects of this challenge are worth noting: the first, the high number of provisions of the Statute they challenged, 187 out of 245; it wasn't so much a challenge to specific aspects but to the whole reform as such. As a result, one of the central elements to be resolved was what were the role and functions of the Statute within the State of the Autonomies, and how far could it go in the reform of the system. The extent of the challenge also sparked a debate on whether the Constitutional Court could (or should) actually review these negotiated reforms which had been agreed on by both orders of government and, in the case of Catalonia, had also been ratified by referendum (Fossas 2011). The second aspect worth noting is that the challenge included provisions that had been copied by other reformed Statutes and in certain cases put forward and endorsed by the PP itself. This led to the challenge being viewed as directed specifically at Catalonia, further increasing its surrounding controversy which continued during the whole proceedings.

The Court's decision, adopted on the 28 June 2010 (STC 31/2010), was much longer than its ordinary decisions, extending to nearly 500 pages. In order to respond to all the challenges, the Court set out an initial set of principles regarding the organization and functioning of the State of the Autonomies, on which it then based the analysis of the specific challenged provisions which it considered and decided on in turn. In resolving these challenges, the court was faced with the difficult task of reconciling the Statute, which had very strong support in Catalonia, with the opposition of a substantial part of the majority nation and of a minority within Catalonia itself. The attempt to find a balance between both sets of demands can be seen in the fact that it declared only 14 provisions (out of the 126 challenged) in violation of the Constitution. In this way, it gave recognition to the claims of Catalonia by "saving" the majority of the challenged provisions and leaving them in force. At the same time, and in response to the demands of the PP, it also put forward a more restrictive "constitutionally compatible interpretation" of 27 of the other challenged provisions, providing that they were not unconstitutional insofar as they were construed in the way stated by the Court. Such an extensive use of this technique is unusual and prompted some commentators to note that it converted the decision into a "handbook" for the interpretation and implementation of the Statute. The decision was also accompanied by five dissenting opinions, four from "conservative" judges, and one from a "progressive" and Catalan judge.

Despite it being included in the preamble, the Court agreed to analyze the compatibility with the Constitution of the reference to the Parliament of Catalonia having "defined Catalonia as a nation" because, as claimed by the applicants, it acknowledged that this had an interpretative value which was then projected on concepts and categories throughout the Statute. Fully aware that this was one of the most controversial aspects of the challenge, the Court began by restricting the scope of its considerations and declaring that: "In effect, one can speak of a nation as a cultural, historical, linguistic, sociological and even religious reality. But the nation that is of relevance here is only and exclusively the nation in a legal-constitutional sense" (STC 31/2010: par. 12). In this way, the Court tried to find a balance between both positions, accepting that Catalonia could be considered a nation in the wider sociological or political sense, and distinguishing this from the strict legal-constitutional sense. It then went on to state that, "in this (legal-constitutional) sense, the Constitution doesn't recognize any other than the Spanish nation" (STC 31/2010: par. 12). The Court also went further and specifically acknowledged that the pursuit of legal recognition of the national identity of the people of Catalonia was legitimate within the context of the democratic state established by the Constitution. It therefore noted that the Constitution allowed for:

> the defence of ideological conceptions which, based on a certain understanding of the social, cultural and political reality, aim to attain for a certain collectivity the condition of national community, even as a principle from which to attain the formation of a constitutionally legitimised will to ... translate that understanding into a legal reality. (STC 31/2010: par. 12)

However, according to the Court, this could only be done, "through the corresponding and inexcusable reform of the Constitution" (par. 12). On these grounds, the Court went on to declare that the judgment should state specifically that the reference to Catalonia as a "nation" in the preamble did not have any interpretative legal effect, and that this should apply to the rest of the provisions challenged.

Turning to the role and functions of the Statutes of Autonomy, the Court was also faced with the complex task of setting out an initial framework which would enable it to carry out a balanced review of the substantial reforms included in the Statute. For this, the Court drew selectively from its previous case law on the organization and functioning of the State of the Autonomies, allowing it to produce a tailored set of principles which it could at the same time present as a continuation of its existing understanding of the State of the Autonomies. The Court started from the basis that "Statutes of Autonomy are norms which are subordinated to the Constitution, as is the nature of provisions which are not the expression of a sovereign power, but of autonomy founded in and guaranteed by the Constitution for the exercise of legislative power in the framework of the Constitution itself" (STC 31/2010: par. 3). It made no reference, therefore, to them being the result of the "exercise of the right to autonomy by nationalities and regions," as provided by the Constitution (Article 2). The Court also seemed to be implying that the Statue was a norm that emanated exclusively from Catalonia rather than a norm that expressed, through a complex and negotiated procedure between both orders of government, the recognition and a specific configuration of its autonomy (Alberti 2010: 83).

Similarly, the Court refused to acknowledge the fundamental role of the Statutes of Autonomy in complementing the Constitution in the articulation of the State of the Autonomies, largely open and undefined, which was generally accepted to determine their unique position with regard to ordinary statutes. While noting that

> It is true that, in any legal system, there are norms apart from the Constitution, *strictu sensu*, carrying out functions in the legal system that can be qualified as materially constitutional, as they serve for ends that conceptually are understood as being within the domain of the first norm of any legal system.

It then went on to add that "this qualification has no wider reach than that that is purely doctrinal or academic. And ... in no case translates to an additional normative value than that which strictly corresponds to all norms located outside the formal constitution" (STC 31/2010: par. 3). In conclusion, the Court limited its characterization of the Statutes to the formal category through which they are given the final endorsement in the State Parliament: "Statutes of Autonomy are integrated in the system of norms as a specific type of state law: the organic law .... Their position in the system of legal sources is, therefore, that which is characteristic of organic laws" (par. 3). And disregarding their generally accepted function as the "basic institutional norms of the Autonomous Community" (Article 147 SC), it went on to define their first constitutional function as simply the "diversification of the legal system" (STC 31/2010: par. 4).

It was on the basis of this restrictive interpretation of the position and functions of the Statute of Autonomy that the Court then went on to review the challenged reforms. As seen above, the Court struck down 14 of the most conflictive provisions (Catalan language, human rights review, judicial branch, financial provisions), agreeing with the applicants that they were in violation of the Constitution, although they had been reviewed and accepted by constitutional experts at both levels during the enactment process. In the case of 27 others (plus 49 more which were discussed in its reasoning but not then included in the final part of the decision), it accepted their compatibility with the Constitution by construing them in such a way as to remove or avoid their more controversial aspects, despite their also having been the object of the above-mentioned scrutiny. In practice, this meant largely transforming their original meaning or depriving them of any binding legal effect, thus conferring absolute freedom on the state Parliament to decide whether or not to implement the new reforms (financing system, competence clauses, participation in state bodies and institutions, judicial branch, among others). Together with the rest of those challenged, the Court "saved the constitutionality" of these provisions, and therefore in principle largely left the statute in force. However, the result was a completely different statute from the one that had been initially enacted.

As has been seen above, while the Court presented its decision as balanced and fair, taking into consideration the demands of both the majority and minority, it largely "de-activated" the two main objectives of the reform put forward by Catalonia. By recognizing that Catalonia was a nation in a political or sociological sense, it refused to acknowledge that this could confer any additional rights or have any legal effects or recognition within the constitutional framework. In doing so, the Court actually disregarded the complex and ambiguous formula the Constitution itself uses to accommodate the plural nature of Spanish state, distinguishing between "nation," "nationalities" and " regions" (Article 2), which was the result of the delicate consensus reached by the drafters in 1978, and which has been largely undermined by the central authorities ever since. Further on in the decision, the Court referred to Catalonia as a "nationality," but made no attempt to define or characterize this term which was included specifically in the text in recognition of the special position of Catalonia, together with the Basque Country and Galicia, in the new constitutional settlement. With this approach, the Court missed a valuable opportunity to set out an authoritative interpretation of these provisions which could have allowed for an inclusive understanding of the constitutional framework in a way which accommodated both the minority and majority nations in recognition of the Spanish plurinational reality. The Court also made clear that any other understanding than the very restrictive one it put forward requires a reform of the Constitution and the attainment of the corresponding super-qualified majority in the Spanish Parliament, involving a process in which Catalonia has no direct participation.

In addition, while saving the constitutionality of many of the challenge provisions through the technique of "constitutional interpretation," the Court converted them into a set of general and redundant political recommendations, completely devaluating the Statute of Catalan Autonomy as a legal norm. This devaluation of the position and functions of the Statute of Autonomy within the constitutional system also resulted in a substantial restriction of the possibilities of participation or impact of Catalonia in the reform and development of its own self-government, and of the system more generally. As has been seen, it is through their role in the initial proposal and their on-going engagement in the enactment and reform of their statute that the Autonomous Communities can contribute to the definition and evolution of the State of the Autonomies, within a very open constitutional framework. On the other hand, they have no direct participation in the reform of the Constitution itself, which also requires a super-qualified majority at the central level. In sum, the message put forward by the Court in this decision was clear: any substantial amendment or development of the State of the Autonomies requires a top-down reform of the Constitution, and until that happens it will not accept to be bound by new interpretations of the provisions regarding the territorial organization of the state, even if they have been enacted in compliance with all the requirements for a bottom-up reform of a Statute of Autonomy. Finally, by de-activating many of the new reforms, in defiance of both the Catalan and state Parliamentary majorities and amidst challenges to its legitimacy to review the Statute, the Court also clearly asserted and reinforced its own position as the final and ultimate interpreter of the Constitution within the system.

The reaction against the Court's decision in Catalonia was unprecedented. In response to initial leaked drafts, 12 Catalan newspapers published a joint editorial in defence of the Statute ("The Dignity of Catalonia"). Days after it was finally published, a massive protest march was held in Barcelona with the slogan "We are a nation, we decide," organized by civil society organizations and with the support of all the Catalan political parties with the exception of the PP and the minority party "Ciutadans." This slogan was a direct response to the Court's statement that "there is no other nation than the Spanish nation," which was one of the ones that received most immediate publicity and largely became the focus for the long and complex decision. The march was headed by the six presidents and ex-presidents of the Catalan Government and Parliament and was attended by a million people. Academic reaction was also immediate, with strong criticism directed not only at the content of the decision, but also at its tone and its lack of clear reasoning (see, in particular, contributions in Bernadi et al.

2010 and Institut d'Estudis Autonomics 2011). In addition, specialist commentaries stressed that it departed from much of its previous case law without clearly acknowledging the fact (Alberti 2010; Fossas 2010). The Court itself was also accused of assuming the role of "prorogued constituent power," and therefore of breaching its constitutional limits (Viver 2011).

At the central state level, the PP largely considered the decision a victory, although some of its members declared it to have been too soft on the Statute and would have liked more of its provisions to be stuck down. The Socialist Party in Government tried to present it as a "balanced decision," and focused its efforts on requesting respect for the Court. Academic commentaries in the rest of Spain also mostly regarded the decision as fair, with some notable exceptions and notwithstanding specific criticism of some of the reasoning or more technical aspects, and this seems to be the general impression that was transmitted to the international sphere (Alvarez and Tur 2010; Diaz 2011). Overall, it can be said that that after years of uncertainty and on-going controversy surrounding the decision, certain normality was restored after it was finally published. Even in Catalonia, although political institutions remained fiercely critical of the decision and the Court, they continued to bring challenges to state statutes before it, highlighting therefore that they still had an expectation that it would respond to their demands. The challenged Statute of Autonomy itself also remained largely in force, and the decision did not have an immediate substantial effect on most of the implementation that was being carried out.

However, this was not the end of the matter. What had without doubt been the biggest crisis of the State of the Autonomies since its establishment in 1978, was followed by a change in the governing parties at both levels, with the more conservative CiU gaining power in the Generalitat (November 2010) and the Partido Popular (November 2011) in the central government. Within the Statutory framework resulting from the Court's decision, CiU continued trying to negotiate a better constitutional accommodation of Catalonia until the celebration of the *Diada* (the national holiday of Catalonia, which commemorates the fight for Barcelona in 1714), on 11 September 2012, when one-and-a-half-million Catalan citizens came out in a march in favor of independence. This led to the holding of new elections and to a new Parliamentary majority, again led by CiU, in favor of holding a referendum on independence and leading the process of national transition to the Catalans' "own state." The first step in this process was the adoption of a "Declaration of Sovereignty and Right to Decide of the People of Catalonia" by the Catalan Parliament, in defiance of the Spanish Government's refusal to even discuss the holding of a referendum. The preamble of the Declaration refers to drawbacks and refusals imposed by the institutions of the Spanish state on measures to transform the political and legal framework, "among which Sentence 31/2010 passed by the Spanish Constitutional Court deserves particular emphasis." More than two years after it was finally adopted, the Court's decision is still at the centre of the conflict between the Catalan authorities and the central state.

## The Supreme Court of Canada's reference on Quebec's secession

Quebec has held two referendums on independence. The first was on 20 May 1980 after the Parti Québécois (PQ) came to power in 1976. The results were unequivocal: 59.56% of voters responded no to a particularly long question, not on independence but on the attainment of a mandate to negotiate a new political arrangement qualified, in brackets, as sovereignty.[2]

The first referendum defeat was followed by major constitutional amendments to the federal framework in 1982: adoption of procedures of constitutional amendment, as previously these were carried out by the British Government – the British North America Act was an imperial law of 1867; entrenchment of a Charter of rights and freedoms; recognition of the rights of aboriginal peoples and inclusion of the principle of distribution of wealth through the commitment to guaranteeing equalization payments. The Quebec National Assembly refused to sign the new Constitution that diminished its powers, most notably with regard to its linguistic regime. The PQ lost the elections in December 1985 and was replaced by the Parti libéral du Québec (or the Quebec Liberal Party), resolutely in favor of maintaining Quebec within Canada.

The PQ was elected again in September 1994 on the promise of holding of a new referendum on sovereignty. This was held on 30 October 1995. The question, a result of an agreement between three parties (two sovereigntist parties, the PQ and the Bloc Québécois, sitting in the federal Parliament; and an autonomist party, the Action démocratique du Québec), asked directly about the attainment of sovereignty without making it conditional on the conclusion of a partnership agreement.[3] A weak majority, that is 50.6 % of the Quebeckers, voted in favor of maintaining Quebec within Canada.

This tight victory of the no camp fuelled substantive criticism of the federal politicians' referendum strategy, principally voiced in English Canada. Most notably, they highlighted the fact that the referendum questions had been deliberately confusing and they had not been understood by a good number of citizens who believed that Quebec would remain a Canadian province even if they voted yes (Pinard 2000).

In September 1996, as part of what was described as the "Plan B" (a set of legal and political measures directed at avoiding a third referendum), the federal government submitted a reference to the Supreme Court of Canada. There is a procedure that allows the Prime Minister to invite the Governor in council to request the opinion of the Supreme Court of Canada (SCC) on an issue of law considered of importance. While this cannot be considered a decision of the Court, it produces the same effects. The Government therefore submitted three questions to the SCC, through the Order in Council P.C. 1996–1497 of 30 September 1996, on which it wished to obtain its opinion:

1. Under the Constitution of Canada, can the National Assembly, legislature or government of Quebec effect the secession of Quebec from Canada unilaterally?
2. Does international law give the National Assembly, legislature or government of Quebec the right to effect the secession of Quebec from Canada unilaterally? In this regard, is there a right to self-determination under international law that would give the National Assembly, legislature or government of Quebec the right to effect the secession of Quebec from Canada unilaterally?
3. In the event of a conflict between domestic and international law on the right of the National Assembly, legislature or government of Quebec to effect the secession of Quebec from Canada unilaterally, which would take precedence in Canada? (SCC 1998)

At the end of August 1998, the Supreme Court of Canada published its Quebec Secession Reference. To the question of whether Quebec had a right to unilateral secession under the Canadian Constitution, the Court said no. To the second question, the Court responded that because Quebec cannot be considered as being "subjugated," "dominated" or "exploited" within the Canadian political framework, which cannot be compared to a colonial empire, the Quebec government does not have a right to secession on the basis of international law. Having said this, the Court did not then need to respond to the third question posed by the Canadian Minister of Justice and Attorney General. In sum, to no-one's great surprise, the SCC considered that a unilateral declaration of independence could not be carried out in accordance with the provisions of the Canadian Constitution. The reasoning of the Court was therefore predictable. It reminded all parties that the constitutional provisions must be respected and, from this perspective, contributed to strengthening the Canadian political system. The Court indicated clearly that a unilateral withdrawal of Quebec from the Canadian federation would be illegal. If this opinion responded to the expectations of a large majority of Canadians from other provinces and of a significant proportion of Quebeckers who had voted no in 1980 and 1995, it also had to ensure that it would not be totally condemned by the Quebec nationalists who would have seen it as a form of imprisonment within Canada, an inability to leave or, at the same time, to make the system evolve.

The opinion therefore did not limit itself to responding to the questions posed by the Canadian Government. The SCC went further and sought to identify the conditions that would allow Quebec to secede in compliance with the Constitution. In order to do this, the Court had to first make use of notable creativity in structuring its reasoning around the norms and principles meant to clarify the understanding of the constitutional text. These fundamental constitutional principles, which were not to be taken in isolation, were: (a) federalism; (b) democracy; (c) constitutionalism and the primacy of law; and (d) the respect for minorities. While not included expressly in the constitution, "the principles dictate major elements of the architecture of the Constitution itself and are such as its lifeblood" (SCC 1998: par 51).

In this way, and in the light of these principles, the Court stated that

> [t]he Constitution is the expression of the sovereignty of the people of Canada. It lies within the power of the people of Canada, acting through their various governments duly elected and recognized under the Constitution, to effect whatever constitutional arrangements are desired within Canadian territory, including, should it be so desired, the secession of Quebec from Canada. (SCC 1998: par. 85)

In sum, if a unilateral secession is illegal, it can nevertheless be carried out through a process of negotiation. The novelty of the opinion is that it established an obligation to negotiate following a democratic expression of Quebec's desire for independence. By doing this, the Court subscribed to the idea that "the clear repudiation by the people of Quebec of the existing constitutional order would confer legitimacy on demands for secession" (SCC 1998: par. 88). Nevertheless, for the obligation of negotiation to arise, two other conditions must be met: "a clear majority of Quebeckers votes on a clear question in favour of secession" (SCC 1998: par. 148).

These negotiations, presented as inevitably difficult and with uncertain results, would have to take into account the interests of all parties (Canadian and Quebec governments, the other provinces and other participants) and would touch on complex issues. The Court listed what these would be on (regional and national economic interests, rights of the linguistic minorities and aboriginal peoples), without, however, being explicit on the content of the negotiations. Finally, the Court did not give an opinion on these issues and returned the debate to the political field. The process would have to be evaluated by the whole of the political actors that "would have the information and expertise to make the appropriate judgment as to the point at which, and circumstances in which, those ambiguities are resolved one way or the other" (SCC 1998: par. 100). It is therefore the political actors and not the voters who, in the final analysis, are the best placed to evaluate the divergent positions adopted by the parties in the negotiations.

One could ask how an opinion that authorizes the secession of Quebec can at the same time preserve the constitutional edifice and the rights and obligations of the national majority and not put into question the very existence of the overarching political community. From the point of view of the representation of the nation, the Supreme Court accomplished the *tour de force* of not denying the existence of a Quebec people while limiting their capacity to question the foundations of the Canadian political community.[4] Despite the judges refusing to pronounce themselves on the existence of a people – "[a]lthough much of the Quebec population certainly shares many of the characteristics of a people, it is not necessary to decide the 'people' issue" (SCC 1998: 7) – their statement of the circumstances that led to the creation of the Canadian federation implicitly recognized the plurality of peoples within Canada. The adoption of a federal structure illustrates the need to accommodate the constitutive diversity of the Canadian political community. It would be an exaggeration, however, to associate the reference to a single binational reading of Canada's political history (some do so, Millard 1999; Leclair 2000) because the creation of the Canadian federation also sought to preserve the culture and autonomy of the two maritime provinces which had been integrated into Canada (Nova Scotia and New Brunswick) (SCC 1998: par. 60).

Because of this recognition and acceptance of the Canadian constitutive diversity, it becomes extremely difficult to leave the overarching political community. The right to self-determination cannot be exercised except if a people are colonized or oppressed. Consequently, if they enjoy an internal autonomy and can proceed freely within this sphere, they cannot claim a right of secession in accordance with international law. In return, every state has a duty to preserve its territorial integrity (SCC 1998: 8). This cannot be broken on the basis of the principles of the primacy of law and of democracy, except if the citizens clearly express their will to do so in response to a clear question in the context of a referendum. But the relationship between the primacy of law (namely, the respect for the procedure of amendment of the constitution) and the principle of democracy is structured hierarchically in favor of the former. This is scarcely surprising, to the extent that the object of the reference, namely the constitutionality of a unilateral secession, directly challenges the integrity of the state and the continuity of the Constitution. Or, in other words, the mandate of the Court is to protect one and the other and, by doing so, to safeguard the reason for its own existence.

If the Supreme Court's reference imposes an obligation to negotiate, it does not facilitate, however, the process leading to the secession of Quebec. It is rather the opposite that seems to prevail in the light of the three major constraints that are spelled out in the opinion. Firstly, as we have highlighted above, Quebec cannot legally proceed unilaterally to its secession from Canada. The requirement of a clear majority to a clear question will result in no more than to force Canada to participate in a process of negotiation. Yet nowhere does the Court qualify this majority or specify how to determine the clarity of the question. It leaves the task of defining the parameters of this double requirement of certainty to the political actors, both of the majority and the national minority, after the fact. This confers a first veto right on the Canadian political authorities following a successful referendum. They can declare that the requirement of clarity has not been attained and that the negotiations should not be initiated. Secondly, if the first obstacle is overcome, the SCC was careful to note that the result of the negotiations should also be an agreement between the representatives of both legitimate majorities, "namely, the clear majority of the population of Quebec, and the clear majority of Canada as a whole, whatever that might be" (SCC 1998: par. 97). In other words, the reference explicitly accords a second veto right to the majority regarding the clearly expressed will of the minority in favor of secession: "Negotiations would need to address the interests of the other provinces, the federal government, Quebec and indeed the rights of all Canadians both within and outside Quebec, and specifically the rights of minorities. No one suggests that it would be an easy set of negotiations" (SCC 1998: par. 151). And if these necessarily difficult negotiations reach an impasse, the reference remains silent as to how to unblock it. In fact, the Court insists on the idea that, for it to be legal, a constitutional amendment would be required (SCC 1998 par. 97). Hence, if the two first obstacles are overcome (agreement on the clarity of the question and the results, and successful negotiations), the process leading to the secession of Quebec will have to be the object of a constitutional amendment. Taking into consideration the complexity of the issues raised, there is no doubt that the unanimous consent of the Canadian Parliament and of the legislative assemblies of each of the provinces would be required.

Despite the constraints imposed on the process of secession, the reference was very well received by a vast majority of commentators and political figures: Quebec's commentators and political actors focused on the obligation to negotiate after a victorious referendum and saw in the decision the recognition of the legitimacy of their claim; in English Canada, the emphasis was placed on the requirement for clarity and the incompatibility of a unilateral declaration of independence with the constitution (Mandel 1999; Rocher and Verrelli 2003; Tierney 2003). It therefore appeared as the result of a well-balanced reasoning. The Court had successfully manage to overcome the feat of declaring Quebec's unilateral secession illegal while opening the door to a process that could, theoretically, lead to its secession following negotiations carried out in good faith. Both audiences targeted by the reference could draw arguments from it that reinforced their position. The Court's status as arbiter was thus not challenged (Lajoie 2000).

Political observers focused especially on the political dimensions of the reference, namely the dimensions located within the logic of containment, rather than on the four principles on which the Court's reasoning was based. Moreover, the federal government made haste to follow up the provisions in the reference by adopting the Clarity Act in June 2000. While the reference remained vague regarding the political actor representing the Canadian majority, the federal government assumed that responsibility. In this sense, the preamble of the act states that "the House of Commons, as the only political institution elected to represent all Canadians, has an important role in identifying what constitutes a clear question and a clear majority sufficient for the Government of Canada to enter into negotiations in relation to the secession of a province from

Canada" (Canada 2000). The act itself does not then contain more than three articles. The first specifies that the Canadian government will give its opinion on the clarity of the question before the holding of a referendum on secession, then disqualifies specifically the questions posed in 1980 and 1995, and indicates that it will refuse to start negotiations if it considers the question to be ambiguous. The second article covers the power of the Canadian government to declare, after the holding of a referendum, if it considers the results to be sufficiently clear to begin negotiations (on the basis of the importance of the majority, the participation rate and of "any other matters or circumstances it considers to be relevant." Furthermore, if the negotiations are finally to take place, they must in particular relate to "the terms of secession that are relevant in the circumstances, including the division of assets and liabilities, any changes to the borders of the province, the rights, interests and territorial claims of the Aboriginal peoples of Canada, and the protection of minority rights" (Canada 2000). What must be retained from the above is that even if the Clarity Act is much more restrictive than what the secession reference permitted, in the sense that it opens the door to an arbitrary interpretation of the results of a future referendum depending on the political interests of the moment, it could not have been adopted if the Supreme Court had not legitimized the idea that it is fair and equitable that the citizens of Quebec should not be the only ones to decide on their future. More important still, while the reference reinforces the obligation of holding eventual negotiations on the basis of the democratic principle which requires a deliberation in good faith by all the political actors, the federal statute seeks to increase the margin of uncertainty by laying the ground for the federal government to set an exorbitantly high barrier before sitting down at the negotiating table (Perelman 1978).

## Conclusion

In both the Catalan Statute Decision and the Quebec Secession Reference, as has been seen, the courts were faced with resolving a political conflict between the majority and minority groups within a plurinational setting that required them to look outside their own existing case law to carry out a more developed and nuanced interpretation of the constitutional framework. The analysis of these cases confirms the main argument in this chapter and shows how the demands of both the majority and minority groups and the evolution of the power relations between them condition the interpretation of the constitutional framework by the courts and, at the same time, how the courts try and construct their decisions in such a way that they will be considered acceptable and legitimate by both groups. In order to do this, the courts were forced to be notably original and creative in drafting their opinions, with the Spanish Constitutional Court distinguishing between the political and legal concepts of "nation" and drawing selectively from its previous case law, and the Canadian Supreme Court going further than the specific questions it was asked and building on the fundamental principles of the Constitution. More importantly, while taking into consideration the demands of both groups and presenting the decision as fair and balanced, in each case the final result of the decision responds clearly to the expectations of the majority group and ensures the respect for the constraints in place to ensure the stability and continuation of the political system ("judicial containment"): in Spain, by "de-activating" many of the new reforms; and in Canada, by establishing very strict conditions for a possible secession.

As well as confirming the main argument put forward in this chapter, the comparative analysis of both cases also highlights a fundamental difference between them, which in turn has consequences for the longstanding effectiveness of the judicial containment carried by the courts. While in the Canadian case the Court succeeded in persuading both sets of audiences with its decision, in the Spanish case a majority of the audience in Catalonia considered the decision to favor the Spanish central level and to therefore contribute to oppression of Catalan expectations and demands. As a result, in Canada the "judicial containment" has been effective and longstanding, and the Supreme Court's decision has contributed to reinforcing the continuation and stability of the overall system and has been largely praised by legal specialists in Canada and elsewhere as a model of respect for democracy and national pluralism. However, in Spain, the "judicial containment" only had a limited and short-term effect of de-activating the controversial reforms and providing a provisional solution to the conflict between the majority in Catalonia and a significant number of the wider Spanish population. Despite the Catalan authorities strongly disagreeing with the decision, they were forced to accept it and comply with it as it had been adopted by the constitutional body established for the resolution of such conflicts, in accordance with constitutional procedures, and was therefore vested with the symbolic effectiveness of being the final word of the ultimate legal authority within the system. A refusal to do so would have resulted in a constitutional crisis. However, the long-term effect of the Constitutional Court's decision has been to further increase the instability of the system and the level of conflict between

Catalonia and the central authorities, as can be seen by the rise in support for independence in the region. Moreover, the decision has also affected the court's own legitimacy and perception of neutrality, and therefore has compromised its position to convincingly mediate in future conflicts between Catalonia and the central state. In the light of the recent "Declaration of Sovereignty," it seems that the full effects of this decision are still to be seen.

## Notes

1. The Statute was also challenged by the Spanish Ombudsman (Defensor del Pueblo) and five Autonomous Communities.
2. The question read as follows:

   The Government of Quebec has made public its proposal to negotiate a new agreement with the rest of Canada, based on the equality of nations; this agreement would enable Quebec to acquire the exclusive power to make its laws, levy its taxes and establish relations abroad – in other words, sovereignty – and at the same time to maintain with Canada an economic association including a common currency; any change in political status resulting from these negotiations will only be implemented with popular approval through another referendum; on these terms, do you give the Government of Quebec the mandate to negotiate the proposed agreement between Quebec and Canada?

3. The question was as follows: "Do you agree that Quebec should become sovereign after having made a formal offer to Canada for a new economic and political partnership within the scope of the bill respecting the future of Quebec and of the agreement signed on 12 June 1995?"
4. As the Court recalled:

   The federal-provincial division of powers was a legal recognition of the diversity that existed among the initial members of Confederation, and manifested a concern to accommodate that diversity within a single nation by granting significant powers to provincial governments. The Constitution Act, 1867 was an act of nation-building. It was the first step in the transition from colonies separately dependent on the Imperial Parliament for their governance to a unified and independent political state in which different peoples could resolve their disagreements and work together toward common goals and a common interest. Federalism was the political mechanism by which diversity could be reconciled with unity. (SCC 1998: par. 43)

## References

Alberti, Enoch. (2010). Concepto y función del Estatuto de Autonomía en la Sentencia 31/2010, de 28 de junio, sobre el Estatuto de Autonomía de Cataluña, Special issue of the *Revista catalana de dret public*, pp. 81–85.

Barceló, Merce, Bernadí, Xavier and Vintró, Joan. (coords) (2010). Especial Sentencia 31/2010 del Tribunal Constitucional, sobre el Estatuto de Autonomía de Cataluña de 2006, Special issue of the *Revista catalana de dret public*.
Bourdieu, Pierre. (1977). "Sur le pouvoir symbolique," *Annales. Économies, Sociétés, Civilisations*, 32: 3, mai–juin, pp. 405–411.
Bourdieu, Pierre. (1986). "La force du droit," *Actes de la recherche en sciences sociales*, 64, septembre, pp. 3–19.
Bourdieu, Pierre. (2012). *Sur l'État. Cours au Collège de France 1989–1992* (Paris: Seuil).
Brouillet, Eugénie and Yves Tanguay. (2011). "La légitimité de l'arbitrage constitutionnel en régime fédératif multinational. Le cas de la Cour suprême du Canada," in Michel Seymour and Guy Laforest (eds), *Le fédéralisme multinational. Un modèle viable?* (Bruxelles: P.I.E. Peter Lang), pp. 133–153.
Canada, *Clarity Act* S.C. 2000 c. 26.
Diaz, Francisco. (2011) "La tipología de los pronunciamientos en la STC 31/2010 y sus efectos sobre el Estatuto catalán y otras normas del ordenamiento vigente," Revista catalana de dret public Vol. 43, pp. 53–86.
Fossas, Enric. (2010). El Estatuto como norma y su función constitucional. Comentario a la Sentencia31/2010, Special issue of the *Revista catalana de dret public* pp. 91–95.
Fossas, Enric. (2011). "El control de constitucionalitat dels Estatuts d'Autonomia," *Revista catalana de dret públic* Vol. 43, pp. 21–51.
Gibson, James L., Gregory A. Caldeira and Vanessa A. Baird. (1998). "On the Legitimacy of National High Courts," *American Political Science Review* Vol. 92, pp. 343–358.
Institut D'Estudis Autonomics. (2011). Special issue "Especial sobre la Sentència de l'Estatut d'autonomia de Catalunya," *Revista d'Estudis Federals i Autonomics* p. 12
Knopff, Rainer, Dennis Baker and Sylvia LeRoy. (2009). "Courting Controversy: Strategic Judicial Decision Making," in James Kelly and Christopher Manfredi (eds), *Contested Constitutionalism* (Vancouver: UBC Press), pp. 66–85.
Lajoie, Andrée. (1997). *Jugements de valeurs. Le discours judiciaire et le droit* (Paris: Presses universitaires de France).
Lajoie, Andrée. (2000). "La primauté du droit et la légitimité démocratique comme enjeux du Renvoi sur la sécession du Québec", *Politique et Sociétés* Vol. 19, pp. 31–41.
Leclair, Jean. (2000). "The Secession Reference: A Ruling in Search of a Nation", *Revue juridique Thémis* Vol. 34, pp. 885–890.
Mandel, Michael. (1999). "A Solomonic Judgment? ", *Canada Watch* Vol. 7, pp. 1–2.
McFalls, Laurence. (2005). "L'État bâtard: illégitimité et légitimation chez Max Weber," in Michel Coutu and Guy Rocher (eds), *La légitimité de l'État et du droit. Autour de Max Weber* (Québec: Presses de l'Université Laval), pp. 47–60.
Millard, Gregory. (1999). "The Secession Reference and National Reconciliation: A Critical Note", *Canadian Journal of Law and Society* Vol. 14, No. 2, pp. 1–19.
Ocqueteau, Frédéric and Francine Soubiran-Paillet. (1996). "Champ juridique, juristes et règles de droit: une sociologie entre disqualification et paradoxe", *Droit et société* Vol. 32, pp. 9–26.

Perelman, Chaïm. (1978). "La motivation des décisions de justice, essai de synthèse" in Chaïm Perelman & Paul Foriers (eds) *La motivation des décisions de justice* (Bruxelles: Émile Bruylant), pp. 415–426.
Pinard, Maurice. (2000). *Confusion and Misunderstanding Surrounding the Sovereignist Option* (Brief submitted to the legislative committee of the House of Commons studying Bill C-20, 24 February).
Radmilovic, Vuk. (2010). "Strategic Legitimacy Cultivation at the Supreme Court of Canada: Quebec *Secession Reference* and Beyond", *Canadian Journal of Political Science* Vol. 43, No. 4, December, pp. 843–869.
Rocher, François and Nadia Verrelli. (2003). "Questioning Constitutional Democracy in Canada: From the Canadian Supreme Court Reference on Quebec Secession to the Clarity Act", in A.-G. Gagnon, Montserat Guibernau and F. Rocher (eds), *The Institutional Accommodation of Diversity* (Montreal: Institute for Research on Public Policy), pp. 207–237.
Supreme Court of Canada. (1998). *Reference re Secession of Quebec*, [1998] 2 S.C.R. 217.
Thornhill, Chris. (2010). "Legality, Legitimacy and the Constitution: A Historical-Functionalist Approach", in Chris Thornhill & Samantha Ashenden (eds), *Legality and Legitimacy: Normative and Sociological Approaches* (Baden-Baden: Nomos), pp. 29–56.
Tierney, Stephen. (2003). "The Constitutional Accommodation of National Minorities in the UK and Canada: Judicial Approaches to Diversity", in A.-G. Gagnon, Montserat Guibernau and F. Rocher (eds), *The Institutional Accommodation of Diversity* (Montreal: Institute for Research on Public Policy), pp. 169–206.
Tur, Rosario and Álvarez, Enrique. (2010). *La consecuencias jurídicas de la Sentencia 31/2010, de 28 de junio, del Tribunal Constitucional sobre el Estatuto de Cataluña. La Sentencia de la perfecta Libertad* (Cizur m enor:    Aranzadi/Thomson Reuters).
Viver, Carles. (2011). "El Tribunal Constitucional: ¿Sempre, nomes.... i indiscutible"? La funcio constitutional dels estauts en l'ambit de la distribucio de competencies scons la STC 31/20101", *Revista d'Estudis Federals i Autonomics* 12, pp. 363–402.

# 3
# The Limits of Constitutionalism: Politics, Economics, and Secessionism in Catalonia (2006–2013)

Hèctor López Bofill

## Introduction

The politics of accommodation in contemporary European multinational democracies is multidimensional. As the Introduction to this volume states, "the notion of accommodation in plurinational polities needs to be unpacked and disaggregated and all of its multiple dimensions need to be analyzed, integrating comparative politics and comparative constitutional law into the analysis" (Lluch 2014). In this chapter, I examine the effect of Spanish constitutionalism on substate nationalist mobilization in Catalonia, but I also examine the impact of economic and political considerations on the latter. I seek to go beyond the constitutional analysis presented by Rocher and Casañas Adam in this volume.

On 11 September 11 2012, on the occasion of Catalonia's National Day (Diada nacional) celebration, hundreds of thousands of people took to the streets of Barcelona calling for Catalonia's independence from Spain. From 2010 onwards, the polls indicate a persistent rise of secessionism to the extent that recent polls maintain that more than 50% of the population entitled to vote would support secession if there were an official referendum (against just around 20% who would oppose it).[1]

In this chapter, I seek to account for this epic political development by first relating it to the failure of the Catalan Statute of Autonomy's amendment process between 2003 and 2010. I then assess the impact of the failure of the fiscal agreement with Spain during 2010–2012, and the impact of a number of court rulings on issues of language and culture. Next I look at the current constitutional and political stalemate by examining the Spanish constitutional framework regarding the right to hold a referendum on independence (the "right to decide"), and assess alternatives for transcending the Spanish constitutional framework.

## The Catalan Statute of Autonomy amendment process (2003–2010)

On 28 June 2010, after four years of deliberation, the Spanish Constitutional Court finally issued its decision on the constitutionality of the 2006 Statute of Autonomy of Catalonia.[2] The Court nullified 14 provisions of this Statute and interpreted another 27 provisions in accordance with the Constitution. The decision undermined the aims and the basic structure of the 2006 Statute of Autonomy.

The recognition of Catalonia as a "nation" was curtailed since the judgment held that the term "nation" used in the Statute's preamble had no legal standing. The Court insisted that according to the Spanish constitutional framework there is only one nation, Spain, which is the unique holder of sovereign power through the will of the Spanish people represented in the Spanish Parliament. The term "nation" mentioned in the Catalan Statute's preamble was therefore rejected by the Spanish Constitutional Court if it contained any attribute of sovereign power. Nevertheless, it was considered compatible with constitutional provisions insofar as it referred to what the Spanish Constitution defines as a "nationality": a community that can exercise a right to autonomy under the framework set by the Spanish Constitution. The interpretation given by the Court to the term "nation" as a "nationality" was extended to any aspect of the Statute in which the national character of Catalonia was mentioned such as the reference to the "national situation" or the regulation of the "national symbols." The struggle for political recognition of Catalonia within a plurinational conception of Spain therefore failed from the very beginning of the Constitutional Court ruling.

With regard to "historical rights" referred to in Article 5 of the Statute, the Court's decision deliberately excluded this provision from the recognition that the Spanish Constitution makes of historical rights in Navarra and the three Basque provinces, on which the independent financing system of these territories is based. Avoiding any possible correspondence between the Catalan "historical rights" and the constitutionally enshrined historical rights of the above-mentioned territories, the Court rejected the Statute's aims not just in regards to the recognition of plural identities within the Spanish state but also in the improvement of its financing system.

Concerning linguistic rights, the ruling abolished the preferential status for Catalan in the Catalan public administration and media. Even though the decision maintained the pre-eminence of the Catalan language in the area of education and its vehicular character, the Court subjected the Statute's provisions to the recognition of the Spanish language as vehicular in education at the same level as Catalan. The decision's holding regarding language policy was the beginning of a sequence of judgments issued by Spanish ordinary courts that have threatened the policy established since 1983 by the Catalan government of making Catalan the main language of communication and learning in Catalonia's public schools. This policy was considered instrumental in order to revive and normalize the Catalan language after 40 years of proscription during General Franco's dictatorship. However, according to the Constitutional Court's ruling, Spanish should increase its presence as a language of learning.

As far as the allocation of powers was concerned, the Constitutional Court's ruling closed the door to the Statute's ambition of modulating the competences framework between the state and the Autonomous Community. Therefore, it obliterated the Statute's attempt to broaden the material content of the exclusive powers of the autonomous community and to ensure that, as far as possible, the central government would not use its own powers to intervene in these areas.

Regarding institutions, the ruling questioned the articles related to the Judicial Power altogether and declared them unconstitutional.

Finally, the financing system was also strongly affected by the Constitutional Court's decision since it reduced the legal effect of the Statute's provisions in this area. The Spanish Constitutional Court ruling on Catalonia's Statute was contested by a huge demonstration that filled Barcelona's center on 10 July 2010 with an estimated attendance of more than one million people.

The subsequent elections to the Catalan Parliament, held on 28 November 2010, were won by the nationalist and center-right coalition Convergència i Unió (CiU). This electoral alliance gained 14 seats in the Catalan Parliament which brought them to a total of 62 deputies (just 5 seats under the overall majority). However, in 2010, CiU and its leader Artur Mas, were still deliberately ambiguous regarding the final political status they sought for Catalonia, as has been CiU's traditional stance since they won the first elections of the regional Parliament in 1980.

CiU's 2010 Parliament election campaign was centered on the so-called "fiscal agreement" proposal, an amendment of the financing system, which would require an agreement with the Spanish government and an amendment of the Spanish statute concerning the financing of the Autonomous Communities (*Ley Orgánica de Financiación de las Comunidades Autónomas,* LOFCA) in order to reduce the fiscal imbalance between Catalonia and the Spanish state. The aim was to obtain a financing system analogous to that recognized by the Spanish Constitution in Navarra and the Basque Country that would allow the Catalan government to collect and manage most of the taxes in Catalonia. Changing the fiscal arrangements between Catalonia and Spain was considered by CiU as the first step to overcome the constitutional crisis provoked by the Constitutional Court's decision on the Statute, and as the most efficient strategy to receive the tax revenues needed to overcome the Catalan government's financial difficulties. The new fiscal relationship, according to the CiU proposals during the 2010 electoral campaign, would have been vital to boost the Catalan economy in the current crisis.

The struggle for the fiscal agreement was the main goal during the first Artur Mas term in office between 2010 and 2012.

## The failure of the fiscal agreement in Spain (2010–2012)

In its fiscal proposal, the Artur Mas Administration was inspired by the Navarra and Basque Country models. It is estimated that the fiscal deficit between the Basque Country and Spain is no more than 2% of the GDP,[3] which is considerably lower than the almost 10% of total GDP that Catalonia maintains with the center. The financing system of the Historical Territories of the Basque Country and the Foral Community of Navarra (Concierto Económico) gives them the authority to establish and regulate their tax systems. This means levying, management, settlement, collection, and inspection of most of the state taxes. These taxes are collected by the said territories, and the Autonomous Community contributes to financing the general expenditures of the state that are not assumed, through an amount called a "quota" or "contribution." Catalonia's tax administration, instead, is included in a centralized revenue collection system and a subsequent regional financing based on per capita allocation of public expenditure, which implies positioning Catalonia as a clear net contributor to other Spanish regions. Thus, Catalonia is ranked third in the amount it pays in taxes to Spain, but is ranked tenth in the amount it receives in return.

In its ruling on the Catalan Statute, as we have seen, the Constitutional Court suggested than any change in the financing system in order to move Catalonia closer to the fiscal models of Navarra and the Basque

Country would require a constitutional amendment. The amendment should count, at the very least, with the support of three-fifths of the Spanish Congress and three-fifths of the Spanish Senate and an eventual referendum. The Catalan proposal sought to transform the financing system in order to produce a similar outcome as the one that benefits Navarra and the Basque Country, but without being based on the same legal foundations, i.e. the "historical rights." According to the Catalan proposal, the fiscal agreement would require an amendment of the Spanish act concerning the financing of the Autonomous Communities (LOFCA), the approval of which only needs the overall majority of the Spanish Congress (it could then be bargained just with the Spanish political group that gained the majority of the House, particularly in a scenario in which the seats of the Catalan nationalist parties would be decisive to form the overall majority). But this plan collided with the outcome of the Spanish general elections that took place on 20 November 2011: the conservative People's Party (PP) not only defeated the ruling Spanish Socialist Workers Party (Partido Socialista Obrero Español, PSOE), but also gained 186 of the 350 seats of the Congress of Deputies and, thus, the overall majority of the House. No negotiation with other political groups would be needed to ensure that the PP leader, Mariano Rajoy, would become the prime minister. The Constitutional Court's decision, which was a consequence of an appeal of unconstitutionality lodged by the People's Party, became the legal framework invoked by Mariano Rajoy in order to legitimate the recentralization of the system by assuming powers in different areas.

Nevertheless, the Catalan Government in July 2012, with the support of more than two-thirds of the Catalan Parliament (ICV and ERC added to the votes of CiU's deputies) passed a proposal of fiscal agreement with the Spanish Government. Unlike the 2006 Statute of Autonomy, the fiscal agreement was a proposal without normative value, a set of principles that should guide the negotiations between the Catalan and the Spanish Governments. But Mariano Rajoy, in a meeting with Artur Mas that took place in September 2012, refused *a limine* the Catalan proposal and any agreement on a specific fiscal status for Catalonia. According to the Catalan prime minister, Artur Mas, the Spanish prime minister reaffirmed during the summit that there was no room for negotiating and that the fiscal agreement was a dead end. The Catalan Government's efforts to change the fiscal relationship with the center became indeed more dramatic given that in August 2012, unable to retain a great deal of the tax revenues produced within Catalan territory, the Mas Administration was forced to ask Madrid for a bailout of almost €5 billion. Current expenditures in basic areas such as health or education were in danger. Taking into account that Catalonia is one of the great net contributors to other Spanish regions (and produces almost 20% of the Spanish GDP), swallowing the bitter pill of asking for a bailout was perceived as a humiliation of Catalan society. The claim for independence was thus deeply imbricated with the fiscal tensions between Catalonia and Spain in the midst of the current economic collapse, and the refusal of the Spanish Government to negotiate made it stronger.

## Court rulings affecting language and cultural policy

As we have seen, the Constitutional Court decision on the linguistic issues regulated by the 2006 Catalan Statute of Autonomy opened the door to challenging the linguistic policy in Catalonia's public schools. The linguistic normalization program introduced in the early 1980s had consolidated the role of Catalan as the vehicle of learning and teaching: students were not segregated into different groups on the grounds of language, and non-linguistic subjects were taught mainly in Catalan. The so-called "linguistic immersion" policy fostered the use of Catalan among new generations and guaranteed its survival within a context in which Spanish still played a dominant role in various social areas. On the other hand, the policy guaranteed equality of opportunities and social cohesion. While during the early 1980s the aim of linguistic immersion was to integrate the children of Spanish-speaking immigrants who had come from other areas of Spain under Franco's rule, at present the purpose of linguistic policy in public schools is to facilitate Catalan as the language of socialization among pupils from 160 different countries speaking around 250 different languages.

However, the Catalan linguistic immersion program has been challenged, first, by a range of ordinary Court decisions that implemented the Constitutional Court judgment and, second, by legislation that the Spanish central authorities have on their legislative agenda.

Following the Constitutional Court, ordinary Courts must establish that Spanish is the co-vehicular language in Catalan public schools. According to the Court, this is because Spanish is the statewide official language.

The particular education design that follows from this approach includes the obligation of the educational centers to teach a percentage of non-linguistic subjects (such as, for instance, sciences or mathematics) in Spanish. Neither the Constitutional Court nor ordinary Courts establish what specific percentage of teaching hours the center must offer in order to consider that the vehicular character of Spanish in Catalan schools has been accomplished. That will be fixed by the normative authorities, whether the Spanish authorities in basic legislation on education or the Catalan ones. The outcome of the policy induced by judicial decisions calls for promoting the use of Spanish as a vehicular language in non-linguistic subjects.

The proposal of the People's Party Government was still more hostile toward the normalization and social use of Catalan. The education minister's draft displaced Catalan language from the principal learning language to the third language taught in the schools of Catalonia, behind Spanish and English. The whole linguistic immersion system is therefore at risk of disappearing and thereby the Catalan process of normalization. Other cultural issues are affected by the education minister's draft plan: 100% of the contents in history, for instance, would be regulated by the central government and not by the Catalan one.

These central state decisions that affect linguistic and cultural policies are an additional factor that explains the growth of the pro-sovereignty orientation.

## The Spanish constitutional framework on the issue of secession

The doctrine on constitutive referenda was established by the Spanish Constitutional Court in its decision issued on 11 September 2008, which declared unconstitutional and void the popular consultation promulgated by the Basque Country prime minister, Juan José Ibarretxe, to the Basque citizens on a new political status for the Basque Country.[4]

According to the Constitutional Court, the Spanish Constitution would not prima facie prohibit the recognition of another subject of sovereignty, i.e. the Basque people, but this would necessitate a structural change in the Spanish constitutional order (which just recognizes the Spanish people founded in the unity of the Spanish nation as the only subject of sovereignty). This constitutional amendment, indeed, would be possible only following the most rigid procedure among the revision procedures foreseen by the Spanish Constitution (Article 168 of the Spanish Constitution). The approval of such an amendment would require: a two-thirds majority of the members of the Spanish Congress and the Spanish Senate; the dissolution of the Cortes Generales; the call for elections to constitute a new Congress and a new Senate; the ratification of the decision passed by the previous Houses by a two-thirds majority of the members of each House; and, finally, the amendment being submitted to ratification by a referendum held by the Spanish people. Spain's Constitution, in force for almost 35 years, has never been amended following the above mentioned procedure. On the other hand, the Constitutional Court, based on the decision in the Ibarretxe enquiry, suggested that merely asking for a different demos from the Spanish demos (like the Basque one) is a question related to sovereignty which would require a Spanish constitutional amendment at the beginning of the process. In other words, no constitutional question addressed to the Basques (or the Catalans) beyond the Spanish constitutional frame could be held without the consent of the Spanish central institutions and the Spanish people under the form of a constitutional amendment.

The described interpretation held by the Constitutional Court has not prevented the emergence of a more heterodox interpretation of the Spanish Constitution defended by scholars cognizant of Spanish jurisprudence. The most remarkable insight has been put forward by Professor Rubio Llorente,[5] who noted the Spanish Constitutional Court's contradiction of requiring the activation of the most rigid Constitutional amendment procedure without previously acknowledging the will of the people that demands the right to self-determination from Spain. For this reason, Professor Rubio Llorente (thinking particularly about Catalan demands expressed in the 11 September 2012 mass protest) argues that there is a need to hold a non-binding referendum within the Autonomous Community that addresses the self-determination claim. According to Rubio Llorente, the Catalan Parliament should make a proposal to the Spanish Cortes Generales in order to reach an agreement on the conditions under which the independence referendum would be held. The Spanish legislative houses would pass the regulation under the form of an organic act (Ley Orgánica), which would require an overall majority in the Spanish Congress. Once the will of the Catalan people is expressed, argues Rubio Llorente, if the majority were to support secession, Spain's constitutional structures would need to be altered according to this circumstance. In any case, a referendum in Catalonia would need the authorization of Spanish central institutions, as well as a constitutional amendment whether at the beginning of the process (as the Constitutional Court argues) or after the Catalan referendum results are known (as suggests Rubio Llorente).

Among the alternative procedures[6] whereby Catalan self-determination demands could be heard are: (a) an act passed by the Catalan Parliament on referendums held within the Catalan legal framework; and

(b) a measure concerning a "popular consultation" pursuant to the Catalan legal framework (that is still pending approval by the Catalan Parliament). The terms of this future popular consultation shaped the core of the agreement between CiU and ERC reached in December 2012 in order to celebrate a self-determination vote.

Some objections can be heard to any effort to hold a self-determination vote.[7] The first is that, according to the mentioned provisions, Catalan authorities can call for a referendum of the people only within the ambit of the powers conferred by the Statute of Autonomy (which would exclude a referendum on the question of sovereignty). Second, in accordance with the Spanish Constitution, the calling of a referendum requires the authorization of the Spanish Government. Thus, while a Catalan initiative respects the exclusive state powers on the holding of referendums (Article 149.1.32 of the Spanish Constitution), an agreement between the Catalan and Spanish authorities has to be reached in order to organize a referendum. This condition is difficult to meet, because the Spanish Government has expressed its frontal opposition to any self-determination process within the state's borders.

Seeking approval of an act concerning a "popular consultation" is even more difficult. The regulation of these citizen consultations would be founded on the exclusive power conferred on the Catalan government by the Statute of Autonomy to regulate and call non-referendary consultations (Article 122 of the Catalan Statute). Taking into account that such consultations would not be referendums, the absence of authorization by the Spanish government would not hinder, according to the Catalan Government interpretation, the holding of the self-determination vote. Among the differences between what is a referendum and what would be considered a popular consultation are the scope of the voters: a referendum would just call the Catalans that have the right to vote according to the Spanish Constitution (the Catalans over 18 years old who have Spanish citizenship), while the popular consultation would open the door to the vote of both those people aged between 16 and 18 years old and the non-Spanish nationals who reside within a Catalan municipality. However, the attempt to use the type of citizenship as a criterion for differentiating a popular consultation from a referendum was explicitly declared unconstitutional and void by the Spanish Constitutional Court in the case of the popular consultation called by the Basque prime minister Ibarretxe. In that decision, the Constitutional Court stated that the popular consultation proposed by the Basque Parliament and the Basque Government was a referendum since it regarded an issue of a manifestly political nature, and was calling the Basque electorate to vote, and was manifested by means of an electoral procedure provided with the guarantees of electoral processes.[8] The Basque law concerning the 2008 popular consultation was seen by the Constitutional Court as a subterfuge to avoid the requirement of Spanish government authorization pursuant to Article 149.1.32 of the Constitution. It is predictable that the Constitutional Court would reach the same conclusion as it did in the Basque case if the Catalan Parliament were to pass an act regulating popular consultations and, specifically, an act on a consultation related to the issue of Catalan self-determination. The fact that a Catalan act extended the electoral body to people aged between 16 and 18 years old or to non-Spanish nationals would probably not be sufficient to elude the unconstitutionality of the act's provisions according to the Constitutional Court's jurisprudence.

## Transcending the Spanish constitutional framework

If the Spanish government were to insist on blocking a Catalan referendum on sovereignty invoking the Constitutional prohibition, then it would open the way to adopting a unilateral declaration of independence by a large majority of the Catalan Parliament.

This would suppose a break with the Spanish Constitutional framework through a decision adopted by the Catalan people's elected representatives. Indeed, a declaration of independence in opposition to the state's constitutional framework has been a common pattern over the last centuries in the creation of new sovereign states. Promulgating a unilateral declaration after free and fair elections in Catalonia would provide a powerful legitimacy factor. The political legitimacy of a unilateral declaration of independence in opposition to the Spanish constitutional framework would be strengthened mainly within a context whereby: (a) a referendum on self-determination is proscribed by the central state; and (b) negotiations with the Spanish government in order to reach an agreement on the conditions of a "popular consultation" have failed.

Yet, the conditions of a hypothetical Catalan unilateral declaration of independence could be analogized with the case of Kosovo's unilateral declaration of independence. As is well known, the International Court of Justice enacted on 22 July 2010 an advisory opinion regarding Kosovo's declaration of independence in which the Court argued that Kosovo's declaration did not violate general international law. However, an advisory opinion does not have the status of precedent that the International Court's reasoning could apply, from a juridical perspective, to other secessionist movements in which the constitutional framework of the state appears rigid and curtails the democratic expression of the majority who are pro-sovereignty. The International Court avoided a statement on the existence of a general right to secession, but it established that international law does not establish general prohibitions to independence declarations,[9] and these are lawful insofar as they are made following democratic and peaceful means.[10]

The Catalan political establishment, and even the pro-independence parties that had reached the overall majority of the Catalan Parliament, are still very far from such a Constitutional break-up scenario. As we have seen, the agreement reached between CiU and ERC reflects an awareness of the need to open negotiations with the Spanish government on the popular consultation's conditions within the Spanish Constitutional framework. On the other hand, an initiative that could set Catalonia outside the Spanish Constitution would most likely exacerbate tensions and promote a conflict, with unpredictable consequences, which Catalan society and their leaders are hardly ready to assume. A Catalan challenge against the Spanish Constitutional framework would eventually entitle the Spanish government to take all measures necessary to compel the Catalan government to fulfill the obligations imposed by the Constitution (Article 155 of the Spanish Constitution). Moreover, an attempt to transcend the constitutional limits could be used by the Spanish government as an argument to erode the legitimacy of the Catalan self-determination efforts before the international community, and particularly, before the European institutions (such as the European Council or the European Union). Unlike the Scottish secessionist pattern, which includes an agreement with United Kingdom authorities and the commitment by both parts to accept the outcome of the independence referendum, a clash between the democratic legitimacy invoked by the Catalan Parliament and the Spanish Constitutional legitimacy would, in all likelihood, involve the European institutions. What procedures would be followed within the European Union framework is not clear since there is no precedent for any secession within a Member State without the consent of the state. The uncertainty provoked by a unilateral independence declaration would probably turn the Spanish constitutional crisis into a European one.

## Conclusion

My approach to explaining the rise of the secessionist orientation in Catalonia has been centered on the description of a number of institutional factors that have developed during the last decade within the Spanish Constitutional framework (the failure of the Statute of Autonomy amendment process, the failure of the financing agreement in the context of the current economic debacle, and the challenge against the language policies in public schools). Stressing the effects of Spanish constitutionalism on the internal dynamics of nationalist politics in Catalonia can help to explain these developments, but it also has its limits. I have shown that we must also consider economic factors (the failure of the fiscal agreement in this economic crisis) and the subtle dynamics of politics in Catalonia. I conclude that these political developments are also strongly connected with the perception among Catalans that Spain has not been capable, during the last decades of Spain's State of Autonomies, of reciprocating and accommodating Catalonia within a multinational and plural constitutional framework.[11]

However, the specific strategy of the newly emerging pro-sovereignty majority within civil society and in the parliamentary sphere is uncertain. Although pro-independence parties won the 2012 Catalan elections (87 seats out of 135), the governing CiU lost significant support (12 MPs, obtaining 50 seats in the 135-seat Parliament). This absence of clarity from CiU seemed, moreover, to help the growth of the left-wing and explicitly secessionist ERC (with 21 seats after they gained 11), which became the second largest party in Parliament and was able to determine the conditions of the process.

The main uncertainties, nevertheless, are institutional: in December 2012, CiU formed a new government led by Artur Mas with the parliamentary support of ERC. The two political groups were able to reach an agreement on the period in which the referendum on Catalonia's sovereignty would eventually be held: during late 2014. This commitment by Catalan parties must face up to the almost insurmountable difficulties that emerge from the Spanish constitutional framework in accepting the democratic principle on the issue of secession. Unlike the Scotland–United Kingdom case, where an agreement between the Scottish first minister, Alex Salmond, and the British prime minister, David Cameron, was signed on 15 October 2012 to provide the legal framework for Scotland's independence referendum to be held, the Spanish Government led by Mariano Rajoy (PP) has expressed a strong opposition to the Catalan proposal to hold a referendum on independence. The Spanish Government's stance is supported by the interpretation of the Constitutional Court defending the most restrictive point of view on the issue of the right to self-determination of other nations currently within the Spanish state. The question is whether a referendum on Catalonia's sovereignty may be held on the basis of the Catalan Parliament's initiative, but in opposition to Spanish constitutional provisions.

## Notes

1. See the polls conducted by Centre d'Estudis d'Opinió (CEO) during 2012: on 27 June 2012, already, 51% would vote for independence in a referendum; while on 8 November 2012, support for secessionism reached 57%. CEO polls available at: http://www.ceo.gencat.cat/ceop/AppJava/pages
2. Spanish Constitutional Court Decision 31/2010 of 28 June 2010.
3. See J. Costa-i-Font, 'Unveiling Vertical State Downscaling: Identity and/or Economy?' (2010) *London School of Economics Europe in Question Discussion Paper series* 20, available at http://www2.lse.ac.uk/europeaninstitute/leqs/leqspaper20.pdf (19).
4. Spanish Constitutional Court Decision 103/2008 of September 11, 2008.
5. F. Rubio Llorente, 'Un referéndum para Cataluña' *El País*, 8 October 2012.
6. On the possible constitutional avenues for holding a referendum, see for example several recent reports by the *Institut d'Estudis Autonòmics* (Institute of Autonomic Studies) of the Catalan Government, such as the "Informe sobre els procediments legals a través dels quals els ciutadans i les ciutadanes de catalunya poden ser consultats sobre llur futur polític col·lectiu", of 11 March 2013. Also, reports by the Consultative Council for the National Transition of the Catalan Government, especially the report entitled "La Consulta sobre el Futur Politic de Catalunya," of 25 July 2013.
7. On legitimacy of referendums over questions of sovereignty for substate territories see S. Tierney, *Constitutional Referendums*, Oxford University Press, Oxford, 2012, pp. 137–52.
8. Spanish Constitutional Court Decision 103/2008 of September 11, 2008 (para. 3).
9. International Court of Justice, Advisory Opinion of 22 July 2010, *Accordance with international law of the unilateral declaration of independence in respect of Kosovo* (paragraph 84). On the consequences of the ICJ Advisory Opinion of 22 July 2010 related to unilateral declaration of independence and the territorial integrity principle, see I. Urrutia Libarona, "Territorial integrity and self-determination: the approach of the International Court of Justice in the Advisory Opinion on Kosovo," *Revista d'Estudis Autonòmics i Federals*, 16 (October 2012): 107–137.
10. International Court of Justice, Advisory Opinion of 22 July 2010, *Accordance with international law of the unilateral declaration of independence in respect of Kosovo* (paragraph 81).
11. The recent developments in Catalonia are explained by Lluch's moral polity thesis (Lluch 2012).

## References

Bel, G., C. Boix, E. Castro and E. Paluzie. (2012). "Spain and the Blame Game", in *Huffington Post*. at: http://www.huffingtonpost.com/carles-boix/spain-economy-catalonia_b_1297516.html.

Buchanan A.E. (1991). *Secession. The Morality of Political Divorce from Fort Sunter to Lithuania and Quebec* (Westview Press: Boulder/St. Francisco/Oxford).
Costa-I-Font, J. (2010). "Unveiling Vertical State Downscaling: Identity and/or Economy?", *London School of Economics Europe in Question Discussion Paper series* 20, at http://www2.lse.ac.uk/europeaninstitute/leqs/leqspaper20.pdf
Guibernau, M. (2004). *Catalan Nationalism: Francoism, Transition, and Democracy* (London: Routledge).
Hale, H. (2008). *The Foundations of Ethnic Politics: Separatism of States and Nations in Eurasia and the World* (Cambridge: Cambridge University Press).
Horowitz, D.D. (2003). "A Right to Secede?", in A.E. Buchanan and S. Macedo (eds.), *Secession and Self-determination*. (New York: New York University Press), pp. 50–76.
Lluch, J. (2012). "Internal Variation in Sub-State National Movements and the Moral Polity of the Nationalist", *European Political Science Review* Vol. 4, No. 3, pp. 433–460.
Meadwell, H. (1989). "Ethnic Nationalism and Collective Choice Theory", *Comparative Political Studies* Vol. 22, pp. 47–68.
Meadwell, H. (1999). "Secession, States and International Society", *Review of International Studies* Vol. 25, No. 3, pp. 371–387.
Muñoz, J. and Tormos, R. (2012). "Identitat o càlculs instrumentals? Anàlisi dels factors explicatius de suport a la independència.", at: http://www.ceo.gencat.cat/ceop/AppJava/export/sites/CEOPortal/estudis/workingPapers/contingut/identitat2.pdf.
Requejo, F. (2010). "Revealing the Dark Side of Traditional Democracies in Plurinational Societies: The Case of Catalonia and the Spanish 'Estado de las Autonomías' ", *Nations and Nationalism* Vol. 16, No. 1, pp. 148–168.
Rubio Llorente, F. (2012). "Un referéndum para Cataluña" *El País*, 8 October 2012.
Tierney, S. (2012). *Constitutional Referendums* (Oxford: Oxford University Press).
Urrutia Libarona, I. (2012). "Territorial Integrity and Self-Determination: The Approach of the International Court of Justice in the Advisory Opinion on Kosovo", *Revista d'Estudis Autonòmics i Federals*, Vol. 16, pp. 107–137.
Varshney, A. (2003). "Nationalism, Ethnic Conflict, and Rationality", *Perspectives on Politics* Vol. 1, No. 1, pp. 85–99.

# Part II
# The Multiple Dimensions of the Politics of Accommodation in Multinational Polities

# 4
# The Accommodation of Island Autonomies in Multinational States

*Eve Hepburn*

## Introduction

A growing body of literature has revealed that islands enjoy some of the most creative and sophisticated forms of governance arrangements in the world (Baldacchino & Milne 2000; Royle 2001; Suksi 2011; Baldacchino & Hepburn 2012). This is especially true in the case of multinational states, where substate islands have been granted unique forms of autonomy to protect their status and identity. Rather than seeking complete separation from the "mainland," islands have often accepted a continuing affiliation with the state. This "loyalty" is often rewarded with particular concessions or dispensations, be they economic, cultural, or political in nature. This represents a successful form of institutional accommodation, though state–island relations are not without their problems.

The aim of this chapter is to explore the politics of accommodation of island regions within multinational democracies. A legislative island region may be defined as a water-bound territorial entity situated at an intermediate level between the local and statewide territorial levels, and which exercises a non-sovereign form of jurisdictional autonomy. As island regions come in many different constitutional forms, the analysis will focus on the accommodation of island autonomies within three different institutional configurations: a federacy (the Åland Islands in Finland), a devolved autonomous region (Sardinia in Italy), and a constituent unit of a federation (Prince Edward Island in Canada). While these cases share a number of similar geographical, social, and cultural traits, there are other significant differences. Sardinia is a relatively underdeveloped region with a strong cultural identity and language, and a range of nationalist parties. Åland constitutes a relatively wealthy region, which shares a number of cultural links with nearby Sweden, and has one small separatist political party. Prince Edward Island (PEI) is one of the Canadian "have-not" provinces, with a strong sense of island identity but lacking any political mobilization of PEI identity and interests. The aim is to compare these cases to identify some general characteristics about the accommodation of island autonomies in multinational states and the strategies employed to manage diversity.

The chapter begins with an overview of island autonomy and accommodation, identifying some general motivations for islands to opt for new models of autonomy rather than seeking full independence. It then undertakes a case-study analysis using the theoretical framework of this edited collection, exploring three dimensions of accommodation: (a) constitutionalism and the institutional frameworks which they create for accommodation; (b) nationalism and political mobilization, i.e. the success of statewide parties in propagating a nationwide nationalism and integration of island politics compared with the demands of substate nationalist movements; and (c) specific state strategies of accommodation. Following this empirical analysis, the chapter concludes with some general remarks about the politics of accommodation in substate island autonomies, linking this back to the general arguments of the book.

## Island autonomy and accommodation

Islands, as a category, have not generally attracted the attention of political scientists or legal scholars. This is surprising given that islands are the classical "periphery" in center-periphery studies. The spatial characteristics of islands as discrete bounded territories (Baldacchino & Hepburn 2012) make them valuable units of analysis for the study of territorial politics. Furthermore, there is good reason to explore what islands can contribute to our discussions on the politics of accommodation. Islands exhibit a considerable variety of autonomy arrangements, whereby autonomy may be understood as a "means for diffusion of powers in order to preserve the unity of a state while respecting the diversity of its population" (Lapidoth 1997: 3). Instead of seeking independence, a large number of island territories have agreed to share their sovereignty with larger states, including Denmark's Faroe Islands, New Zealand's Cook Islands, France's Martinique, the US Virgin Islands and the UK's Turks and Caicos Islands. This has resulted in an abundance of different measures of self-government, including associate statehood, overseas territory, commonwealth territory, autonomous province, crown dependence, and overseas department. Many of these unique constitutional arrangements lie outside the "traditional" understandings of autonomy that involve federalism, confederalism, and decentralization (Lapidoth 1997). Furthermore, island peoples have demonstrated that they prefer to maintain linkages to a larger state, by rejecting independence in popular referendums in Mayotte (1994), the Dutch Antilles (1994), Puerto Rico (1967, 1993, and 1998), US Virgin Islands (1993), Bermuda (1995), and Tokelau (2006, 2007). Instead, islands have chosen to develop creative forms of jurisdictional autonomy that involve degrees of affiliation with host states. This is not to say that political movements have not emerged on these islands to contest relations with the host state. Successful nationalist movements have secured independence for Anguilla, Papua New Guinea, Fiji, and the Comoros. Furthermore, nationalist movements have also emerged in Tobago, Kiribati, the Solomons, Sardinia, the Canary Islands, New Caledonia, Nevis, Greenland and Puerto Rico to name a few. However, some scholars have argued that island independence movements are "withering on the vine" (Clegg 2012), with many of them moderating their goals to include varying degrees of linkages with states.

So why do islands often choose special autonomy arrangements rather than full sovereignty? Let us consider three possible factors, which are historical, economic, and (geo)political. First, many islands have a colonial inheritance, and were subject not only to foreign military domination but also integration into the colonizing state's economic and social system. A history of integration into a colonizing state may encourage islands to maintain political and economic ties rather than complete separation (Royle 2001). For example, Saint-Barthélemy and Saint-Martin in the Caribbean were administratively attached to Guadeloupe (a French overseas department), but preferred closer ties to Paris and so, in 2002, became overseas collectivities of France (see Clegg 2012).

Second, there may be economic motivations to maintaining a special autonomy status. Small islands are typically understood as being poor, remote, and disadvantaged in development terms due to high transport costs and insufficient natural resources. Economic weakness may encourage islands to forge ties with larger states that can guarantee trading markets and potentially lucrative fiscal transfers (Baldacchino & Milne 2000). A prime example is Niue and the Cook Islands, which enjoy an enviable form of "free association" with New Zealand, but where "the financial assistance provided by New Zealand is required simply for the governments of these two states to meet their budgetary needs" (Levine 2012). Indeed, Nieu and the Cook Islands have chosen wisely: a recent quantitative survey of the socio-economic profiles of 30 sovereign island states and 25 autonomous island regions found that the latter group enjoys a "consistently superior performance" (McElroy & Parry 2012).

Finally, there may be (geo)political reasons for seeking to establish a partnership with a larger state. In federal systems, islands may exercise greater political capacity through their influence over the decision making of a large state, rather than being a small independent player in a globalized arena. Or, for islands that are situated in a precarious geopolitical or geographical situation, they might benefit from the protection of the larger host state. This was evident in the aftermath of the devastating volcanic eruptions in Montserrat in the late 1990s which required direct support from the UK, and in the case of the Falklands, which were provided with extensive British security in the face of the Argentine invasion. In short, the various economic and political benefits of maintaining forms of association with a host state are often seen to outweigh the risks associated with secession (Baldacchino & Hepburn 2012). And the benefits to states seem equally compelling. Island regions may be seen as useful to central governments as remote geographical spaces in which to conduct nuclear testing (Sardinia), as important geostrategic defense locations (Hawaii) or as offshore tax havens (Macau). In the next section, we will consider in greater detail how three diverse forms of island autonomy were developed in the Åland Islands, Sardinia, and Prince Edward Island, and how the state has sought to accommodate island specificities.

## Åland Islands

The Åland Island in Finland constitute a relatively wealthy self-governing legislative region of an otherwise unitary state. Åland may be categorized as a federacy, which enjoys asymmetrical autonomy that is not granted to any other part of Finland. For over 650 years, Åland belonged to the Kingdom of Sweden (along with Finland) until the war in 1808–09, at which point Åland and Finland were ceded to Russia. When Finland declared independence in 1917, the question emerged as to whether Åland should fall to Finland or Sweden. Åland initially rejected Finland's offer of autonomy, and a petition was signed demanding reunification with Sweden (Suksi 2011). However, this strong popular desire for Ålandic reunification with Sweden fell on deaf ears. The Finnish authorities refused to give up Åland and the following year the League of Nations stepped in to resolve the conflict, decreeing by international law that Åland's future should lie as an autonomous region within the Finnish state.

*Constitutional and institutional framework*

Åland's constitutional status as a self-governing, demilitarized, and monolingually Swedish-speaking region was laid out in the Act on the Autonomy of Åland in 1921 (subsequently revised in 1951 and 1991). While Finland was granted formal sovereignty over the islands, the Act stipulated important restrictions that were designed to protect the Swedish language, customs, and traditions of Åland. One scholar calls it the "most radical form of international guarantee for a national minority ever to have been drawn up" (Modeen 1969: 183). Åland was granted a government and a legislative assembly (Lagting). Meanwhile, Finnish interference is limited to the existence of a state governor and state delegation in Åland, tasked with resolving disputes. In return, Åland's formal representation in Helsinki is restricted to a single elected representative in the Finnish parliament. For Ålanders, the most important goal has been to achieve *self-rule*; influence in Finnish affairs has received little attention.

To protect Åland's extensive competences, the Autonomy Act guarantees the Åland autonomous institutions a veto against competence reallocation. Yet while Åland was granted extensive legislative powers, these were allocated in such a way that they were *residual* to the enumeration of the Finnish parliament's powers, which included foreign affairs, international treaties and customs and taxation (Suksi 2011: 140). Following the emergence of a patriotic movement in Åland in the 1950s, the Ålandic authorities embarked on a nation-building project, primarily through creating national symbols, such as a national flag, national museum and postage stamps, in addition to revising the Autonomy Act to give constitutional form to this new sense of Ålandness (Interview with Barbro Sundback, leader of the Åland Social Democrats, 16 June 2010). The Finnish authorities agreed to revise the Autonomy Act so that the exclusive competencies of both parliaments were listed. For Åland, these included competencies in education, culture, health, social welfare, promotion of industry, housing, municipal administration, public order, the postal service, radio and television, farming, forestry, agriculture, fishing, protection of the environment, and mining rights (Palmgren 1997: 86–88). The 1951 Autonomy Act also introduced the notion of an Ålandic citizenship, which foreigners moving to Åland are eligible to apply for, including the rights to own real estate, to operate a business, or to vote or stand as a candidate in

Lagting elections (Hannum 1990; Daftary 2000). With the agreement of Finland, the Autonomy Act was revised again in 1990 to further increase Åland's competences in certain areas, including rights of negotiation on international treaties (including those relating to the European Union). The Ålandic citizenship was also strengthened, which added proficiency in the Swedish language as another condition of regional citizenship. And to protect Åland's competences, the Autonomy Act guarantees that Åland's powers cannot be revoked without two-thirds majorities from both parliaments.

*Statewide and substate nationalism*

Political parties are often forces of national integration responsible for aggregating and representing the interests of the people of a given state. However, if part of a state enjoys a separate party system that is completely cut off from national politics, this makes it virtually impossible to "integrate" the region into the state or to propagate the ideologies and nation-building sentiments of the state at the regional level. This is the situation in Åland. The island's party system developed along completely separate lines from the Finnish party system, so that there is no overlap in political parties. Finnish parties are therefore unable to spread their message across the Åland archipelago (which in any case does not speak the language of the Finnish parties) while the Swedish-speaking Åland parties have no impact on the Finnish national scene.

This means that Finnish political actors are incapable of disseminating a Finnish nationalist ideology in the Swedish-speaking archipelago. Since the 1970s, Åland politics has been dominated by two regionally based centrist parties: the Liberals in Åland and Åland Centre, which have tended to form coalition governments, with the Åland Social Democrats forming the main Opposition. Åland Centre is the most pro-autonomy party, and strongly argues for enhanced fiscal autonomy. This is also supported by smaller parties such as the Moderates and Non-Aligned Coalition. Although the Åland Social Democrats have some links to the Finnish Social Democrats, these are largely informal and irregular, and there is no cooperation on deciding a joint party "message" or policy program on the islands (Hepburn 2014, forthcoming).

This lack of a Finnish nationalist presence on the islands does not mean, however, that Åland wishes to break all of its ties with the mainland. Recently, Stepan et al. (2011: 217) concluded that "no significant political movement has emerged in Åland since the federacy was created in 1922 that might have led Åland to break its federacy commitments, join Sweden or become independent." However, this statement may be a little premature. A nationalist party was founded in 2001, with the aim of making Åland a "sovereign, neutral and demilitarized microstate." Ålands Framtid (Åland's Future) has increased its electoral support from 6.5% in the 2003 Lagting elections, to 8.1% in the 2007 elections and 9.7% in 2011 (resulting in three seats in the Lagting). Party members argue "we're not really a part of Finland ... We need to be independent from the Finnish Government because our way of getting back our taxation is not fair" (Interview with Rolf Granlund 15 June 2010). Economic interests are not the only motivation for independence; the party also seeks to further protect Åland's distinct cultural identity, fearing that Finnish has become too dominant and that not enough protection has been given to Finland's other official language – Swedish.[1] But although the party has increased its share of the vote in recent years, some commentators believe that the independence movement is merely "an expression of discontent ... with regard to life on Åland I think that there aren't really that many frustrations" (Interview with Sia Spiliopoulou Åkermark 16 June 2010). This may be because any of the demands of the autonomy movement have been met – such as the protection of Swedish and increased control over social and cultural policy – with the full support of the Finnish government.

*State accommodation strategies*

Finland is viewed very much as a benign "patron" in Åland, having agreed to give the island as much self-rule as was demanded and ratifying extensions of the Autonomy Act in the 1950s and 1990s. In particular, Finland fully supports Åland's monolingual policy and agreed to solely conduct any negotiations with the island in Swedish. As such, scholars have argued that relations between Helsinki and Åland have been largely harmonious, and indeed that a degree of consensus and reciprocity were built into the Autonomy Act (Åkermark 2009). This is evident in the joint agreement of the governor of Åland and the balanced composition of the Åland delegation (the dispute resolution body composed equally of Åland and Finnish representatives). The Finnish authorities have also granted Åland representation in Finnish political institutions – which is unusual for a federacy – including a seat on the Finnish Parliament and permanent representation on the powerful Constitutional Committee. And while Finland is responsible for foreign affairs, Finland has encouraged Åland's "substate diplomacy." Åland has a small external representation in Stockholm (Sweden), a representative in the Finnish Permanent Mission to the EU, it holds one of the Finnish seats in the EU Committee of the Regions, and it has its own delegation to the Nordic Council (Suksi 2011: 141). Yet despite these political concessions, some tensions have arisen with Finland. The first is in fiscal matters. Åland's GDP per capita surpasses both the Finnish and Swedish averages, and ranks among the highest in Europe (Interview with Bjarne Lindstrom, Director of Åland Statistics Office 17 June 2010). However, because Åland's lump sum is regulated by Finland, public finances in Åland suffer whenever the Finnish economy is underperforming. Due to this, there have been calls for fiscal autonomy to enable Åland to fully control its own finances (currently Åland has local taxation powers and some additional income tax powers that have never been used). Second, there have been demands for direct representation in European institutions, owing to several recent spats between Åland and the EU on issues such as mouth tobacco (an Åland pastime that the EU has banned) and seabird hunting (an Åland cultural tradition that goes against EU laws on the protection of birds). In both matters, Ålanders felt that Finland did not stand up for Åland's interests. Furthermore, Åland parties have argued that *the powers lost to the* EU/Finland have not been compensated by being represented in the European Parliament. But rather than give Åland one of its few seats in Strasbourg, Finland gave Åland more access influence over the national preparation of Finnish EU policy. For island actors, this concession is inadequate, and they have continued demanding their own seat in Europe (Hepburn 2014 forthcoming).

**Prince Edward Island**

An example of a federation is provided by PEI, which is the smallest province in Canada. PEI lies on Canada's eastern flank in the Maritime provinces, separated by some eight miles from mainland New Brunswick, which has been helped by the creation of a new "confederation bridge" in 1997 (Baldacchino 2007). As an independent colony of Britain with its own elected legislative assembly since 1769, PEI resisted joining the Canadian confederation in 1867, as it found the terms of union economically and politically unfavorable (Connor 2008: 35). As such, it chose to remain a colony of the UK and even explored the possibility of becoming a discrete dominion of its own, as well as entertaining the notion of joining the USA (Bolger 1961: 27). Yet, following an economic crisis in PEI resulting from mounting railways debts, the deal was sweetened by the willingness of the Canadian federal government to absorb these debts and to finance a deal to free the island of leasehold tenure. Canadian financial assistance, combined with various pressures from the British government, therefore pushed the island into Confederation in 1873.

*Constitutional and institutional framework*

PEI is the smallest of ten provinces that make up the Canadian federation. As a fully fledged provincial unit, PEI has its own government, legislature and lieutenant-governor. In addition, PEI is fully represented in the Canadian federal parliament and senate. The island therefore enjoys both self-rule through its provincial autonomy, and shared-rule through its influence in Canadian federal affairs.

While giving up certain parts of its independence during its accession to Canada, PEI was able to maintain a considerable degree of autonomy (which is also enjoyed by Canada's other provinces). PEI's membership of the Canadian federation was constitutionally embedded in the British North America Act (subsequently the Constitution Act 1982). This Act laid down an extensive list of provincial and federal powers, with some indication as to those that should be concurrent/shared (Connor 2008). In particular, PEI was granted: the powers of direct taxation within the province; the management and sale of public lands belonging to the province; municipalities; education; health and social services; economic development; prisons; property and civil rights; administration of civil/criminal justice; incorporation of companies; and natural resources (ss. 92–93 Constitution Act). At no time has there been a sense that these competences were inadequate and that PEI's autonomy should be enhanced. Instead, according to the speaker of the PEI legislative assembly, the general feeling is that despite its tiny size and population, PEI is lucky to have the same powers as the larger provinces: "we do have all of the privileges that Ontario, BC, Alberta would have. We're responsible for healthcare, education, we get to look after that" (Interview with Kathleen Casey 18 May 2010). In addition, PEI enjoys substantial representation in Canadian federal institutions. The island is represented by four members of parliament in the House of Commons, in addition to four members of the upper parliamentary chamber, the Senate. When PEI entered Confederation in 1873, it was originally entitled to six MPs, but a declining population reduced this figure to only three MPs in 2011. Following popular protests, the BNA Act was subsequently revised to ensure that no province should have fewer MPs than senators, increasing PEI's total to four. According to one commentator, "PEI has about four times as many MPs as we're entitled to if you go strictly representation by population. So in that sense PEI is represented well" (Interview with Harry Baglole 19 May

2010). Furthermore, PEI by tradition has also enjoyed at least one representative in the Canadian federal cabinet (Watts 2000: 27). This representation is due to a federal government convention that each province should have representation in the federal executive – giving PEI disproportionate influence over federal affairs.

*Statewide and substate nationalism*

PEI is dominated by Canada's two largest political parties – the Liberals and Conservatives – in what is described as the purest two-party system in Canada. Unlike Åland, there are no nationalist parties in PEI, no PEI-only regional parties, and no regional mobilization around issues of culture. Third parties have never been a factor in PEI politics, and indeed the only times a non-Liberal or Conservative politician won a seat in the provincial legislature was in 1919 when an Independent won a seat and in 1996 when the New Democratic Party leader was elected (MacKinnon 2007: 72). PEI's positive attitude toward being part of Canada, coupled with dominance of Canadian Liberal-Conservative ideologies on the island, seems to preclude the emergence of any nationalist party. As MacKinnon (2007: 72) argues, "because of its 'have-not' status, the province has always favored maintaining close ties with Ottawa. That desire to maintain friendly relations with the federal government had resulted in Prince Edward Island predominantly electing governments of the same political stripe as that of the federal government throughout most of the 20th century, earning the distinction of leading all other provinces in keeping its governments in line with its federal counterpart." Given that some 39% of PEI's revenue is funded by the federal government, "its viability as a jurisdiction, without the support of the federal government, is in question" (Connor 2008: 36). This widely acknowledged economic dependency on Ottawa means that there is no appetite in PEI for pursuing a course of independence or increasing the autonomy of the island.

However, despite the formidable influence of the Canadian party system on PEI politics (Stewart 1986) and the strong desire to maintain influence and concessions within the federal polity, this is not to say that PEI hasn't experienced some degree of local patriotic mobilization. In 1973 – the year of the centennial of Confederation – an island movement called "The Brothers and Sisters of Cornelius Howatt" was founded in response to the elaborate celebrations. Howatt had been one of the two assemblymen to oppose Confederation in 1873. The purpose of the movement was "to remind Islanders of their distinctive heritage and to urge them to consider their contemporary situation in this light" (Robertson 1975). Harry Baglole, one of the founders of the movement along with David Weale, describes it as "a society formed both to poke fun at the Centennial celebrations ... but more than that it was an organisation to try to look at our history and to make the case that we had a period of much more independent thinking as a society and as a political entity" (Interview 19 May 2010). The movement presented briefs to the PEI government, premier and land commission, and at the end of the year it disbanded. Today, the influence of the movement is still palpable, as many of the leading Brothers and Sisters are currently serving as members of the provincial legislature. However, it is important to stress that these members represent Canadian parties and are happy to combine their local patriotism with a strong sense of Canadian values and identity.

*State accommodation*

While provincial–federal disagreement and tensions are often the hallmarks of a federal state, and indeed several provinces in Canada have fought in recent years with Ottawa over economic or constitutional issues (such as Alberta and Quebec), PEI's relationship to the federal level has generally been one of harmony and goodwill. There are several reasons for this. The first is Canada's successful accommodation of PEI demands during the island's entry into Confederation in 1873. Owing to PEI's opposition to entering the federal union, the dominion government "realized that it would have to make a more generous settlement to offset these declared disadvantages if it were to succeed in inducing the Island to enter Confederation" (Bolger 1961: 28). These generous provisions included a promise to establish efficient steam services, telegraphic infrastructure and "constant communication" between PEI and the mainland, to absorb the railway liabilities that had brought the island to bankruptcy, and to provide a special subsidy in consideration of PEI's lack of Crown lands (ibid). PEI therefore gained tremendous benefits over other provinces that had joined prior to 1973.

In addition to the economic and materials benefits provided by the federal government, Ottawa also granted PEI substantial rights of political representation that were disproportionate to the island's small population. Islanders had previously been concerned about "a reduction in the significance of their local institutions. They realized, moreover, that they would have an insignificant voice in a centralized legislature, and as a result they feared that their local needs would be disregarded" (Bolger 1961: 25). In response, Ottawa guaranteed an additional member for PEI in the House of Commons, which today translates into four MPs and four senators, as well as a seat on the Federal Cabinet. Furthermore, the federal government currently makes a special allocation of funding to PEI, whereby 25% of the island's provincial finances come from equalization payments, in addition to a per capita share from the Canada Health and Social Transfers, which amounts to approximately 40% of the province's budget coming from the federal government (Interview with Sandy Stewart, Deputy Minister of Intergovernmental Relations 25 May 2010).

Provincial status has therefore exaggerated the prominence of this community of approximately 140,000 people, and there are few complaints that PEI is not represented enough at the federal level or that it fails to receive its adequate share of fiscal equalization. As the Minister for Finance says, "One of the greatest things that our Premier always talks about is the fact that we're such a small province, yet we have the same voice around the table" (Interview with Wesley Sheridan 28 May 2010). Yet some have acknowledged that PEI's position within the federation is not ideal: "we've had a dependent sort of relationship with Ottawa which has made us feel supplicant, a client" (Interview with Edward MacDonald 27 May 2010). Furthermore, having only four MPs in a House of Commons of 308 "makes it very difficult for federal representatives to make a strong case for the province" (Interview with Wayne MacKinnon 27 May 2010). Yet there are no demands to increase PEI's federal representation. Instead, the dominant sense is that PEI has an influence far beyond its size.

## Sardinia

Our third example is of island autonomy within an asymmetrically regionalized state. The island of Sardinia, which lies over 100km from mainland Italy, had a history of independence through its position in the Kingdom of Sardinia (which contained the possessions of the House of Savoy) and was one of the first provinces to become part of a united Italy in 1860. The island was granted "special status" in the Italian constitution of 1948, along with Valle d'Aosta, Trentino Alto-Adige, and Friuli-Venezia Giulia. Sardinia's special status largely resulted from the formidable inter-war nationalist movement, which won 36% of the vote in Sardinian elections in 1919 (Hepburn 2009). The Partito Sardo d'Azione (Psd'Az) demanded self-determination within a federal Italian state and the recognition of Sardinia's distinctiveness. But although the Psd'Az was a catalyst for institutional recognition of Sardinia's *specialità*, its electoral fortunes have since declined and other parties in Sardinia have taken up the autonomy banner.

## Constitutional and institutional framework

When Sardinia was offered a special statute with extensive powers based on that of the recently approved Sicilian model in 1946, island political parties refused it (Mattone 1982: 31). This was due to internal disputes among Sardinian parties as to what powers the island should have. The final text of the Sardinian statute was eventually drawn up by the Constituent Assembly in Rome, which severely moderated the powers that the Sardinian Consultative Council had eventually proposed. For instance, Sardinian legislative power could be superseded by national law, many important matters were "concurrent" powers with Rome, and there was no reference to the Sardinian language. Thus, unlike Åland and Prince Edward Island, Sardinia's autonomy was ultimately decided and dispensed by state – and in a considerably diluted form.

Sardinia's autonomy was based on a particular statute (Constitutional Act of 26 February 1948) and comprised exclusive legislative powers in certain areas such as: health; education; employment; industry and banking; municipalities; agriculture and forests; police; land reclamation; construction and development; transport and shipping; and public utilities and waters (Articles 3–5). The region was also granted a degree of financial autonomy and limited tax-raising powers. Most importantly, the Statuto contained a specific reference that was not contained in any other statute: a commitment by the state to "the economic and social renaissance of the island" (Art.13). Sardinia's claim to special treatment – more resources from the state – has dominated Sardinia's relations with the central state. Sardinia's powers were further enhanced during the reform of Title V of the Italian Constitution in 2001. The constitutional powers of all of the regions in Italy – including the 15 "ordinary regions" – were enhanced, and Sardinia was granted greater control over town-planning, tourism, public works, agriculture, forestry, fishing, and arts and crafts (Fabbrini & Brunazzo 2003: 101).

In addition to self-rule, Sardinia also enjoys some representation in Italian institutions. This includes members the Italian parliament (which will be reduced from nine to eight in 2013) and deputies in the senate (which will be reduced from 18 to 17 in 2013) (*Sardinia Post* 27 December 2012). The reason for the reduction is that the number of representatives for each region is proportional to the resident population, and Sardinia's population has been decreasing. However, even before this reduction, there were concerns that Sardinia's voice was marginalized in Italian politics: "we are 1,600,000 inhabitants and we do not have the same power that Sicily has because they are 5 millions and in the Parliament this makes a big difference ... if the Sardinian

Deputies vote, they are so few it does not make a difference" (Interview with Gianmario Demuro 14 July 2010). In addition, Sardinia enjoys representation in the State-Regions Conference, which is an Italian organ chaired by the prime minister and composed of the presidents of all the regions. However, within this organ, Sardinia is treated like any other region; so while it has a degree of access to the center, this is on a multilateral basis whereby it must work with others to try and influence state policy.

*Statewide and substate nationalism*

Many of the Italian parties (in particular, parties on the left) have historically been opposed to decentralization and regional autonomy. But this view changed in the 1980s during the "regionalization" of the Italian state. Furthermore, with the constitutional reform in 2001, some Italian parties – such as the Democrats of the left – reorganized their party structures along federal lines, thereby endowing regional branches – including those in Sardinia – with more autonomy yet keeping them firmly within the Italian party family. So, although for parties "in Sardinia we're all federalists, autonomists or separatists" (cited in Hepburn 2010), there is also a strong degree of integration into Italian politics and ideologies. This is most evident in the center-right Sardinian People of Freedom Party (which currently forms the government in Sardinia), which is closely tied to Berlusconi's National Party. In addition to this, the influence of Italian ideologies has been disseminated through political patronage (Clark 1996). During the second half of the 20th century, there was a strong sense that the regional institutions did not represent the people, but were in fact controlled by Rome through these systems of patronage, so that the "culture" of the regional governments ended up being the same as that of the state (Melis 1982: 1). The lack of an autonomous Sardinian elite meant that the rhetoric of "autonomy" was used to disguise a dependence on Rome.

So while Sardinia's impoverished status ensured its economic dependence on the Italian government, it was its political dependence on Roman patronage that remobilized the previously moribund nationalist movement in the 1960s. During this period, the Italian state had begun carrying out a modernization plan for the Sardinian economy according to the terms of Sardinia's statute. In 1962, the Italian parliament allocated 100 billion lire to Sardinia's *piani di rinascita* ("plans of rebirth"). Based on the concept of growth poles, the plans sought to create high-technology industries such as petrochemicals, steelworks, and oil refineries on the island, administered by the Italian-run Cassa per il Mezzogiorno with little consultation of Sardinian authorities. The imposition of an alien form of industrialization on an island spelt disaster, and the Sardinian people turned against the "cathedrals in the desert" (Mattone 1982).

They did so by supporting a nationalist movement, called *neo-sardismo*, which was based on the valorization of Sardinia's culture and identity. The cultural movement was subsumed under the nationalist party Partito Sardo d'Azione, whose electoral fortunes rose to almost 15% in regional parliament elections in the 1980s (Hepburn 2009). However, the Psd'Az became a victim of its own success: as the party of government, it too came to be seen as culpable for poor economic planning, as well as being perceived as a "puppet" of Rome, and so entered another period of decline. However, the principles of *neo-sardismo* have recently re-emerged in Sardinian politics. Parties have begun calling for the "valorization" of the Sardinian nation, and the strengthening of its identity, language, and culture (Hepburn 2010). In particular, a new Sardinian party, which was linked to the Italian center-left and headed by the media billionaire Renato Soru, governed the region from 2004–09. The "Sardinian Project" passed laws to "save the coasts," to increase the potential of tourism, to protect the environment, and to bolster the Sardinian identity through plans for bilingualism and other cultural initiatives. However, following a change in government that saw Soru's party lose office to the center-right People of Liberty Party, demands for increasing Sardinia's autonomy have been put on the back burner and Sardinia's institutions are once more dominated by Italian concerns.

*State accommodation*

The nature of Sardinian–Italian relations and accommodation of island needs was very much formed during the creation of the Special Statute in 1948, which was a watered-down form of autonomy that was decided by Rome with no Sardinian consultation. As a result, it is widely acknowledged by all political parties that the Statute does not fully reflect Sardinia's identity or sense of distinctiveness, and, by extension, that the Italian state does not fully recognize Sardinia's *specialità*. Furthermore, as the local *classe dirigente* were reluctant to break their ties to Rome, they opted to give up a strong framework for self-determination in favor of receiving funds from the central state. As a result, nationalist parties have accused the Italian government of "duping" Sardinia into a dependent relationship without giving the island the full levers of autonomy (Hepburn, 2010).

Certainly, at times, Sardinian political actors from outside the traditional *classe dirigente* have sought to contest these dependent relations, leading to tensions with Italy. In the 1970s, popular agitation against the installation of military bases in the north of the island provoked "the first official protest by the Sardinian Establishment against government policy" (Clark 1996: 96). Sardinia hosted an American nuclear submarine base in the Santa Stefano area where nuclear testing was carried out, that was the result of negotiations between Italy and the USA. The base was creating enormous damage to the environment and economy, and, in 2005, President Renato Soru's objections to America's continued military presence were successful (see Hepburn 2010). In addition, Soru demanded that Berlusconi's finance minister hand back some of the money that Sardinia overpaid in Italian taxes, amounting to €4.5 million euros (*La Repubblica* 28 October 2005). After Soru refused to go through the usual institutional channels such as the State-Regions Conference to make his claim, the two parties were able to reach a compromise and Rome agreed to return some of the money.

While Soru's politics of contestation with the Italian government have today been replaced by a more harmonious relationship between the new center-right Governments in Sardinia and Italy, there has also been an acceptance of the need to strengthen the island's autonomous institutions. This was catalyzed by the constitutional reform of 2001 that increased the autonomous powers of the 15 "ordinary" regions and precipitated a crisis of identity in the five "special regions," which were stripped of their *specialità*. In response, all parties in Sardinia began advocating Sardinian "sovereignty" and the need for more autonomy to distinguish themselves from the ordinary regions. However, there are considerable challenges in rewriting the Statute. In particular, "one obstacle is the Roman Parliament in the sense that [the Statute] must be approved by the Parliament of Rome and the Parliament will not approve ... a bilingual situation; equality between Italian and Sardo" (Interview with Ilenia Ruggiu, 14 July 2010). Until Italy does recognize Sardinia's language, culture, and distinctiveness in the rewriting of the Statute, accommodation of Sardinia's interests and identity is far from being achieved.

## Conclusion

This chapter has examined the accommodation of island interests and identities in three multinational states: Finland, Canada, and Italy. In line with the general hypotheses presented at the start of the discussion, the findings have shown that islands have preferred to pursue autonomy within states rather than seek independence. In particular, island political actors have been accommodated through specific concessions from states in return for their continuing loyalty. However, when central governments have at times been perceived as failing in their representation of island interests, this has led to dissatisfaction among island actors, and increased demands for autonomy.

In particular, the discussion explored three aspects of the accommodation of island regions: institutions, nationalism, and specific state strategies. Generally, it was found that units of federations enjoy much stronger guarantees of representation in central state structures than federacies or units of regionalized states. This was evident in the remarkable access to state structures and (potential) influence on federal politics that PEI enjoys despite its tiny size and population. In contrast, while "shared rule" is not a goal of Åland political actors, it is clear that the island is unable to effectively defend its territorial interests in the face of Finnish or European laws, due to its limited representation and weak voice in Helsinki and Brussels. Equally, Sardinia has no way to constitutionally influence Italian policy in a bilateral setting (Clark 1989; Elazar 1994; Hepburn 2012).

Another factor that may facilitate or impede the accommodation of island regions is the extent to which the constitutional framework governing self-rule and island–state relations is flexible and open to revision. Åland enjoys a highly reflexive model of autonomy, which can effectively satisfy demands for increasing the archipelago's powers, evident in the relatively straightforward way in which the Autonomy Act was revised in 1951 and 1991. Contrarily, the difficulties in rewriting the 1948 Special Statute of Sardinia have led to considerable frustration among island political actors. Finally, the degree of autonomy awarded to the island region in relation to other units of the state also affects accommodation strategies. While Åland and Sardinia were granted special status within their respective states (which in Sardinia was compromised in 2001 when all other regions were given similar powers), PEI has only the same rights as other provinces in Canada. However, there is also a widespread sense that PEI is lucky to have the same powers and privileges as much bigger provinces such as Ontario, and as such PEI does not want to be seen as "different"; it is more interested in being viewed as equal.

Secondly, the party system and nationalist mobilization has an important role to play in determining autonomy demands, whereby a separate or distinctive island party system reduces island "integration" with mainland politics and may lend itself to stronger demands for autonomy, especially where a strong substate nationalist party exists. In Sardinia, nationalist parties in Sardinia were once successful in mobilizing demands for independence; however, their goals have to a large extent been taken over by regional branches of Italian parties in Sardinia (such as the Sardinian Project), which have all called for a strengthening of Sardinia's constitutional autonomy. In Åland, while all of the parties support autonomy – be they Christian Democrats or Liberals – they have no ties to the Finnish mainland and are thus less "integrated" into mainstream politics than parties in Sardinia or PEI. Indeed, in the latter case, the two largest Canadian statewide parties dominate PEI politics to such an extent that there is no desire to have a home-grown PEI regional or autonomist party. This demonstrates that political parties may be used as instruments of integration and accommodation.

Thirdly, specific state accommodation strategies have tended to focus on economic concessions – which were the main reasons that PEI and Sardinia chose to join/remain part of the state when their constitutional treaties were being negotiated. In both cases, the state assumed responsibility for special economic rehabilitation of the islands, which cemented their long-term dependence on central funds. Demands for independence are bolstered when there is a sense that the island is not benefiting economically from state integration. This was evident in Sardinia (whose former president has been demanding a return of funds to Sardinia) and Åland (which is economically wealthier than Finland and is demanding greater fiscal autonomy). But while one of the accommodation strategies of states is economic, another is political, whereby the central state may grant the island special representation of island actors in state structures, thereby giving them disproportionate influence over state politics in relation to what their size may warrant – which was the case in PEI.

Perhaps above all, this discussion has shown that states must regularly express an interest in, and respect for, island issues, if accommodation is to be successful. While this may be an obvious – and even clichéd – assertion, in two of the cases analyzed, the central state government has spectacularly failed on both counts. In Sardinia, there was a sense that regional interests were not being taken into account by the Italian government, especially during decisions that involved no consultation or participation of island representatives – such as the design of the economic "plans of rebirth" and the decision to put American military installations on the island. It was also evident in Åland, where there is a growing sense than Helsinki is indifferent to Åland's interests, which was demonstrated during the debates on Åland's non-compliance with

European laws on mouth tobacco and seabird hunting. In contrast, the Canadian government may be held up as a paragon of virtue in accommodating island identity (at least in relation to PEI, though perhaps not Quebec as Rocher and Casañas Adam in this volume argue!) where there is a general sense that the island has a stronger voice than its size warrants, and whose claims for equality – rather than distinctiveness – have been easily met by the state.

## Notes

I would like to thank all interviewees for their time, generosity and insights into this research project, which was funded by an Economic and Social Research Council (ESRC) grant on "'The Politics of Island Regions: A Framework for Comparative Research"' (RES–000–22–3699).

1. "A Brief Summary", Ålands Framtid website: http://www.alandsframtid.ax/content/view/319/88888889/. [Accessed 8 January 2013]

## References

Åkermark, S.S. (2009). "L'example des Îles Åland on les vicissitudes d'un concept en flux", in M. Chillaud (dir.) *La question des Îles Åland. Hier, aujourd' hui et demain* (Paris: L'Harmattan).
Baldacchino, G. (ed.) (2007). *A World of Islands: An Island Studies Reader* (Malta & Canada: Agenda Academic & Institute of Island Studies).
Baldacchino, G. and E. Hepburn. (eds) (2012). "Independence, Nationalism and Subnational Island Jurisdictions", Special Issue of *Commonwealth and Comparative Politics* Vol. 50, No. 4.
Baldacchino, G. and D. Milne. (eds) (2000). *Lessons from the Political Economy of Small Islands: The Resourcefulness of Jurisdiction* (Basingstoke: Macmillan).
Baldacchino, G. and A. Spears. (2007). " The Bridge Effect: A Tentative Score Sheet for Prince Edward Island", in G Baldacchino (ed.), *Bridging Islands: The Impact of Fixed Links* (Charlottetown: Acorn Press), pp. 49–68.
Bolger, F. (1961). " Prince Edward Island and Confederation 1863–1873", CCHA, *Report* Vol. 28, pp. 25–30.
Clark, M. (1989). "La Storia Politica e Sociale 1915–1975", In B. Bandinu et al. (eds), *L'età contemporanea dal governo piemontese agli anni sessanta del nostro secolo* (Cagliari: Jaca Book).
Clark, M. (1996). "Sardinia: Cheese and Modernization", in C. Levy (ed.) *Italian Regionalism: History, Identity and Politics* (Oxford: Berg).
Clegg, P. (2012). "Independence Movements in the Caribbean: Withering on the Vine?" *Commonwealth and Comparative Politics* Vol. 50, No. 4, pp. 422–438.
Connor, H. (2008). "The Capacity for Sub-National Island Jurisdictions to Increase Autonomy: The Example of Prince Edward Island", in G. Baldacchino and K. Stuart (eds), *Pulling Strings. Policy Insights for Prince Edward Island from other Sub-National Island Jurisdictions* (Charlottetown: Island Studies Press).

Daftary, F. (2000). "Insular Autonomy: A Framework for Conflict Settlement? A Comparative Study of Corsica and the Åland Islands", *European Centre for Minority Issues (ECMI) Working Paper* Vol. 9.

Elazar, D. (1994). *The American Mosaic: The Impact of Space, Time, and Culture on American Politics* (Boulder: Westview Press)

Fabbrini, S. and M. Brunazzo. (2003). "Federalizing Italy: The Convergent Effects of Europeanization and Domestic Mobilization", *Regional and Federal Studies* Vol. 13, No. 1.

Hannum, H. (1990). *Autonomy, Sovereignty and Self-Determination. The Accommodation of Conflicting Rights* (Philadelphia: University of Pennsylvania Press).

Hepburn, E. (2009). "The Ideological Polarisation and De-polarisation of Sardinian Nationalism", *Regional and Federal Studies* Vol. 19, No. 5.

Hepburn, E. (2010). *Using Europe: Territorial Party Strategies in a Multi-Level System* (Manchester: Manchester University Press).

Hepburn, E. (2012). "Recrafting Sovereignty: Lessons from Small Island Regions?", in A.-G. Gagnon and M. Keating (eds), *Political Autonomy and Divided Societies: Imagining Democratic Alternatives in Complex Settings* (Basingstoke: Palgrave Macmillan).

Hepburn, E. (forthcoming—2014). "Forging Autonomy in a Unitary State: The Åland Islands in Finland", *Comparative European Politics*.

Lapidoth, R. (1997). *Autonomy: Flexible Solutions to Ethnic Conflicts* (Washington, DC: United States Institute of Peace Press).

Levine. (2012). *Commonwealth and Comparative Politics*, 50(4), pp. 101–134.

MacKinnon, W. (2007). "The 2007 Provincial Election in Prince Edward Island", *Canadian Political Science Review* Vol. 1, No. 2, pp. 69–74.

Mattone, A. (1982). *Le radici dell'autonomia* in *La Sardegna, Enciclopedia, Vol. 2*, a cura di M. Brigaglia, Cagliari, Edizioni della Torre.

McElroy, J. and C. Parry. (2012). "The Long-Term Propensity for Political Affiliation in Island Microstates", *Commonwealth and Comparative Politics* Vol. 50, No. 4, pp. 403–421.

Melis, G. (1982). "L'autonomia regionale della Sardegna: una chiave di lettura" in M. Brigaglia (ed.), *La Sardegna, Enciclopedia, Vol. 2* (Cagliari, Edizioni della Torre).

Modeen, T. (1969). *The International Protection of National Minorities in Europe* (Turku: Åbo Akademi).

Palmgren, S. (1997). "The Autonomy of the Åland Islands in the Constitutional Law of Finland", in L. Hannikainen and F. Horn (eds), *Autonomy and Demilitarisation in International Law: The Åland Islands in a Changing Europe* (The Hague: Kluwer Law International), pp. 85–97.

Robertson, I. (1975). "Recent Island History", *Acadiensis* Vol. 4, No. 2, pp. 111–118.

Royle, S.A. (2001). *A Geography of Islands: Small Island Insularity* (London and New York: Routledge).

Stepan, A., J. Linz, Y. Yadav. (2011). *Crafting State-Nations: India and Other Multinational Democracies* (Baltimore: Johns Hopkins University Press).

Stewart, I. (1986). "Friends at Court: Federalism and Provincial Elections on Prince Edward Island", *Canadian Journal of Political Science* Vol. XIX, No. 1.

Suksi, M. (2011). *Sub-State Governance Through Territorial Autonomy: A Comparative Study In Constitutional Law of Powers, Procedures and Institutions.*(Heidelberg: Springer).
Watts, R. (2000). "Islands in Comparative Constitutional Perspective", in G. Baldacchino and D. Milne (eds), *Lessons from the Political Economy of Islands. The Resourcefulness of Jurisdiction* (Basingstoke: Macmillan), pp. 23–29.

# 5
# From Autonomism to Independentism: The Growth of Secessionism in Catalonia (2010–2013)

*Jordi Argelaguet*

## Introduction

As the Introduction to this volume notes, "the implementation of constitutional strategies of accommodation has led to the rethinking and reformulation of creative models of accommodation within existing states, although with varying degrees of success". Since 1978, Spain has implemented a constitutional strategy of territorial pluralism to accommodate its substate national societies, with varying degrees of success.

In this chapter, we will analyze the changes in Catalan public opinion on the issue of the political relations between Catalonia and Spain; and we will provide some keys to understand its causes and to assess its consequences for the future. First, we will show the growth of secessionism in recent years and we will explain the change. We will see that the most powerful explanatory variable is the so-called "subjective national identity." Secondly, we will analyze if the changes in the latter could be seen as a main factor for explaining the growth in pro-sovereignty opinion, and we will demonstrate that one of the most important elements to take into account is the impact of the political context in individuals' opinions. Third, we will review the major political events that have occurred during this period, and we will see how the attitudes and behavior of the Spanish authorities have played an important role in this change. Fourth, we will show in detail how pro-secessionism has grown, and we will present a social and political profile of the supporters of the various options in an eventual referendum. Finally, we will end this chapter with some remarks about the evolution of this political conflict between Catalonia and Spain.

The chapters by Rocher and Casañas Adam, and by Lopez Bofill, in this volume make a juridical and political analysis of the effects of Spanish constitutionalism on politics in Catalonia. This chapter is mindful and attentive to the effects of Spanish constitutionalism as well, but seeks to make an additional contribution: we will examine the rich data on public opinion in Catalonia to understand the interaction between politics and constitutionalism, and how it is a critical dimension of the politics of accommodation in multinational democracies. This chapter seeks to understand the causes and motivations of substate nationalism in Catalonia in relation to recent developments in Spanish constitutionalism.

On 25 November 2012, in the elections to the parliament of Catalonia,[1] CiU received 30.7% of the votes and 50 seats (out of 135); ERC, 13.7% and 21 seats; PSC, 14.4% and 20 seats; PP, 13.0% and 19 seats; ICV-EUiA, 9.9% and 13 seats; Cs, 7.6% and 9 seats; and, finally, CUP, 3.5% and 3 seats.[2] These results show that in Catalonia a clear majority of the parties are defending the so-called "right to decide" (CiU, ERC, ICV and CUP), that is, they believe that the people of Catalonia have the right to decide its political future and, moreover, they are committed to holding a referendum on independence.

One of the first decisions of the new Parliament was to approve, on 22 January of 2013, the Resolution 5/X, whose title was "the Declaration of sovereignty and right to decide of the people of Catalonia."[3] Its centerpiece states that "The people of Catalonia has, for reasons of democratic legitimacy, the nature of a sovereign political and legal subject." This resolution – adopted by 85 votes in favor (CiU, ERC, ICV-EUiA and a member of CUP), 41 against (PSC PPC and C's) and two abstentions (CUP)[4] – came into collision with the Spanish Constitution, which establishes that the Spanish people are sovereign.

The new Parliament of Catalonia of 2012 reflects the growth of the secessionist orientation in Catalan society in recent years, especially since the Constitutional Court passed a sentence, in July 2010, on the 2006 Statute of Autonomy of Catalonia. The growth in secessionism occurred in the context of a dynamic process of increasing confrontation between the will of large segments of Catalan society and the actions taken by the Spanish government, which has, since 2011, had the support of an absolute majority of the rightist Popular Party.

## The preferences on the constitutional relationships between Catalonia and Spain through history and public opinion

The construction of the Spanish nation-state is a long and complex process because of the existence of various substate nationalisms (De la Granja et al. 2001; Fernández García & Petithomme 2012). There was always a conflict, more or less intense depending on the period, between the Spanish government and the majority of the Catalan population while the Spanish state was being built: from its distant background (the union of the crowns of Castile and Aragon between the 15th and 16th centuries); through the composed monarchy of the Habsburg's dynasty (16th–17th centuries); the absolute monarchy of the Bourbons' dynasty (from the beginning of the 18th century), the establishment of a sort of liberal centralist state (after the first third of the 19th century) and its subsequent precarious development; through the two dictatorships of the 20th century (General Primo de Rivera's one 1923–1931, and General Franco's 1939–1975); the Second Republic (1931–1939); up until the current State of Autonomies, embodied in the democratic Constitution of 1978 (De Riquer 2000; McRoberts 2002).

During the 20th century, this conflict adopted the struggle between two nationalisms (the Castilian one transformed into a Spanish one versus Catalan nationalism) and it became a tie: Spain was not strong enough to assimilate Catalonia and Catalonia has not had sufficient force to achieve full independence from Spain. Catalan nationalism has been plural since its early theoretical formulations (during the last third of the 19th century). In this sense, starting from the notion that Catalonia is conceived as a nation, political Catalanism has been advocated by various social sectors, which have also promoted a considerable diversity of policy proposals for Spain, and developed several strategies to make them feasible, such as regionalism, autonomism, federalism or, even, separatism (Acosta 1981; Balcells 1996; Guibernau 2004).

Depending on the historical period, each of these options has had a higher or lower projection on Catalan society, represented by political parties (Caminal 1998; Molas 2000). Also, within each party, one can also find different approaches on the national question. Moreover, today, this debate can be detected in public opinion surveys, asking which is the preferred option for articulating the political and constitutional relations between Catalonia and Spain (see Table 5.1).[5]

In Table 5.1, there are data from the Centre d'Estudis d'Opinió of some of the polls conducted in recent years, from which one can appreciate the considerable changes that have taken place on this issue,

*Table 5.1* Constitutional preferences of the relationships between Catalonia and Spain according to Centre d'Estudis d'Opinió surveys (2006–2013)

| | Region | Autonomous community | A state within a Federal Spain | An independent state | DK/NA | N | Source |
|---|---|---|---|---|---|---|---|
| 2006 (1) | 8.1 | 38.2 | 33.4 | 13.9 | 6.3 | 2.000 | REO, 346 |
| 2006 | 6.8 | 40.0 | 32.8 | 15.9 | 4.5 | 2.000 | REO, 367 |
| 2007 | 5.1 | 37.8 | 33.8 | 17.3 | 6.0 | 2.000 | REO, 404 |
| 2008 | 7.1 | 38.3 | 31.8 | 17.4 | 5.4 | 2.000 | REO, 466 |
| 2009 | 5.9 | 37.0 | 29.9 | 21.6 | 5.6 | 2.000 | REO, 544 |
| 2010 | 5.9 | 34.7 | 30.9 | 25.2 | 3.4 | 2.500 | REO, 612 |
| 2011 | 5.7 | 30.3 | 30.4 | 28.2 | 5.4 | 2.500 | REO, 651 |
| 2012 | 4.0 | 19.1 | 25.5 | 44.3 | 7.1 | 2.500 | REO, 705 |
| 2013 | 4.4 | 20.7 | 22.4 | 46.4 | 6.1 | 2.000 | REO, 712 |

*Note*: This is the first survey of the CEO's Barometer Series, in March 2006. The other surveys are the last wave of the Barometer in each year. In 2013, it is the first wave of the Barometer.

especially the great change that affects the "independent state" option, rising from 13.9% in 2006 to 46.4% in 2013.

On the other hand, the two minority options ("a region of Spain" and "DK/NA") have had similar (although fluctuating) figures over the years. And the data for the other three remaining options present appreciable changes, especially the "independent state" one, as already stated.

The "Autonomous Community" (the current arrangement) has been the most preferred one until 2011, when it was overtaken by a "state within a federal Spain" option. In fact, the "autonomous region" has had a downward trend since almost the beginning of the series. The "federal" alternative has always been the second one, except in 2011, when it got a little more support than all the other options. However, since then it has recorded a downward trend, too. Finally, the option that has changed more, the "independent state," has had a clear upward trend since 2006, although it shows a variable slope. Between 2006 and 2008, there was a smooth growth, which was accelerated between 2008 and 2011; a huge increase in 2012 was followed by a reduced slope by 2013. At the present time, the data seem clear: the choice of the "independent state" is the most preferred one and it had an inflexion point in 2011.

Apart from confirming the evolution of these data, we need to explore the reasons for the recorded changes; that is, what are the factors that would explain the change in the individual political attitudes toward the different options about the constitutional relations between Catalonia and Spain. A recent and interesting contribution comes from Prat (2012), who has analyzed the individual support for the independence of Catalonia from various explanatory variables that are considered relevant by the literature: the age; the generation; the cultural frame based on the assumption that the media are builders and shapers of identity, which frame the differentiation between citizens depending upon whether they are Spanish-centered or Catalan-centered (Fernandez-i-Marín & López 2010); the impact of economic motivations and their interaction with identity (Munoz & Tormos 2012); and, finally, all the issues related to the subjective national identity. After a complex multinomial analysis, which includes the subjective national identity, the age group, the sympathy towards a political party, the satisfaction with the functioning of democracy, the trust in politicians, the fact of being informed about politics by TV3 (the Catalan public television channel), the assessment of the economic and political situation in Catalonia, the list of the main problems in Catalonia, the size of the municipality, and also including several control variables such as gender, own language and most used language, place of one's birth, the place of birth of his/her father and mother, level of education, religion and ideology (in the left–right dimension), Prat concludes that the subjective national identity is the variable with the greatest impact on the preferences about the institutional arrangement of Catalonia with Spain.

This variable comes from the "Moreno-Linz question," which builds a bidirectional indicator that summarizes the identification of individuals with two political communities which claim to be nations, such as Catalonia and Spain. This indicator, originally conceived by Linz (1973, 1981), compels individuals to take a position with respect to the national cleavage in an axis with five positions: only Catalan, more Catalan than Spanish, as Spanish as Catalan, more Catalan than Spanish and only Spanish (Moreno 2006). There is plentiful available data on this question. Some of them are shown in Table 5.2.

The data collected in the previous table show trends of change and continuity in each of the five main options. The most important elements of continuity are three: the percentage of DK/NA is usually very low; the biggest group has always been the "dual identity" ("as Catalan and Spanish"); and, third, the other large groups are always those where the weight of Catalan identity is higher. Likewise, there are elements of change that should be noted: the Catalan component has tended

Table 5.2  Subjective national identity in Catalonia (1979–2013)

| | Only Catalan | Cat > Spa | Cat = Spa | Spa > Cat | Only Spanish | DK/NA | (N) | Source and study number |
|---|---|---|---|---|---|---|---|---|
| 1979 | 14.9 | 11.7 | 35.4 | 6.7 | 31.3 | | 1.079 | DATA |
| 1982 | 9.3 | 11.7 | 41.2 | 8.7 | 23.1 | | 1.176 | DATA |
| 1984 | 7.1 | 22.4 | 46.2 | 8.8 | 12.5 | 3.0 | 4.872 | CIS, 1413 |
| 1988 | 11.1 | 28.2 | 40.4 | 8.4 | 9.1 | 2.7 | 2.896 | CIS, 1750 |
| 1992 | 15.6 | 23.4 | 35.7 | 8.3 | 14.9 | 2.0 | 2.489 | CIS, 1998 |
| 1995 | 13.4 | 23.1 | 41.0 | 7.0 | 13.8 | 1.7 | 1.593 | CIS, 2199 |
| 1999 | 14.0 | 21.8 | 43.1 | 6.1 | 11.5 | 3.3 | 1.368 | CIS, 2374 |
| 2001 | 15.4 | 25.8 | 35.9 | 6.2 | 14.7 | 2.0 | 2.778 | CIS, 2410 |
| 2003 | 13.9 | 24.7 | 43.2 | 6.7 | 9.8 | 1.8 | 3.571 | CIS, 2543 |
| 2006 | 13.8 | 24.7 | 41.6 | 7.6 | 8.8 | 4.5 | 1.965 | CIS, 2660 |
| 2006 | 14.2 | 27.7 | 42.5 | 5.2 | 6.6 | 3.9 | 2.000 | REO, 346 |
| 2006 | 14.5 | 27.2 | 44.3 | 4.7 | 6.1 | 3.2 | 2.000 | REO, 367 |
| 2007 | 17.1 | 29.4 | 41.2 | 5.1 | 3.9 | 3.4 | 2.000 | REO, 404 |
| 2008 | 16.4 | 25.7 | 45.3 | 5.4 | 4.7 | 2.5 | 2.000 | REO, 466 |
| 2009 | 19.1 | 25.6 | 42.7 | 4.5 | 5.7 | 2.4 | 2.000 | REO, 544 |
| 2010 | 20.3 | 25.5 | 42.5 | 3.9 | 5.5 | 2.3 | 2.500 | REO, 612 |
| 2011 | 20.5 | 29.5 | 39.3 | 3.3 | 5.0 | 2.4 | 2.500 | REO, 651 |
| 2012 | 29.6 | 28.7 | 35.0 | 2.5 | 2.0 | 2.3 | 2.500 | REO, 705 |
| 2013 | 29.1 | 27.9 | 35.1 | 2.7 | 2.9 | 3.2 | 2.000 | REO, 712 |

*Note*: DATA and CIS surveys are based on personal interview; CEO, CATI.
*Sources*: DATA. Quoted by Shabad and Gunther (1982); CIS, Centro de Investigaciones Sociológicas, available at www.cis.es; CEO, Centre d'Estudis d'Opinió, available at www.ceo.gencat.cat

to grow while the Spanish component has declined significantly. The changes, however, have been structural and short-term, too.

Regarding the former, it has been shown that, indeed, the effect of the main agents of the political socialization process in Catalonia have had an impact on the spread of Catalan identity in recent years: generation (Argelaguet 2006), family (Rico & Jennings 2012), whether the school teaches in Catalan (Clots-Figueras & Masella 2012) and the media (Fernández-i-Marín & López 2010). As for circumstantial elements, Hierro argues that national identity can be altered in the short term as a result of changes in the political context, such as changes in government or as a result of political mobilization (Hierro Hernández 2010). Finally, recent research – which examines the effects of age, period, and generation on the support for Catalan independence between 1991 and 2011 – has also identified a link with the changes that have taken place in subjective national identity and it concludes that, although the generational effect has a slight influence, the period effect has more influence in order to understand the change in support for independence. This last variable and the subjective national identity would have been evolving, although with different intensity, in the same direction (Civit 2013).

Therefore, based on these findings, let us explore the elements of the political context that would have had an effect on promoting the growth of the "Catalan" component within the subjective national identity and, also, the growth of the secessionist option in these last few years.

## The effect on the political context of constitutional moments in Catalonia and Spain

The shift over recent years in Catalan public opinion about constitutional preferences is mainly due to the impact of various events that have occurred during this period. Since 2006, and even more especially since 2010, Catalan politics entered an intense dynamics of confrontation of ideas on how to interpret what was happening with regard to self-government of Catalonia. Therefore, it is imperative to give a brief account of the main political events that have contributed to the change in the opinions and attitudes of substate nationalists. These episodes are diverse and they affect strictly political issues such as election results and formation of new governments, or they are related to public policy (bills, public investment in the area); constitutional moments (for instance, the controversial rulings of the Constitutional Court in Madrid); or economic factors (the economic crisis and its impact on the finances of the government of Catalonia, with all its consequences); or, even, they affect some symbolic elements (expressions of opposition to the action of the head of state, for example). Also, this process is completed with the structuring of a mass social movement in favor of independence, which showed a high capacity for action in the public sphere and for exerting pressure on political parties.

It can be helpful to follow a chronological approach. The starting point of this period is the referendum to approve the new Statute of Autonomy of Catalonia, held on 18 June 2006.

After a long process of political negotiations, first in Barcelona and later in Madrid, the degree of self-government that a big plurality of the

Catalan Parliament had wanted was severely reduced under the pressure of veiled military threats and under a strong campaign led by the PP against this process.[6] The PP was accused of promoting catalanophobia (Capdevila & Gomez 2011). Finally, there was a referendum about the proposed reform of the Statute. It was approved by 73.9% of votes in favor, 20.8% against, with 5.3% blank votes. The turnout was low: only 48.85% of the Catalan electorate voted. Some days later, the new Statute of Autonomy became effective and the PP presented an appeal of unconstitutionality before the Constitutional Court.[7]

This situation reconfirmed the belief of many people that the proposal approved by the majority of the Catalan people to build a new relationship within Spain was not accepted at all by a large part of the Spanish population.

While the appeal to the Constitutional Court was being debated in Madrid, the perception that Catalonia did not receive fair treatment from the Spanish government in all the issues related to infrastructure was being consolidated among many Catalans.[8] In this sense, at the end of 2007, there was a massive demonstration in Barcelona against this perceived unfair public investment policy. It had the support of CiU, ERC, ICV-EUiA and CUP. They demanded the transfer of the transport network and infrastructures to the government of Catalonia, the publication of fiscal balances between Catalonia and Spain, and that the Catalan government should collect and manage all taxes paid in Catalonia. However, two months later, in February 2008, the connection between Barcelona and Madrid by high speed train was completed.[9] However, this popular mobilization could not transform itself into electoral results. In the following Spanish elections of March, PSOE won in the whole of Spain, and it reached the simple plurality of 169 out of 350. And in Catalonia, PSC also won the elections, with 45.39% of votes and 25 seats; CiU, 20.9% of votes and 10 seats; PP, 16.4% and 8 seats; ERC, 7.83% and 3 seats; and ICV-EUiA, 4.92% and 1 seat.

The new Spanish government was in a minority in the Congress, and it was compelled to submit data on the so-called fiscal balances of the Autonomous Communities with the public sector for 2005. That year, the fiscal balance between Catalonia and the central administration of the state was negative, meaning 8.7% of Catalan GDP.[10] It was the first time that official data confirmed the Catalan fiscal deficit; that is, the state was collecting more taxes in Catalonia than all its investments and payments there. These data were so impressive and controversial that the Spanish government has not provided similar figures since, fearing they could fuel the Catalan secessionist movement.

On 13 September 2009, an unofficial referendum was held on the independence of Catalonia. It was organized by cultural associations with the support of the local authorities in a small village near Barcelona, Arenys de Munt. The success of this initiative, measured in popular participation and media coverage, propelled others to repeat the exercise around Catalonia, through several waves of popular consultations during the following months. The last referendum was held in Barcelona on 11 April 2011. Throughout this process, nearly 3 million people were invited to participate in the consultations, thanks to the initiative of a civic network made up of local volunteers (but coordinated with each other and often with the support of local councils). The final turn-out was 23%, of whom 93.3% were in favor of Catalan independence.[11] This experience had important consequences, since it served to mobilize sociological nationalism and it received important media coverage, especially when a restrictive sentence of the Constitutional Court about the Statute was expected.

Finally, on 28 June 2010, the Constitutional Court released the expected ruling, and it declared unconstitutional 14 articles of the Statute of Autonomy, and 27 more were reinterpreted. It presented a minimalist interpretation of Catalonia's right to self-government, compared to the will that had been expressed by the Parliament of Catalonia at the beginning of the reform process; and, also, when compared to the text that the people of Catalonia had approved in the 2006 Referendum. For almost all the Catalan political parties, the decision of the Constitutional Court certified the end of an entire political autonomy project within the framework of a democratic Spain.

The immediate effect was the holding of a demonstration against the ruling in Barcelona on 10 July. Hundreds of thousands of people took part in it and it became the largest demonstration ever held in Catalonia. The confrontation of the people of Catalonia and the Spanish institutions was underway and it had several points of friction. For instance, a few days later (on 28 July), the Parliament of Catalonia approved the elimination of bull-fighting in Catalonia, at the request of a Popular Legislative Initiative (PLI).[12] Afterwards, the PP filed an appeal against this measure before the Constitutional Court.

In late November 2010, elections were held in the Parliament of Catalonia, and there emerged a new political plurality. CiU, the moderate Catalan nationalist coalition, won 62 seats out of 135. However, it had to govern in minority, hoping to receive some support from other parties. The political commitment of the new president, Artur Mas, was to get a new fiscal pact and try to cope successfully with the economic crisis which had had two important effects: it was eroding the living conditions of many families and it was jeopardizing the finances of the government, threatening the implementation of welfare policies.

In late December, the Supreme Court publicized three rulings that questioned the foundations of the Catalan language policy in schools because, under the recent Constitutional Court decision on the Statute of Autonomy, the Catalan language could not be considered preferential in Catalonia. From here, there were other judicial decisions that went in the same direction, in schools or in other areas of public service.

The real scope of the Constitutional Court's ruling was having a deep impact, and many Catalans showed their displeasure about it. In the local elections of May 2011, CiU registered significant progress at the expense of the PSC, and it reached a historic victory in Barcelona. In addition, the political climate was tense as a result of the growing economic crisis. In late August 2011, the reform of Article 135 of the Spanish Constitution of 1978 was approved, thanks to an agreement between the PSOE and the PP, and without the involvement of Catalan and Basque nationalist parties. This reform was required by the European Union, and it brought in the concept of "budgetary stability" and set the absolute priority of payment of the debt's interest and the debt itself.

A few months later, on 20 November, the Spanish general elections were held and the PP won an absolute majority. This party not only proposed right-wing solutions to the economic crisis, but it wanted to reformulate the State of Autonomies via its centralization policies. On the other hand, in Catalonia, for the first time in history, CiU became the majority party in this type of election.

Gradually, pro-independence sectors were organizing to begin an open conflict with Spain. Thus, at the institutional level, the Association of Municipalities for Independence (AMI), in order to promote the exercise of the right to self-determination, was formally established in December 2011.[13] In the area of civic organizations, in March 2012, the National Assembly of Catalonia (ANC) was founded, and it quickly spread its local branches across all Catalonia. To foster its cause, it made conferences and debates about the right to self-determination and independence of Catalonia and it began to prepare a huge demonstration in Barcelona for 11 September, the Catalan National Day (Martí 2013). To encourage popular mobilization in favor of their political postulates, the Catalan secessionists used one of their historically most preferred arguments: the fiscal deficit between Catalonia and Spain (Pons-i-Novell & Tremosa-i-Balcells 2004, 2005; DEC 2012).

In March 2012, the government of Catalonia presented the fiscal balance of the central government in Catalonia (2006–2009). It was estimated that by the year 2009, this had represented a negative fiscal balance of 8.9% of GDP.[14] Despite this, it is a very controversial issue because there are strong disagreements on methodology for making these calculations, and the results generally show clear elements of inequity in funding various regions (Ruana 2003).

In the Catalan case, the magnitude of the "fiscal deficit" – alongside evidence that the state is discriminating against Catalonia with low public investment because it is following a policy to articulate Spain under a French-inspired centralist nation-state model (Bel 2010) – gives arguments to the secessionist groups to feed their protests, for example, against the tolls on the Catalan motorways.

Meanwhile, the highest institutions of the state had serious problems of public image, which reinforced the argument of the secessionists that Spain was in a deep political crisis.[15] In late May, the Parliament of Catalonia approved by a large majority a proposal for a fiscal agreement that the President of Catalonia should negotiate with the Spanish government. This proposal set a new funding model in which the Catalan government had: the management of all taxes through a fully operative Taxation Agency of Catalonia; and total regulatory power over all government taxes. This model would include a contribution (in accordance with the Spanish government) to pay the services provided by the state in Catalonia and, finally, another contribution to fund the solidarity of Catalonia with other regions, although it would delimited by objective criteria.

But the economic crisis was causing serious problems to society and to the finances of the government, which was forced to ask for help from the Spanish government in August 2012. It requested a loan of €5.023b to pay the debt and the interests assumed by the Catalan government. Three realities emerged: Catalan-self-government was diminished; the funding of Catalonia was not satisfactorily resolved; the Catalan government had no choice but to cut its spending capacities. The option in favor of Catalan independence had a strong argument ("without this big fiscal deficit, the budget adjustment would not be necessary") and it was repeatedly used by the secessionists to prepare the way for the announced demonstration during the next Catalan National Day. A few days earlier, in September, the council of a small town, Torelló, had proclaimed itself as a "free Catalan territory" and it decided that the Spanish legal framework would rule there in a provisional way, until the Parliament of Catalonia set a new sovereign legal framework.[16]

The process of mobilization by secessionist groups reached its peak in the demonstration that was held in Barcelona on 11 September, the National Day of Catalonia, under the slogan "Catalonia, new state in Europe." This demonstration, with hundreds of thousands of participants, became the largest ever held in Catalonia and it had a great impact on the international media.

Days later, a planned meeting between the Spanish and Catalan presidents was held to discuss the proposed "fiscal pact" that the Parliament of Catalonia had approved at the beginning of the summer. It ended without any agreement because the Spanish government not only rejected the Catalan proposed model, but it refused to negotiate a new funding scheme for Catalonia bilaterally, apart from the other Autonomous Communities. This attitude of strong opposition to the proposals coming from the Parliament of Catalonia was reinforced when, in the following October, the Minister of Education of the Spanish government said in the Spanish Parliament that he was committed to "Hispanicize the Catalan students."[17] This was one of the main reasons he had for promoting the writing of a new education bill. He intended, in addition to a substantial change in the overall schooling model, to modify the current uses of languages for teaching in Catalonia; and he wanted to increase up to 65% (instead of 55%), the percentage of curricular content determined by the Spanish government, with the aim of unifying and controlling the subjects taught throughout the Spanish state. In practice, this move meant an almost complete erosion of Catalan self-government in education.

On 25 November, Catalan elections were held. Almost all the main parties, except PP and Cs, concurred with a more or less explicit defense of the Catalan people's "right to decide" on their connection with Spain. The results gave a clear plurality to the parties most committed to this democratic right: CiU, ERC, ICV and CUP.

On 18 December according to the electoral results, the "Pact for Freedom" was signed between CiU and ERC. It facilitated the formation of a government led by CiU with the Parliamentary support of ERC. In the next month, on 22 January, the Parliament of Catalonia approved the "Declaration of Sovereignty and the right to choose of the people of Catalonia." The Spanish government announced that the state's Justice Minister would appeal this resolution before the Constitutional Court because he believed that both the recognition of the sovereignty of the Catalan nation and the notion that Catalonia has the right to decide about its future, violated several articles of the Constitution.[18] Also, the report determined that the same Declaration of the Catalan Parliament has an "ad extra" legal effect, because it is trying to direct the institutions of Catalonia toward a clear unconstitutional end.

The political process lived in Catalonia over recent years has shown that the existing substantive discussion is the possible access of Catalonia to its political independence. For this reason, it is necessary to draw a profile of the social and political bases of the different options in a referendum on this issue (Rokkan 1973; Estrade and Tresserras 1990).

## The social bases of the different options in a referendum for secession in Catalonia

Although the goal of independence had been present in Catalonia for decades (Colomer 1995), it was not until the 1990s that it had a real and quite important political-electoral expression, with the Republican Left of Catalonia (ERC) (Argelaguet 2012). Since then, the secessionist option has had a Parliamentary referral, despite the fact that there are secessionist voters in nearly all the other Catalan political parties. Gradually, this option has been gathering more support among larger parts of the Catalan electorate: while in the mid-1990s it stood at about a third, in 2013, it had risen to 54.7%.[19] The evolution registered in recent years is shown in Table 5.3.

Table 5.3 Evolution of the options about Catalan independence

|  | 2001 | 2011 (June) | 2011 (Oct.) | 2012 (Jan.) | 2012 (June) | 2012 (Nov.) | 2013 (Feb.) |
| --- | --- | --- | --- | --- | --- | --- | --- |
| Yes, in favor | 35.9 | 42.9 | 45.4 | 44.6 | 51.1 | 57.0 | 54.7 |
| No, against | 48.1 | 28.2 | 24.7 | 24.7 | 21.1 | 20.5 | 20.7 |
| Non-voting | — | 23.3 | 23.8 | 24.2 | 21.1 | 14.3 | 17.0 |
| Other answers | — | 0.5 | 0.6 | 1.0 | 1.0 | 0.6 | 1.4 |
| DK | 13.3 | 4.4 | 4.6 | 4.6 | 4.7 | 6.2 | 5.2 |
| NA | 2.8 | 0.8 | 1.0 | 0.9 | 1.1 | 1.5 | 1.0 |
| (N) | 2.777 | 2.500 | 2.500 | 2.500 | 2.500 | 2.500 | 2.000 |
| Source | CIS | CEO | CEO | CEO | CEO | CEO | CEO |
| Study number | 2410 | 652 | 661 | 677 | 694 | 705 | 712 |

Notes: Centro de Investigaciones Sociológicas (CIS) survey is an interview face to face. Centre d'Estudis d'Opinió (CEO) survey is a CATI one.

In 2001, according to the CIS, the pro-independence group represented 35.9% of the Catalan population. Those in favor of Catalan independence outnumber those who are against it in the following categories: those with a higher level of education; those whose mother tongue is Catalan; those who were taught in Catalan or mainly in Catalan; those whose level of knowledge of Catalan is high; those who place themselves on the left wing of the political spectrum; those who see themselves as "Catalan only" or "more Catalan than Spanish"; those who were born in Catalonia or have their family's origins in Catalonia; and those who vote for CiU or ERC (Argelaguet 2003). In 2011, the percentage in favor of independence was 42.9%. In mid-2012, the 50% barrier was overcome. By 2013, in the first CEO barometer, the percentage stood at 54.7%. Logically, the independence option is linked to social and political variables, as shown in the cross-tabulation between these and the option in a referendum, which are presented in the following tables. From them, a sociopolitical profile of each group could emerge.

Taking as reference the percentage favoring independence in the whole sample, 54.7%, Table 5.4 shows that its figure is higher: for the group of inhabitants of small villages (67.6%), small towns (58.6%) and medium-sized towns (58.0%); among those born in Catalonia (64%); for those who were born in Catalonia, with both parents also born in Catalonia (77.5%) or both parents also born in Catalonia (60.1%) and those who say that Catalan was their first language (78.3%) or who say, in the subjective national identity, they were Catalan and Spanish (55.3%). However, it is interesting to note that 20.7% of those born outside Catalonia or 32.7% of those who have Spanish as their first language are also in favor of independence.

*Table 5.4* Socio-political variables and the referendum on independence (1)

|  |  | yes | no | abs | other | DK | NA | (N) |
|---|---|---|---|---|---|---|---|---|
|  | Overall sample | 54.7 | 20.7 | 17.0 | 1.1 | 5.4 | 1.0 | 2,000 |
| Gender | Male | 59.3 | 19.3 | 15.6 | 1.0 | 3.6 | 1.1 | 965 |
|  | Female | 50.5 | 21.9 | 18.4 | 1.2 | 7.1 | 1.0 | 1,035 |
| Age group | 18–34 | 58.0 | 19.2 | 17.1 | 1.5 | 4.2 |  | 480 |
|  | 35–49 | 56.1 | 19.8 | 15.1 | 1.0 | 6.0 | 1.9 | 580 |
|  | 50–64 | 50.0 | 24.2 | 18.9 | 1.3 | 4.1 | 1.5 | 466 |
|  | More than 64 | 54.5 | 19.7 | 17.5 | 0.6 | 7.2 | 0.4 | 474 |

(*continued*)

*Table 5.4* Continued

| | | | | | | | | |
|---|---|---|---|---|---|---|---|---|
| Size of town | <2.000 inhabitants | 67.6 | 9.8 | 10.8 | 1.0 | 8.8 | 2.0 | *102* |
| | 2.001–10.000 inhabitants | 58.6 | 17.5 | 14.7 | 1.4 | 5.3 | 2.5 | *285* |
| | 10.001–50.000 inhabitants | 58.0 | 17.9 | 16.2 | 0.7 | 6.0 | 1.1 | *535* |
| | 50.001–150.000 inhabitants | 51.2 | 22.1 | 19.9 | 1.5 | 4.7 | 0.5 | *403* |
| | 150.001–1.000.000 inhabitants | 44.9 | 30.1 | 21.2 | | 3.8 | | *237* |
| | Barcelona | 53.7 | 22.1 | 16.2 | 1.6 | 5.5 | 0.9 | *438* |
| Born in … | Catalonia | 64.0 | 14.9 | 14.0 | 1.0 | 4.9 | 1.2 | *1,552* |
| | Rest of the Spanish state | 20.7 | 42.7 | 27.8 | 1.5 | 6.6 | 0.8 | *395* |
| | European Union | 40.0 | 33.3 | 13.3 | | 13.3 | | *15* |
| | Rest of the world | 35.5 | 16.1 | 35.5 | 6.5 | 6.5 | | *32* |
| | Doesn't answer | 33.3 | 33.3 | | | 33.3 | | *6* |
| Family's origins | Born in Catalonia with both parents also born in Catalonia | 77.5 | 7.2 | 9.6 | 0.1 | 4.3 | 1.3 | *766* |
| | Born in Catalonia with one parent born in Catalonia | 60.1 | 17.3 | 13.8 | 2.4 | 5.3 | 1.1 | *377* |
| | Born in Catalonia, both parents born outside Catalonia | 43.1 | 26.9 | 22.5 | 1.0 | 5.6 | 1.0 | *413* |
| | Born outside Catalonia and both parents too. | 22.2 | 40.7 | 27.6 | 1.6 | 7.2 | 0.7 | *445* |
| First language spoken at home | Catalan | 78.3 | 6.4 | 9.0 | 0.8 | 4.8 | 0.9 | *926* |
| | Both languages: Cat. and Spanish | 55.3 | 12.9 | 20.0 | 4.7 | 7.1 | | *85* |
| | Spanish | 32.7 | 34.8 | 24.3 | 0.8 | 6.0 | 1.3 | *950* |
| | Other lang. or other combinations | 31.6 | 28.9 | 26.3 | 10.5 | 2.6 | | *38* |
| | DK | | 100.0 | | | | | *1* |
| | NA | | 100.0 | | | | | *1* |

*Source*: Own calculations from CEO's 2013 barometer, study number REO 712.

Table 5.5 shows how the level of education is also associated with the vote for independence: a higher education level tends to be linked to a higher percentage in favor of independence. The consumption of political information through the media in Catalan is also associated with the acceptance of the independence of Catalonia: 76.2% of those who are informed through TV3 prefer independence; this percentage is 78.5% in the case of Canal 33 (the second channel in Catalan public TV) and 71% for 8TV (a private TV channel in Catalan). However, this percentage is much lower among those informed through the television channels that broadcast in Spanish.

Finally, Table 5.6 shows the cross-tabulations of some political variables with the options in a referendum. The percentage of "yes" is very high among supporters of Catalan nationalist parties: ERC (94.5%), CiU (78.0%) and CUP (86.3%). It is also the majority percentage in ICV (43.8%). However, it is a clear minority in PSC (14.4%) and in PP (5.1%).

*Table 5.5* Socio-political variables and the referendum on independence (2)

|  |  | yes | no | abs | other | DK | NA | (N) |
|---|---|---|---|---|---|---|---|---|
|  | Overall sample | 54.7 | 20.7 | 17.0 | 1.1 | 5.4 | 1.0 | 2,000 |
| Level of Education | Illiterate | 50.0 |  | 50.0 |  |  |  | 5 |
|  | Fewer than five years in School | 35.1 | 13.5 | 35.1 |  | 16.2 | 0.0 | 37 |
|  | Incomplete Primary School | 45.0 | 21.1 | 25.7 |  | 7.3 | 0.9 | 109 |
|  | Primary School | 45.8 | 25.3 | 22.0 | 0.8 | 5.7 | 0.4 | 487 |
|  | Secondary School | 64.6 | 16.9 | 13.7 | 1.3 | 3.2 | 0.3 | 315 |
|  | Professional Formation (medium) | 44.3 | 28.7 | 24.1 |  | 2.9 |  | 174 |
|  | Professional Formation (superior) | 58.3 | 20.3 | 15.1 | 1.8 | 1.8 | 2.6 | 270 |
|  | University Grade (3 years) | 57.3 | 23.4 | 8.7 | 1.8 | 6.9 | 1.8 | 217 |
|  | University Grade (4 or more years) | 63.2 | 14.6 | 12.2 | 1.4 | 8.3 | 0.3 | 287 |
|  | Post grade, Master | 66.3 | 11.3 | 10.0 | 2.5 | 7.5 | 2.5 | 79 |
|  | Doctorate | 50.0 | 15.0 | 15.0 |  | 10.0 | 10.0 | 19 |
|  | No answer | 100.0 |  |  |  | 0.0 |  | 1 |

(*continued*)

*Table 5.5* Continued

| | | | | | | | | |
|---|---|---|---|---|---|---|---|---|
| Preferred TV to get the political information | TVE 1 (Public TV in Spanish) | 11.3 | 48.7 | 36.0 | 1.3 | 2.7 | | 150 |
| | TVE 2 (Public TV in Spanish) | 50.0 | 0.0 | 50.0 | | | | 5 |
| | TV3 (Public TV in Catalan) | 76.2 | 6.0 | 12.3 | 0.5 | 4.5 | 0.5 | 922 |
| | Canal 33 (Public TV in Catalan) | 100.0 | | | | | | 2 |
| | Tele 5 (Private TV in Spanish) | 22.7 | 45.5 | 20.9 | 3.6 | 7.3 | 0.0 | 110 |
| | Antena 3 (Private TV in Spanish) | 12.4 | 56.6 | 22.1 | 3.5 | 5.3 | | 113 |
| | Cuatro (Private TV in Spanish) | 7.7 | 53.8 | 38.5 | | | | 14 |
| | La Sexta (Private TV in Spanish) | 26.0 | 42.0 | 21.0 | 2.0 | 7.0 | 2.0 | 100 |
| | Canal 3/24 (Public TV in Catalan) | 78.5 | 8.9 | 5.1 | 5.1 | 1.3 | 1.3 | 79 |
| | 8TV (Private TV in Catalan) | 71.0 | 14.5 | 6.5 | | 6.5 | 1.6 | 62 |
| | Intereconomía (Private TV in Spanish) | 0.0 | 83.3 | 16.7 | | | | 6 |
| | Other channels | 22.7 | 50.0 | 18.2 | | 4.5 | 4.5 | 22 |
| | Without a usual channel | 30.3 | 36.9 | 22.1 | | 6.6 | 4.1 | 123 |
| | Doesn't know | 0.0 | | 50.0 | | 50.0 | | 5 |
| | No answer | 0.0 | 100.0 | | | | | 3 |
| | With no information through TV | | | | | | | 285 |

*Source*: Own calculations from CEO's 2013 barometer, study number REO 712.

And it is non-existent in Cs. The self-assessment on the ideological axis in the left–right continuum is associated with the options in the referendum, so that the percentage for independence is highest among those who are at the extreme far left (81.8%) and descending gradually to the extreme right (18.2%). However, note that more than 50% are in favor of independence in all positions ranging from the center to the left.

The self-assessment on the national axis, which is the basis of the aforementioned indicator of the subjective national identity, also shows that there is an association between increased presence of the Catalan identity and the percentage of affirmative votes for independence, and vice versa. Finally, a cross-tabulation between the various constitutional options for the relationships between Catalonia and Spain and the eventual behavior in a referendum are also linked. While among

Table 5.6 Socio-political variables and the referendum on independence (3)

|  |  | yes | no | abs | other | DK | NA | (N) |
|---|---|---|---|---|---|---|---|---|
|  | Overall sample | 54.7 | 20.7 | 17.0 | 1.1 | 5.4 | 1.0 | 2,000 |
| Sympathy for a party | CiU | 78.0 | 7.6 | 9.0 | 0.0 | 5.1 | 0.2 | 409 |
|  | ERC | 94.5 | 1.2 | 3.2 |  | 1.0 |  | 401 |
|  | PSC | 14.4 | 59.5 | 22.2 |  | 3.9 |  | 152 |
|  | PPC | 5.1 | 87.2 | 7.7 |  | 0.0 |  | 40 |
|  | ICV-EUiA | 43.8 | 17.0 | 21.6 | 3.6 | 13.4 | 0.5 | 194 |
|  | C's | 0.0 | 83.3 | 16.7 |  |  |  | 54 |
|  | CUP | 86.3 | 4.1 | 9.6 |  |  |  | 73 |
|  | Other parties | 63.9 | 20.0 | 17.1 |  |  |  | 35 |
|  | None of them | 26.7 | 28.9 | 34.3 | 3.0 | 6.6 | 0.6 | 499 |
|  | Doesn't know | 41.4 | 17.1 | 20.0 |  | 18.6 | 2.9 | 69 |
|  | Doesn't answer | 52.7 | 12.2 | 8.1 |  | 8.1 | 18.9 | 74 |
| Self location at the ideological axis | Extreme left | 81.8 | 3.0 | 9.1 | 6.1 |  |  | 32 |
|  | Left | 62.9 | 16.8 | 12.8 | 0.8 | 5.6 | 1.2 | 775 |
|  | Left of center | 62.3 | 19.3 | 14.8 |  | 3.3 | 0.5 | 400 |
|  | Center | 50.2 | 23.9 | 18.4 | 2.6 | 3.9 | 1.0 | 310 |
|  | Right of center | 48.6 | 33.1 | 12.7 |  | 5.6 |  | 142 |
|  | Right | 32.9 | 42.5 | 20.5 | 0.0 | 2.7 | 1.4 | 73 |
|  | Extreme right | 18.2 | 45.5 | 36.4 |  |  |  | 11 |
|  | Doesn't know | 35.2 | 18.1 | 34.2 | 2.1 | 10.4 | 0.0 | 193 |
|  | Doesn't answer | 22.2 | 22.2 | 28.6 | 3.2 | 15.9 | 7.9 | 64 |
| Subjective National Identity | Only Spanish | 3.4 | 70.7 | 15.5 | 6.9 | 3.4 |  | 58 |
|  | Spanish >Catalan | 5.5 | 58.2 | 29.1 |  | 7.3 |  | 55 |
|  | Spanish = Catalan | 17.7 | 42.8 | 31.0 | 1.1 | 6.7 | 0.7 | 702 |
|  | Catalan >Spanish | 74.4 | 5.4 | 11.5 | 0.7 | 7.2 | 0.9 | 559 |
|  | Only Catalan | 92.8 | 0.3 | 3.6 | 0.3 | 2.1 | 0.9 | 581 |
|  | Doesn't know | 28.1 | 15.6 | 37.5 | 6.3 | 6.3 | 6.3 | 32 |
|  | Doesn't answer | 7.7 | 15.4 | 15.4 | 15.4 | 15.4 | 30.8 | 13 |

(continued)

*Table 5.6* Continued

|  |  |  |  |  |  |  |  |  |
|---|---|---|---|---|---|---|---|---|
| Relationship between Catalonia and Spain | A region of Spain | 4.5 | 66.3 | 23.6 | 2.2 | 3.4 | 0.0 | 88 |
|  | An autonomous community in Spain | 6.5 | 54.3 | 31.5 | 1.9 | 5.3 | 0.5 | 414 |
|  | A state within a Federal Spain | 36.3 | 26.5 | 25.6 | 2.2 | 8.2 | 1.1 | 449 |
|  | An independent state | 94.7 | 0.2 | 3.0 | 0.0 | 1.8 | 0.2 | 928 |
|  | Doesn't know | 21.4 | 5.1 | 42.9 | 3.1 | 26.5 | 1.0 | 97 |
|  | Doesn't answer | 4.2 | 12.5 | 16.7 |  | 16.7 | 50.0 | 24 |

*Source:* Own calculations from CEO's 2013 barometer, study number REO 712.

secessionists the alternative of "independent state" is the most preferred one (94.7%), it should be emphasized that among those who prefer "federalism," more than a third would opt for independence in a referendum. The observation of the dynamics in this cross-tabulation makes possible the identification of two types of secessionist groups (Muñoz & Tormos 2012): the "hardliners" and the "softliners," depending on whether they choose "yes" in the referendum and their first option is an "independent state" or they choose "yes" in the referendum but their first option is any other constitutional arrangement (like federalism, for instance). In this sense, these authors analyze whether there are differences between them in terms of explaining factors. They detected significant heterogeneity: while the group with strong secessionist preference shows a bigger impact of an identity factor (language, family's origins, and so on), members of the other group with a weaker secessionist preference are more likely to cite instrumental considerations, specifically, the perceived unfair fiscal treatment of Catalonia.

## Final remarks

Data from surveys in recent years are showing an important growth in the percentage of Catalans who would support the independence of Catalonia. This wish (or will) is reflected in the electoral results: the parties that endorse this goal are a clear majority in the Parliament of Catalonia. Since Franco's death in 1975, Catalan leaders have tried to negotiate with the Spanish government with the aim of constructing a constitutional, political, and economic model allowing Catalans to preserve their freedoms and their identity within the Spanish state. Many have come to the conclusion that this is impossible. As a consequence, this conviction has fueled the diffusion of a secessionist agenda among large sectors of the Catalan population (Mañoz and Guinjoan 2013).

The growth of secessionism can be explained by the confluence of several factors. Among them, we should note the generational change, and especially the reaction of an important part of the Catalan population to the political process that started with the reform of the Statute of Autonomy and the negative response of the principal Spanish political actors. These actors have opted to limit the scope of the self-government that Catalonia had envisaged within the framework of the democratic transition after Franco's dictatorship (Parés 2011).

In view of the evidence that Spain cannot accommodate the will of the majority of the Catalans, the secessionist groups have articulated a movement that, emerging from civil society, has pushed the Catalan nationalist parties to do everything possible so that the people of Catalonia can decide for themselves what political status they want for Catalonia. Whether this challenge will undermine the foundations of Spain is uncertain. Surveys are showing there is a clear majority of secessionists among Catalans, but this majority is partially based on grievances that could be appeased without secession if this were the will of the Spanish government. These concessions by the Spanish government could include: offering Catalonia a fiscal agreement that was similar to the one nowadays enjoyed by the Basques or the Navarrese; ensuring a scrupulous respect for the current use of the Catalan language in schools, according to the model that has been implemented for the last 30 years, consonant with the will of the majority of the Parliament of Catalonia; making a more "autonomist" interpretation of the Spanish Constitution and the Statute of Autonomy; and, finally, accepting that it could be in the interest of the whole of Spain to change its current policy on infrastructures which is really hurting the economic development of Catalonia. These are some of the measures that could be taken by the Spanish government to reduce the will for independence. However, there are powerful reasons to be skeptical about the chances for this change of course by the Spanish government, because it would affect the very political and economical foundations of the modern Spanish State. The historical conflict between Catalonia and Spain is thus at a point of no return: either Catalonia becomes a new state, or Catalonia will face a slow decline as a distinct society under a newly recentralized Spanish State.

## Notes

1. Source: Departament de Governació, government of Catalonia.
2. CiU, Convergència i Unió [Convergence and Union], is a moderate center to right Catalan nationalist coalition. ERC, Esquerra Republicana de Catalunya [Republican Left of Catalonia], is a pro-independence and leftist party. PSC, Partit dels Socialistes de Catalunya [Party of the Socialists of Catalonia] is a Catalan socialist party with narrow links with PSOE (PSOE). PPC, Partit Popular Català [Catalan Popular Party] is the regional branch of the Popular Party (PP). ICV-EUiA, Iniciativa per Catalunya Verds – Esquerra Unida i Alternativa [Initiative for Catalonia Greens – Alternative and United Left] is a coalition between a postcommunist and green party with a coalition of leftist groups led by the Party of the Communists of Catalonia (PCC). Cs, Ciudadanos – Partido de la Ciudadanía [Citizens – Citizenship's Party], is a Spanish nationalist and populist party. CUP, Candidatura d'Unitat Popular [Popular Unity Candidature] is an extreme left and pro-independence party. SI, Solidaritat per la Independència [Solidarity for Independence] is a pro-independence party.
3. This complete declaration is available at http://www.parlament.cat/web/documentacio/altres-versions/resolucions-versions
4. Five PSC members of parliament did not participate in the vote because they did not want to vote against the "right to decide" as had been suggested by their party. Two deputies belonging to CUP abstained because they rejected the references to EU and some other aspects of this Declaration.
5. The Centre d'Estudis d'Opinió (Opinion Studies Center), of the government of Catalonia, has asked this question in its surveys since 2006. The CEO's surveys are available at www.ceo.gencat.cat
6. At the initial stages of the Statute of Autonomy reform process, Lieutenant General José Mena, top commander of the Spanish army, was arrested and relieved of his duties for having threatened the Army's intervention. He made this assertion in an official speech during one of the most important days of the Spanish army (see *El Pais*, 8 January 2006).
7. On 31 July 1999, MPs and senators belonging to PP signed the appeal against 187 articles and other additional provisions of the Statute of Autonomy. Some days later, the Ombudsman, a former member of PSOE, also presented its own appeal against the Statute. Finally, some regional governments led by PP did the same.
8. The feelings of grievance were already so intense that the same Statute of Autonomy, in its Third Additional Provision, states that "1. With the exception of the Inter-Territorial Compensation Fund, State investment in infrastructure in Catalonia shall be equal to the relative participation of Catalonia's gross domestic product in the gross domestic product of the State for a period of seven years. These investments may also be employed in eliminating tolls or for construction of alternative expressway roads."
9. The high-speed train joined Madrid and Seville in 1992. The connection between Barcelona and the French border was inaugurated in January 2013. The railway connecting Barcelona, Tarragona and Valencia (the three main Spanish ports in the Mediterranean) still has 50km of a single track in the south of Catalonia which becomes a real bottleneck for the

"Mediterranean Corridor," a railway line that goes from southern Spain to northern Europe.
10. For the Spanish official figures, see http://www.lamoncloa.gob.es/ServiciosdePrensa/NotasPrensa/MAPYA/_2008/ntpr20080715_balanza.htm and http://www.lamoncloa.gob.es/NR/rdonlyres/7799A507-C58E-4572-BE29-EC87EE6CBDDA/89951/150708Balanzasfiscales.pdf
11. These referenda were held in 518 municipalities in four different waves, despite some towns having their own "referendum day." For an analysis of this process, see Muñoz et al. (2011).
12. This Popular Legislative Initiative collected the support of 180,169 signatures. The decision to abolish bull fighting was taken by 68 yes, 55 no, 9 abstentions and 3 absentees. There was a strong debate among citizens, with animal rights arguments and nationalist ones converging.
13. In February 2013, the members of this association are 1 provincial government (out of 4 existing in Catalonia), 28 county councils (out of 41) and 652 local governments (constituting 68.8% of all Catalonia). These local governments represent 35.7% of the Catalan population. See http://www.municipisindependencia.cat/
14. This report updates the report done for the 2002–2005 period. It is available at http://www20.gencat.cat/docs/economia/70_Economia_SP_Financament/arxius/estadistiques-informes/resultatsbalancafiscal2006_2009.pdf .
15. In April, the King of Spain had an accident while he was in Botswana in safari killing elephants. He was there with his lover. In May, the King was loudly booed by the public at the King's Cup final. In this football match, FC Barcelona played against Athletic Club of Bilbao, the main Basque football team. One month later, in June, the President of the General Council of the Judiciary Power and President of the Supreme Court, Carlos Dívar, had to resign because of an investigation about improper use of public money.
16. Since then, almost 200 local governments have declared themselves to be "free Catalan land." The Spanish government began to take these declarations before the courts.
17. *El Pais*, October, 10, 2012.
18. The articles referred to would be: Article 1, which states that sovereignty resides in the people of Spain; Article 2, which fixes the indissoluble unity of the Spanish nation, the common and indivisible homeland of all the Spaniards; Article 9, which says that all public powers, regardless of their scope, are subject to the Constitution; and, finally, Article 168, which specifies the process of constitutional reform.
19. The first big survey about the independence issue was conducted and analyzed by Estradé & Tresserras (1990). The press has also published surveys about this question. See a review in http://ca.wikipedia.org/wiki/Estudis_del_suport_social_a_la_independència_de_Catalunya.

## References

Acosta, Rafael. (1981). *La España de las Autonomías: pasado, presente y futuro* (Madrid: Espasa Calpe).

Argelaguet, Jordi. (2003). *Catalonia: Autonomous Community or nascent State?* In Ruane, Todd and Mandeville.

Argelaguet, Jordi. (2006). "Subjective National Identities in Catalonia", *Nationalism and Ethnic Politics* Vol. 12, No. 3–4, Autumn–Winter 2006, pp. 431–454.
Argelaguet, Jordi. (2012). *Les fondements idéologiques d'un parti indépendantiste de gauche: le cas d'Esquerra Republicana de Catalunya (ERC)*, in Fernández García, Alicia and Mathieu Petithomme. (dirs.), *Compétition politique et identités nationales* (Paris: Armand Colin).
Balcells, Albert. (1996). *Catalan Nationalism* (London: MacMillan).
Bel, Germà. (2010). *España* (Paris. Barcelona: Destino).
Caminal, Miquel. (1998). *Nacionalisme i partits nacionals a Catalunya* (Barcelona: Empúries).
Capdevila, Arantxa. and Lorena Gómez. (2011). "La articulación territorial de Cataluña y España en las estrategias persuasivas de los partidos políticos y de las instituciones autonómicas durante la campaña del Estatut", *Anàlisi* Vol. 41, pp. 13–25.
Civit, Roger. (2013). *Anàlisi dels efectes de l'edat, la generació i el període en el suport a la independència de Catalunya 1991–2011*. (Barcelona: Institut de Ciències Polítiques i Socials), Working Papers, 312. Avaialable at www.icps.cat.
Clots-Figueras, Irma and Paolo Masella. (2012). *"Education, language and identity"*, *Economic Journal* ISSN 0013–0133 (In Press) http://sro.sussex.ac.uk/42501/
Colomer, Jaume. (1995). *La temptació separatista a Catalunya (1895–1917)* (Barcelona: Columna).
De la Granja, José Luis, Justo Beramendi and Pere Anguera. (2001). *La España de los nacionalismos y las autonomías* (Madrid: Editorial Síntesis).
Departament d'Economia i Coneixement. (DEC) (2012). *Resultats de la balança fiscal de Catalunya amb el sector públic central 2006–2009* (Barcelona: Generalitat de Catalunya, Monografies), p. 14.
De Riquer, Borja. (2000). *Identitats contemporànies: Catalunya i Espanya*. Vic: Eumo (University of Vic).
Eisenstadt, Samuel and Stein Rokkan. (eds.) (1973). *Building States and Nations: Models, Analyses and Data across Three Worlds* (Beverly Hills, CA: Sage).
Estradé, Antoni and Montserrat Tresserras. (1990). *Catalunya independent? Anàlisi d'una enquesta sobre la identitat nacional i la voluntat d'independència dels catalans* (Barcelona: Fundació Jaume Bofill).
Fernández García, Alicia and Mathieu Petithomme. (dirs.) (2012). "Les nationalisms dans l'Espagne Contemporaine (1975–2011)", *Compétition politique et identités nationales* (Paris: Armand Colin).
Fernández-i-Marín, Xavier and Jaume López. (2010). *Marco cultural de referencia y participación electoral en Cataluña*, Revista Española de Ciencia Política, nr 23, July 2010, pp. 31–57.
Guibernau, Montserrat. (2004). *Catalan Nationalism: Francoism, Transition and Democracy* (London: Routledge).
Hierro Hernández, María José. (2010). *Canvis a curt termini en la identificació nacional a Catalunya* (Barcelona: Fundació Jaume Bofill). *Informes breus*, nr. 32
Linz, Juan José. (1973). *Early State-Building and the Late Peripheral Nationalisms against the State: The case of Spain*, in Eisenstadt, Samuel and Rokkan, Stein (eds.).

Linz, Juan José. (1981). *"La crisis de un Estado unitario, nacionalismos periféricos y regionalismo"*, In R. Acosta, *La España de las Autonomías: pasado, presente y futuro* (Madrid: Espasa Calpe).
Martí, Pere. (2013). *El dia que Catalunya va dir prou* (Barcelona: Columna).
McRoberts, Kenneth. (2002). *Catalunya. Una nació sense estat* (Barcelona: Proa Edicions).
Molas, Isidre. (dir.) (2000). *Diccionari dels Partits Polítics de Catalunya. Segle XX* (Barcelona: Enciclopèdia Catalana).
Moreno, Luis. (2006). *Scotland, Catalonia, Europeanization and the "Moreno question", Scottish Affairs*, No. 54, Winter 2006, pp. 1–21.
Muñoz, Jordi and Marc Guinjoan. (2013). *Accounting for internal variation in nationalist mobilization: unofficial referendums for Independence in Catalonia (2009–11) Nations and Nationalism* Vol. 19, No. 1, pp. 44–67.
Muñoz, Jordi, Marc Guinjoan and Ricard Vilaregut. (2011). "Les consultes sobre la independència: context, organització i participació", in Parés (2011).
Muñoz, Jordi and Raül Tormos. (2012). *"Identitat o càlculs instrumentals? Anàlisi dels factors explicatius del suport a la independència"* (Barcelona: Centre d'Estudis d'Opinió). Col·lecció Papers de Treball. Available at www.ceo.gencat.cat
Parés, Marc. (dir.) (2011). *Informe sobre l'estat de la democràcia de Catalunya 2010.* (Barcelona: Fundació Bofill. Institut de Govern i Polítiques Públiques, Universitat Autònoma de Barcelona).
Pons-i-Novell, Jordi, and Ramon Tremosa-i-Balcells. (2004). *L'espoli fiscal. Una asfíxia premeditada* (València: Eliseu Climent editor).
Pons-i-Novell, Jordi and Ramon Tremosa-i-Balcells. (2005). "Macroeconomic effects of Catalan fiscal deficit with the Spanish state (2002–2010)", *Applied Economics*, Vol. 37, pp. 1455–1463.
Prat, Sebastià. (2012). *El suport a la independència de Catalunya. Anàlisi de canvis i tendències en el període 2005–2012* (Barcelona: Centre d'Estudis d'Opinió. Monografies). Available at http://www.ceo.gencat.cat
Rico, Guillem and M. Kent Jennings. (2012). "The Intergenerational Transmission of Contending Place Identities" *Political Psychology*, Vol. 33, pp. 723–742. doi: 10.1111/j.1467-9221.2012.00894.x
Ruane, Joseph, Todd, Jennifer and Anne Mandeville. (eds.) (2003). *Europe's Old States in the New World Order* (Dublin: University College Dublin Press).
Shabad, Goldie and Richard Gunther. (1982). "Language, Nationalism, and Political Conflict in Spain", *Comparative Politics*, Vol. 14, No. 4, July, pp. 443–477.

# 6

# The Multilevel Politics of Accommodation and the Non-Constitutional Moment: Lessons from Corsica

*André Fazi*

The politics of accommodation in multinational democracies has been studied mainly through a limited number of cases. Research has tended to focus on states with strong cultural and/or religious heterogeneity, and on territorialized minority groups.[1] When we consider nationalist movements within Western democracies, the spectrum is even smaller. Most studies deal with Canada, Spain, Belgium and the United Kingdom, even though many other states have strong movements.[2]

France, which has long been seen as an example of a rigidly unitary state, is too often overlooked. First, its experience with imperialism and decolonization has led it to develop territorial accommodation strategies. The state's political and institutional structures have remained unitary on the mainland, but they are considerably more decentralized and asymmetric overseas.[3] As early as 1946, the Constitution of the Fourth Republic provided that overseas territories (*territoires d'outre-mer*, TOM) would have "a status reflecting their respective local interests within the Republic." Not only have the TOM obtained increasingly broad competency in the legislation domain, but this evolution has been enshrined in two constitutional amendments. The 1999 amendment established New Caledonia's institutions based on an agreement negotiated between the government and the territorial parties. The 2003 amendment overturned the principles of the unitary state, making status differentiation an implicit right.[4] Second, since the 1960s, there have been many regional movements, including mainland-based ones. The linguistic dimension is the most well known, but the political dimension of the Breton, Basque, and Corsican movements should not be underestimated. These movements have claimed political recognition for groups identified with a region and culture different from the state's majority culture (often called "ethnonational" groups), and specific power-sharing between the state and the region.

Third, the political mobilization potential of these groups can range from extremely high to virtually non-existent. While the Corsican, Kanak, and Polynesian languages are at the heart of the actions of powerful nationalist parties, a language such as Picard is a "completely depoliticized issue" (Harguindéguy & Cole 2009).

Within the French Republic, Corsica is of interest for several reasons. From a geographical point of view, insularity is a significant predictor of secessionism and regionalism (Sorens 2012), and it is a factor conducive to original political and legal arrangements (Watts 2000).

From a cultural point of view, Corsica became French in 1769, after having been under Italian influence since the end of the first millennium, and it remains an exception. In 1999, 43.3% of adults said that they "spoke Corsican with those close to them," which makes Corsican the most used regional language – in relation to the regional population – in mainland France (Filhon 2005).[5] However, this in no way implies that Corsican society is divided into different linguistic communities.[6] The French language dominates linguistic exchanges on the island to such a point that it would be risky to distinguish Corsican-speaking from French-speaking communities.

From a comparative politics standpoint, Corsican nationalism is an original case. On the one hand, it involves clandestine organizations that have perpetrated thousands of attacks and a few dozen assassinations, but whose violence is much less radical than that deployed in the Basque Country and Northern Ireland (Crettiez 1999). Moreover, there are no political parties in Corsica devoted to the defense of the continental French, which could influence the strategies of state-wide parties (SWP). On the other hand, while nationalist parties obtained over 35% of the vote in 2010, they have never managed to win major public positions.

Finally, local elected officials have played a crucial yet ambiguous role in the process of national integration, which was achieved through a form of indirect rule in which local notables were the indispensable intermediaries between the government and society. This was generally described as a clan system, and was defined by the "perfection of the combination" of "four inseparable elements:" a two-party system, compulsory affiliation, clientelism, and arbitrariness (Lenclud 1986). On the one hand, collusion between the government and its island partisans led to the latter receiving the resources necessary to ensure political support, social consensus, and national loyalty. There was no substate nationalist movement before the 1920s, and Corsica experienced very few violent political protests until the 1960s (Tilly 1998). On the other hand, despite a government that was supposed to inculcate diametrically opposed practices, elected officials allowed the perpetuation of violence, clientelism, arbitrariness, etc. They thus obstructed the process of nationalization of society in general, and especially of politics.

This chapter examines the analytical framework relating to the politics of accommodation in Western democracies through the case of Corsica. I argue that most research has mainly considered the largest nationalist movements, and it has ignored important political features of a significant number of such movements. We thus hope to contribute to constructing a more global framework of analysis, which favors comparative research by identifying the most pertinent variables, and exploiting the nexus between political science and constitutional law.

The study of the politics of accommodation generally refers to the following features: a nationalist movement that is very powerful in substate elections; the main political groups seeking a general solution to the conflict; one of the groups being the government of the state; legal instruments with constitutional dimensions being negotiated and adopted. This configuration is descriptive of the 1998 Good Friday Agreement (Ulster), the 1998 Noumea Accord (New Caledonia), the 2009 Act on Greenland Self-Government, etc.

Clearly, this generalization should not be taken too far. First, with the exception of the government, it is rare for political groups to be homogenous. Generally, nationalist movements are divided into radical and moderate wings, or even into enemy factions, and this has significant consequences (Pearlman and Cunningham 2012). Next, the politics of accommodation cannot be reduced to the constitutional reform processes and constitution making. There are other dimensions of the politics of accommodation, and they are usually studied by considering history, political culture, nationalist mobilization, interpartisan relationships, etc. For example, Keating (2008) has shown that the Basque and Catalan situations flow more directly from more informal mechanisms.

However, a case such as that of Corsica clearly requires a different approach. In Corsica, accommodation policies are dominated by the following features: (1) significant nationalist mobilization that nonetheless wins only a minority of the vote in elections; (2) more heterogeneous groups because (a) some leading actors reject the idea of accommodation, (b) the agenda may cover an extremely limited range of issues, (c) resolution of the conflict is not always the primary objective; (3) the state government is not necessarily involved; (4) the measures or accords adopted almost always have a subconstitutional scope. Importantly, one of the most significant features of the France–Corsica relationship is that Corsica has never had a "constitutional moment." A constitutional moment is a:

> higher order constitutional event, which impacts the relationship between the central state – largely controlled by the majority nation – and the minority nation embedded within the same state ... It is of a higher order than ordinary legislative activity. Such constitutional moments are relatively rare, and they represent a critical event that crystallizes the nature of the relationship between the central state and the embedded minority nations. (Lluch 2010: 42)

After presenting our analytical framework, we will describe the evolution of the Corsican political system, which has led to the development of the politics of accommodation. Finally, we will present and interpret the main accommodation strategies implemented on the island since 1974.

## Developing an analytical framework

In this section, we will begin by proposing a framework designed to better approach the great diversity of substate nationalist movements. Next, we will focus on the factors favoring the development of accommodation policies in the case of Corsica.

### Tackling diversity of accommodation strategies

According to Lijphart, (1975: 104), the purpose of the politics of accommodation is to provide pragmatic means of resolving conflictual issues on which we can foresee only minimal consensus. In relation to substate nationalist movements, this should involve: explicit or implicit recognition of the legitimacy of the demands by both substate and state national groups, inclusion of these demands on the political agenda, and adoption of policies designed to provide a positive response to these demands.

Using Meguid's typology (2005), we consider that, faced with a nationalist movement, the central government and SWPs can adopt: a dismissive strategy, which consists of ignoring nationalist claims, so as to indicate that the movement is not significant; an accommodation strategy, which consists of more or less broadly adopting the movement's claims so as to undermine its support; an adversarial strategy, which consists of radically opposing the movement's demands. A number of precautions have to be taken when using this typology because its primary purpose is to maximize votes, whereas ours is to manage national diversity in multinational democracies using a strategy of territorial pluralism:

1. The latter raises broader issues than the former, such as state unity, equality of opportunities, etc.
2. Management of territorial conflicts concerns actors in different political arenas – regional, and even international – and thus their goals are all the more likely to be different.
3. The three types of strategies can be used simultaneously by the same actor by taking a different stance on each of the major nationalist themes.
4. Nationalist parties also make strategic choices (Elias 2011). In particular, their degree of radicalism has major consequences.
5. There is not one but *several* very different accommodation strategies.[7] At least seven major variables can be identified:
   (a) At the level of orientation: accommodation strategies may aspire to greater separation between the region and the state, or to integrate regional representation into the national government.
   (b) At the level of objectives: their target may be global or focus on a sector, and it may concern the short, medium or long term. It is just as necessary to identify issues that do not appear on the agenda as those that do.
   (c) At the level of the actors involved: they can be different depending on regional powers, objectives, the international dimension, etc.
   (d) At the level of decision making: decisions can be made in more or less centralized ways; be part of the normal institutional framework or belong to extra-institutional negotiations, etc.
   (e) At the level of normative impacts: the effects can range from symbolic declarations to constitutional – or even European treaties[8] – revisions.
   (f) At the level of political impacts: political effects can strengthen the nationalist movement or weaken it; lead to the institutionalization of a fraction of nationalists and to the radicalization of others, etc.
   (g) At the level of context: such strategies can be correlated with different kinds of political contingencies, in particular with the electoral agenda.

## The calls for accommodation: A preliminary approach to the Corsican case

Our initial basic hypothesis is simple: the more salient the nationalist movement, the less political authorities can choose a dismissive strategy. In theory, responses can range from full satisfaction of nationalist demands to their total rejection and repression of their supporters. In practice, in Western democracies, when there is significant support for substate nationalist demands, it is virtually impossible to imagine the complete exclusion of accommodation strategies (Rudolph & Thompson 1985).

Certainly, violent mobilization seems likely to legitimate an adversarial strategy. However, the influence of the violence factor can be measured only in light of two other variables: the level of support for the violence by the community on behalf of which it is committed; and the forms of violence employed. If there is strong support for the violence – as in Ulster – and/or it does not reach levels justifying brutal repression – as in Corsica – it is just as likely to generate accommodation strategies as adversarial strategies. Even in the Basque Country, where there was a high level of violence but it was almost universally condemned,[9] accommodation strategies have been implemented, generally in the context of discussion with moderate nationalists.

According to Sorens's findings (2012), five factors probably stimulated secessionist and/or regionalist movements in Corsica: the experience of independence; the fact that there is a language specific to the community; geographic isolation; economic backwardness: and political fragmentation. However, despite the combined and constant presence of the first four factors, the nationalist mobilization is recent. This brings us to a more contingent, but decisive, factor: discrimination against native people. This is frequent in the modernization process, which generates competition for and distribution of wealth favoring one cultural group at the expense of another (Melson & Wolpe 1970: 1115–1117).

## Beyond nationalism and regionalization: A new political system

The Corsican political system was traditionally based on steadfast commitment to the state and absolute domination by two clans. However, from the emergence of nationalism in the early 1970s until the first regional elections with proportional representation in 1982, there was a transformation that led to the development of the politics of accommodation in Corsica.

## Corsican nationalism: an outcome of the modernization process

A number of factors would lead one to believe that Corsican nationalism has been a constant since the 18th century:

(1) The historical roots are strong. The Corsican struggle for liberation against the Republic of Genoa began in 1729. Its aspiration was to establish an independent state. However, Genoa conceded its "sovereign rights" to France in 1768, and Corsican state building was interrupted by military conquest.
(2) There was major cultural heterogeneity. It was not until 1852 that official acts ceased to be translated into Italian. From 1915–1919, the "transmission rate" of Corsican as the "mother tongue" to children aged five was still nearly 85% (Héran et al. 2002).
(3) The geographical isolation is an obstacle to national integration with France on the political, economic, and cultural levels.

Yet, no regionalist movement developed in Corsica between the end of the 18th century and the 1920s. It should be added that the "Corsists" of the interwar period did not form real parties and refrained from running in elections (Leca 1994).

Contemporary nationalism is the product of a modernization process initiated in 1957 by the regional action program (Programme d'action régionale, PAR) (Delors & Muracciole 1978: 114–165). Based in the farming and tourism sectors, this process gave rise to deep anxiety and frustration on a wide range of issues.

First, let us look at the economic and social dimension. The ability of islanders to reap the benefits of modernization was very uncertain. The PAR revealed yet again Corsica's major economic lag, stigmatized "local customs," and was described as "internal colonialism." Thus, it promoted segregation. In farming, the preference given to people who had been repatriated from North Africa was obvious, through very favorable bank loans and land distribution (Dottelonde 1987: 87–89).

Second, there is the dimension related to identity. Over 23,000 Corsicans left the island between 1954 and 1962, while 15,000–17,000 people who had been repatriated from North Africa began to move there (Renucci 1974). In parallel, development of the tourism industry attracted many immigrants, and outside investors were designing projects involving tens of thousands of beds. The 1971 development plan for Corsica forecast that by 1985 the population would have gone from 210,000 to 320,000. These phenomena contributed to spreading the perception that the Corsican language, land and identity were in mortal danger; this bolstered the politicization of cultural difference.

Third, we should turn to the political dimension. Traditionally, political competition was extremely closed, dominated by two major parties of notables, and this was rendered all the easier because France used majority vote systems. This closure was increasingly resented. In 1972, a survey found that 48% of the population supported the "regionalists' position against the clans."[10] Yet, the modernization process revealed a new limitation, through a highly centralized state decision-making process. When the 1971 plan was adopted, the French state ignored the 27 amendments by the Corsican elected representatives, and did not respond to their request to revise the document (Silvani 1976: 189).

### Birth, radicalization and institutionalization of nationalist organizations

The anxiety and frustration led to a rebirth of regionalism in the early 1960s. The largest organization was the Action Régionaliste Corse (ARC), which abandoned the election route after a few failures.[11] The year 1973 was marked by (1) endorsement of the idea of nationalism by the public organizations, first through the demand for autonomy; and (2) the emergence of the first, real, violent, clandestine organizations.

A major turning point occurred on 21–22 August 1975. The ARC carried out an armed occupation of a vineyard run by a farmer repatriated from Algeria. The government repressed it by sending in military forces,[12] and then outlawing the ARC. This intransigence fostered radicalization. In 1976, the National Liberation Front of Corsica (Fronte di Liberazione Naziunale di a Corsica, FLNC) united the clandestine organizations to promote achievement of independence through armed violence. The first party publicly defending its positions came into being in 1980.

A second turning point occurred with the nationalists' decision to run in elections. The first were the autonomists, heirs of the ARC, who participated in the first regional elections in 1982. The independentists adopted the same position a year later. Note that Corsican nationalism is very fragmented (De la Calle & Fazi 2010), but that the cleavage between legalist autonomists and independentists supporting violence did not prevent them from forming coalitions in around half of the legislative and regional elections.

The nationalists' electoral outcomes depend on the type of election. They have been major actors in regional elections since 1992, but have never been associated with a majority coalition, despite strongly asserted willingness to do so in 2004 and 2010. In contrast, they have only exceptionally been successful in municipal, cantonal and legislative elections. Nonetheless, generally, their electoral influence is undergoing significant growth. In 2012, for the first time (moderate) nationalist candidates managed to get into the second round of legislative elections (Table 6.1).

At the same time, the impact of violence has dropped considerably. The action of clandestine organizations is increasingly directed towards easier targets, such as isolated secondary residences.[13] In 2011, there were two attempts to bomb public properties, whereas in 1995 there were 85 (Crettiez 2007).

### Fragmentation and territorialization of the party system

Corsica's special status, which was adopted in 1982, did not give it institutions or powers that were very different from those of mainland French regions. However, use of a proportional voting system generated a revolution through fragmentation of the party system and territorialization of politics. At the level of political debate, Corsica has remained virtually impervious to French national issues, except during presidential votes, which are the only ones in which the island's actors are not in competition. Moreover, despite the nationalist movement, the electoral platforms of the SWPs contain very few positive references to Corsica's place in France. At the level of partisan structures, we have to take into account more than the cleavage between substate nationalist parties and the SWPs. First, the relations between moderate and radical nationalists are ambiguous. On one hand, nationalists have always nurtured a unitary dream, made concrete by their joint candidates. On the other hand, the various groups are in competition,[14] which can, in particular, favor radical stances (Elias 2011).

Second, there are many, highly varied substate non-nationalist parties. In the first round of the 1982 regional elections, only two lists out of 17 were nationalist. During the 1980s, most of these lists were dissident ones, which still claimed to represent their SWPs. In contrast, since the 1990s, it was mainly a question of actors basing their approach on the regional level alone. These were neither SWPs nor nationalist parties, but substate territorial parties, and they played major roles in regional elections. Furthermore, they were integrated into regional executives in 1992 and 2010.[15]

Often it has been important elected officials, SWP members, who have left their partisan framework either because they were dissatisfied

Table 6.1 Nationalist parties and elections in Corsica (1982–2012)

| | 1982 | 1984 | 1986 | 1988 | 1992 (1st round) | 1992 (2nd round) | 1993 | 1997 | 1998 (1) | 1998 (2) | 1999 (1) | 1999 (2) | 2002 | 2004 (1) | 2004 (2) | 2007 | 2010 (1) | 2010 (2) | 2012 |
|---|---|---|---|---|---|---|---|---|---|---|---|---|---|---|---|---|---|---|---|
| Regional elections | 12.73% | 11.4% | 9% | | 21.1% | 24.8% | | | 17.3% | 9.85% | 23.4% | 16.7% | | 14.9% | 17.3% | | 27.8% | 35.7% | |
| Legislative elections (1st round) | | | 7.2% | 7.1% | | | 20.6% | 6.2% | | | | | 7% | | | 13.2% | | | 22.8% |

Table 6.2 Political equilibrium in Corsica: regional elections (1982–2010)

|  | 1982 | 1984 | 1986 | 1992 (1) | 1998 (1) | 1999 (1) | 2004 (1) | 2010 (1) |
| --- | --- | --- | --- | --- | --- | --- | --- | --- |
| SWP | 51.4% | 78.1% | 73.8% | 58.7% | 64.6% | 47.7% | 42% | 65.1% |
| Nationalist parties | 12.7% | 11.4% | 9% | 21.1% | 17.3% | 23.4% | 14.9% | 27.8% |
| Territorial parties | 35.9% | 10.5% | 17.2% | 20.2% | 18.1% | 28.9% | 43.1% | 7.1% |

with their position, or because they considered it advantageous to do so. The present president of the Executive Council of Corsica, Paul Giacobbi, is a representative of the Radical Left Party (Parti radical de gauche, PRG), but he did not run under that label in the 2004 and 2010 elections (Table 6.2).

However, non-nationalist parties have to be understood essentially as two very different categories. The one that is the most influential comprises the heirs of the former clans. With De la Calle (2010), we call them strong-network parties (as opposed to weak-network parties, which are the second category), and identify them through the composition of their lists in regional elections: more than 25% of their candidates are members of parliament, mayors, and departmental council members. Strong-network parties are largely based on the two major SWPs: the Union pour un Mouvement Populaire (UMP, right) and the PRG. Of the 20 highest elected positions on the island, 15 are held by persons who belong to one of these two parties.

On the one hand, the division between strong and weak network parties cuts across lines that are different from those between the SWPs and territorial parties. Joining a SWP is not indispensable to building a powerful network of elected officials and gaining electoral success. In 2010, 53% of the list led by Paul Giacobbi was composed of members of parliament, mayors, and departmental council members.[16] On the other hand, strong network parties are no longer unconditional enemies of particularism. Only the Mayor of Bastia, Émile Zuccarelli, and Senator Nicolas Alfonsi (PRG) continue to deny the opportunity for institutional debates.

In contrast, since the end of the 1990s, Paul Giacobbi, who is also a member of the PRG, has regularly asserted that he is in favor of regional legislative powers for Corsica. At an intermediate level, the UMP is increasingly open to the idea of deeper regional competencies. Naturally, this development is relevant to the application of accommodation strategies.

## Forty years of politics of accommodation

Faced with Corsican nationalism, the French government and SWPs in Corsica have had to make strategic and tactical choices. Here, we are going to outline the main accommodation policies initiated at the state level, highlight the diversity of the players' strategies, and then describe strong network parties in greater detail through the linguistic policies initiated in Corsica.

### Introducing the state policies of accommodation in Corsica

Six policy periods (PP) are to be considered at the level of state accommodation policies.

1. In the 1974–1975 period (P1), there was the first real consideration of nationalist demands, but it was limited to the economic and cultural dimensions. The main result was the adoption of a charter of economic development by the Corsican regional council, and then by the government.
2. The 1981–1982 period (P2) resulted in the adoption of Corsica's first special status, promised by the socialist candidate Mitterrand. It was part of the general framework of decentralization, and excluded any regional legislative power.
3. The 1989–1991 period (P3) led to the adoption of the Joxe Statute, which had not been announced by Mitterrand when he was a candidate. The text increased specificity by creating an executive council separate from the Corsican assembly and broadening the range of regional competencies. The Constitutional Council suppressed the symbolically decisive recognition of the Corsican people.
4. The 1996–1997 period (P4) was marked by the adoption of ambitious economic and cultural policies. After a major campaign of attacks and an attempt at dialogue between those who had committed them and the minister of the interior, the Prime Minister Juppé decided to combine repression with a free economic zone and development of bilingual education.
5. The 1999–2002 period (P5) led to the adoption of the Act of 22 January 2002 amending the status of Corsica. Four months after having refused any institutional changes, Prime Minister Jospin opened a dialogue which only excluded independence. For the first time, acceptance of the reform process was general, and there was a plan to revise the Constitution. This also led to a schism in government, with the resignation of Minister of the Interior Chevènement. This

in fact has been the only case of a strong intrastate dispute on the Corsican conundrum. However, the Constitutional Council suppressed the main change, and the left lost the 2002 elections.
6. The 2002–2003 period (P6) was the time of the drafting and proposal to Corsican voters of a merger of departmental and regional authorities. The reason a referendum was chosen flowed from the lack of sufficient consensus among Corsican elected officials. The "No" side won 51% of the vote (Table 6.3).

Table 6.3 presents these six policy periods in a synoptic manner.
We will use this table as a basis to deepen our analysis.

**Moderate aims and uncertain impacts**

Studying the politics of accommodation certainly begins with consideration of the state and substate political contexts. Among the six policies, four were initiated in the framework of a change in government orientation, and four were initiated in the context of radicalization of the substate nationalist movement. However, it does not seem to be possible to draw definitive conclusions from this.

In contrast, only the changes in the P2 period were announced during an electoral campaign, which indicates how much governments favor pragmatism. Regarding the Corsican issue, the following issues generate a lot of suspicion among voters: the presence of violent clandestine organizations; the challenge to the unitary foundations of the Republic; and Corsica's strong financial dependency on the state. With respect to the government's political identity, the three experiences conducted by right-wing governments (P1, P4 and P6) have been the most limited in their objectives and normative impacts. However:

1. Real changes can be seen. In 2002–2003 (P6), for the first time, the right supported a reform of institutions, and it has been alone in having consulted Corsican voters directly.
2. From 1981 to 2011, the left and right each governed France for 15 years. The left adopted an adversarial strategy for four years (1983–86 and 1998–89), while the right took that tack for only two years (1986–88).

When we look at objectives, we find that in P1 and P4 any institutional dimension was excluded, and in P6 there was a rejection of any increase in regional competencies, themes that are of central importance to nationalists. In contrast, the teaching of the Corsican language, another

Table 6.3 Principal state policy periods and the politics of accommodation in Corsica

| | 1974–1975 | 1981–1982 | 1989–1991 | 1996–1997 | 1999–2002 | 2002–2003 |
|---|---|---|---|---|---|---|
| Government | Right-wing | Left-wing | Left-wing | Right-wing | Left-wing | Right-wing |
| National political context | Political shift | Majority shift | Political shift | Political shift | Political shift | Majority shift |
| Regional political context | Radicalization | Radicalization | Latency | Radicalization | Radicalization | Latency |
| Position of the national opposition | Criticism | Adversarial | Adversarial | Adversarial | Adversarial | Support |
| Position of Corsican strong-network parties | Support | Adversarial | Adversarial | 1/2 support 1/2 adversarial | Support | 2/3 support 1/3 adversarial |
| Position of nationalists | Criticism | Criticism | Criticism | Criticism | Support | Support |
| Decision making | Institutional and societal consultation by a government official; governmental definition | Institutional and societal consultation by a government official; governmental definition | Institutional consultation by government officials; governmental definition | Governmental definition; consultation of the Corsican assembly | Institutional discussions between governmental officials and Corsican representatives; societal consultation by the Region; governmental proposals validated by Corsican assembly | Institutional consultation by minister of Interior; governmental definition after lack of consensus; regional referendum |

(continued)

Table 6.3 Continued

| | 1974–1975 | 1981–1982 | 1989–1991 | 1996–1997 | 1999–2002 | 2002–2003 |
|---|---|---|---|---|---|---|
| Main official goals | Reorientation of economic policy; unofficial recognition of the Corsican People; Corsican language teaching; University | Specific powers and institutions; withdrawal of violence; unofficial recognition of the Corsican People; Corsican language teaching | Specific powers and institutions; legal recognition of the Corsican People; withdrawal of violence; Corsican language teaching; overhaul of the electoral register | Bilingual education; free economic zone | Withdrawal of violence; extending sphere of competencies; legislative powers; exceptional investment plan; Corsican language teaching | Administrative organization (fusion of regional and departmental authorities) |
| Issues ruled out | Institutional reform; official recognition of the Corsican People; compulsory teaching of Corsican language | Legislative powers; compulsory teaching of Corsican language; legal recognition of the Corsican People | Legislative powers; compulsory teaching of Corsican language | Institutional reform; compulsory teaching of Corsican language; legal recognition of the Corsican People | Compulsory teaching of Corsican language; legal recognition of the Corsican People | Normative powers; compulsory teaching of Corsican language; legal recognition of the Corsican People |
| Expected normative impacts | Regulative | Legislative | Legislative | Legislative | Constitutional | Legislative |
| Achieved normative impacts | Regulative | Legislative | Legislative | Legislative | Legislative | None |
| Main political impacts | Radicalization of nationalism | Opening of political competition; fragmentation of party system; Institutionalization of nationalism | Fragmentation of party system; reinforcement of nationalism; Institutionalization of nationalism | Marginalization and radicalization of nationalism | Institutionalization of nationalism; integration of nationalist organizations; division of national parties | Reinforcement of antinationalist actors; Radicalization of nationalism |

theme crucial to nationalists, was at the center of the first five policy periods.

When we look at normative impacts, we find that Corsica has never had a "constitutional moment," which makes it impossible for it to have regional legislative power, compulsory education in the Corsican language, etc.[17] Revising the Constitution was considered only once (P5), and it was subject to many conditions, of which the first (the victory of the left) could not be met. Yet, this limitation does not flow only from the strength of unitary principles in France. The Constitution is regularly amended, and this has made it possible for some overseas territories to adopt positive discrimination measures. To a large extent, the limitation results from the balance of power, which is very favorable to strong network parties and leads the government to define moderate objectives.

Finally, the political impacts have been decisive. Legislation concerning Corsica's status (P2, P3 and P5), which was adopted by left-wing majorities, has promoted the process of institutionalization of nationalism, and nationalist themes have been central in elections. Violence has not ceased, but this process – combined with repression – makes it possible to speak of a weakening of clandestine organizations. Whether they become more marginal or more prominent will depend on the ability of the parties that support them to conquer positions of power.

In contrast, the policies of right-wing governments have tended to favor nationalist radicalization. This was unequivocal in P1. In P4 and P6, it was obvious although a number of self-evident factors – competition among clandestine organizations, repression, partial rejection of the 2002 legislation, etc. – also influenced the radicalization processes. The prominent symbol of these periods is the assassination of Prefect Érignac in February 1998. Indeed, the moderate objectives of all these policies were likely to repel nationalists, and their impact has never satisfied all actors. Nonetheless, support for the principle of accommodation has increased substantially.

## The ambiguous consecration of accommodation strategies

Since 1974, the politics of accommodation have been received in many different ways by the main political actors in Corsica. Gradually, the latter have begun participating more strongly in their drafting, which is a result of both state choices and strategic endorsement.

Above all, centralized decision making has been abandoned. First consulted in an informal way (P1, P2 and P3), elected Corsican officials have been playing increasingly noticeable roles.[18] In P5, the only important proposal that was rejected was compulsory Corsican language teaching in primary school. During P6, it was the lack of consensus among elected Corsican officials that led the state to propose a referendum. The national opposition has not been very concerned by this change. It runs fewer political risks by criticizing the government than by fostering national union. Only once did the opposition support a government-led reform plan (P6), knowing that its orientation had already been approved (P5).

In contrast, the evolution of the main Corsican political players has been significant. For 20 years, the strong network parties rejected all institutional reform. In the two last periods, their attitude was very different. Above and beyond the change in generation of the leaders, there were three main causes for this:

1. Varying levels of dependency on national authorities. During P5, regional UMP leaders supported the process despite the opposition of national authorities. However, in P6, a number of local elected UMP members rejected the government's plan, though the regional authorities expressed no reservations.
2. A desire to maximize their vote share. Since the end of the 1990s, Corsicans have been more sensitive to nationalist themes. In January 2000, 62% of inhabitants were in favor of compulsory teaching of the Corsican language; in July 2000, 30% wanted "an autonomous status that allows elected officials to vote on legislation specific to Corsica," and 6% wanted independence,[19] etc. Strong network parties are thus tempted to regionalize their discourse in order to avoid electoral losses and win new voters.
3. The evolution of decision making. In the first three periods, the government seemed to favor moderate nationalists and weak network parties, while in P4 consultation was minimal. During P3, the government even tried to handicap strong network parties by reworking the electoral rolls. Yet, in P5 and P6, through the importance given to votes in the Corsican assembly, the government implicitly acknowledged the domination of such parties.

The evolution of nationalist positions is similar. In the first four cases, they denounced the shortcomings of the measures proposed. There are also a number of different reasons behind the accommodation strategies adopted in P5 and P6:

1. An overall change in the movement. The tension between the integrative and differentiating tendencies has always been decisive. Even

violence does not target destruction of the political system, but a transformation that makes it possible for its supporters to play a key role (Crettiez 1999). On one hand, voter participation has produced good results. On the other hand, confrontations between clandestine organizations (1995–1996) have weakened them. Thus, the adoption of an accommodation strategy reveals the process of the institutionalization of nationalism. It confirms that even independentist parties supporting violence are "accommodating" anti-system parties (Capoccia 2002).
2. Objectives more consistent with their expectations. Nationalists could not support P1 and P4, which excluded any institutional dimension. They also could not support P2 and P3, which excluded any delegation of legislative power and compulsory teaching of the Corsican language. In contrast, in P5, no limits were set a priori. In P6, the issues involved only the merger of the departmental and regional authorities. Nonetheless, nationalist support was guaranteed because elimination of the general councils was one of their main demands.
3. The evolution of decision making. Discussions between nationalists and state representatives had always been discreet, even secret (P1, P2, P3). This changed in P5 and P6 since elected independentists supporting violence became the government's official interlocutors.

In sum, the participation of Corsican political actors in defining the politics of accommodation has been guided by a wide range of factors. We will now try to identify the motivations of strong network parties through policies conducted at the substate (regional) level.

## Substate (regional) politics of accommodation: the prevalence of opportunism?

Even taking only normative impact into account, substate accommodation policies cannot be as influential as state policies. However, they concern issues as essential as identity, territorial planning, the environment, etc. We will focus on the area in which the accommodation dimension is most highly developed: language.

During the 1970s, nationalists who advocated making Corsican an official language were strongly against the state, which rejected the idea. While they excluded giving it official status and it was against the law, elected officials on the island supported the principle of teaching the Corsican language.[20] In contrast, since the 1982 statute, strong network parties have depolarized the issue of identity by adopting positions that are often close to those of nationalists. Five events have been especially significant:

1. Less than a year after its first election, on 8 July 1983, the Corsican assembly unanimously adopted a motion calling for general implementation of bilingualism and compulsory teaching of the Corsican language.
2. On 26 June 1992, the Corsican assembly adopted a motion stating that "the Corsican language is official throughout all of the territory under the jurisdiction of the Corsican assembly."
3. On 10 March 2000, 48 – out of 51 – councilors in the Corsican assembly approved motions calling for compulsory teaching of Corsican in kindergarten and primary school.
4. On 26 July 2007, the Corsican assembly unanimously adopted a strategic plan designed to spread bilingual teaching and normalize the use of the Corsican language in society.
5. On 28-29 July 2011, the Corsican Executive Council ruled in favor of a "territorial official status" for the Corsican language, and the assembly adopted, 36 to 47, a motion enshrining the idea of co-official languages.[21]

Context seems to be the crucial factor: all of these decisions and stances were adopted in circumstances of strong political uncertainty, in which the regional majority was relative, or it was very divided on another issue.[22] The regional majority thus seems inclined to develop accommodation policies highly favorable to the Corsican language when it is in a fragile position. On the one hand, surveys show that this is not politically dangerous; on the contrary, it can reassure voters who are sensitive to identity issues. On the other hand, investing in this very symbolic area by seeking consensus can make voters forget fiercer debates and paint oneself as guardian of the general interest.

Some reversals seem to have been very tactical. Whereas the 2000 motions were clear as to the compulsory nature of teaching the Corsican language, this possibility was set aside by the government with no real challenge. The Corsican elected officials were aware of the need for a constitutional reform and the reluctance to go down that path, while the Government in question had made major commitments on the level of normative powers. Thus, during the parliamentary process, a number of these elected officials renounced the position asserted by the two motions (Assemblée nationale 2001).

In sum, the main inspiration for these policies does not seem to have been the desire to meet the substate nationalist challenge. Instead, the stimulus seems more likely to have been a desire to appropriate the issues that, initially, were closely correlated with nationalism, but which had become important to a much broader range of voters. The primary concern would thus be to maximize voter support without losing the trust of state actors.

## Conclusion: Corsica and the multilevel politics of accommodation

The politics of accommodation is often studied through negotiation processes, the purpose of which is the ratification of an accord establishing a constitutional mechanism for the management of the ethnonational divide. Such pacts have a constitutional scope, and even establish such asymmetries and exceptions that we can speak of constitutional antinomies, as in New Caledonia.[23]

The particularities of Corsica suggest a completely different approach. First, many regions that have strong nationalist movements have never known or made concrete such a constitutional accommodation policy for the management of the ethnonational divide. One of the most significant features of the France–Corsica relationship is that Corsica has never had a "constitutional moment." The analysis in the case of Corsica has to be based on debates and decisions with much more limited scope:

1. The purpose of discussions has not been to deal with all of the issues raised by the nationalist movement.
2. The objectives have not necessarily been to find a global constitutional resolution for the problem or problems raised.
3. All actors have not necessarily been included. The central power is not necessarily involved.
4. Decision making has not involved discussions held outside of the normal institutional framework.

Second, entirely territorialized party systems are scarce, and even more rare are those that reflect a communal division. Normally, SWPs are crucial actors in the politics of accommodation. They play fundamental roles in all processes involving the national government, and they themselves can initiate and/or administer such policies.

Third, beyond the interrelations among the three main groups of actors (the national government, regional SWP federations, and nationalist parties), we have to take into account the heterogeneity of these three groups. This is a decisive factor in the definition of accommodation strategies, and can flow just as easily from ideological factors as from a desire to win the maximum number of votes in an election.

Clearly, the attractive power of "constitutional moments," and of constitutional mechanisms for the management of the ethnonational divide can become a prejudicial bias for observers. Accommodation is an everyday political issue, in which symbolism often reigns. Bilingual street signs, the flying of the regional flag, audiovisual works giving a bad image of the region, municipal council meetings held in the regional language, names given to streets and university amphitheaters, etc. are all topics that have been – and still are – important issues in politics and the media in Corsica. Conversely, a number of nationalist mayors adorn themselves with the tricolor sash, symbolizing France, so as to avoid displeasing a section of their supporters.

To overlook these issues would be unwise. On the one hand, the macro-politics of accommodation initiated at the state level are partly consequences of the failure of everyday politics – in other words, the micro-politics of accommodation. On the other hand, the fact that there have been no "constitutional moments" does not mean that there is an intractable, highly conflictual situation. In Corsica's case, it means that the conflict is still manageable, and that the balance of power between the nationalists and anti-nationalists has not yet justified territorial exceptions to constitutional principles because the political cost of such exceptions would be high in a country where unitary ideology remains strong.

Yet, the idea of an autonomous region with legislative powers, which would require constitutional reform, is now stronger than ever in Corsica. This idea does not really frighten people. In September 2008, a survey showed that 51% of people living on the island wanted "more autonomy" for Corsica.[24] This seems to be confirmed by the progress in nationalists' election results. In 2010, the UMP government decided that its legislation on territorial reform would not apply to the departmental and regional authorities of Corsica, and it asked its elected officials on the island to define their own vision. This required reopening an institutional debate that had been closed since 2003. Now, the Corsican assembly has shown immediately a broad consensus on the goal of institutional change. Strong network parties are increasingly open to the possibility of constitutional reform. On the one hand,

Corsica's Executive Council, chaired by Paul Giacobbi, supports such a reform in order to solve issues concerning normative powers, taxation, the Corsican language and land ownership. On the other hand, in the 2012 legislative elections, none of the eight candidates supported by the two major SWPs (the UMP and the PRG) stated official opposition to this. Finally, the adversarial strategy is in decline. In 2010, its partisans obtained only 8.05% of votes. Of course, the opponents of constitutional revision enshrining autonomy for Corsica remain powerful on the island, and even more so at the state level. Despite everything, while the lost referendum of 2003 ended a cycle initiated in 1982, it is plausible that Corsican society is experiencing the beginning of a new cycle of the politics of accommodation, in which the range of constitutional possibilities may be noticeably wider.

## Notes

1. The reference work edited by Choudhry is a prime example of this bias.
2. For Europe: Csergő and Wolff (2009).
3. The most comprehensive study seems to be Michalon (1982).
4. Since 1999, Article 77 of the Constitution has provided that the statutory law of New Caledonia must be "in accordance with the guidelines set out in" the Noumea Accord. Since 2003, (1) Article 72-4 has set out the terms of a change of status for the overseas communities, and requires a territorial referendum to ratify such a change; (2) Article 73 allows the Parliament to empower some overseas departments to adopt (materially) legislative acts "in a limited number of matters."
5. Despite its island geography, Corsica is considered to be a part of mainland France.
6. Here we are referring only to Corsicans of origin and other French people living on the island.
7. We do not confuse them with the "forms of accommodation" characterized by McGarry, O'Leary and Simeon (2008): consociation, centripetalism, multiculturalism, and territorial pluralism.
8. As can be seen in the case of the Åland Islands.
9. ETA may be guilty of 834 deaths, including 297 civilians. Before it announced it was giving up violence in October 2012, around 1 percent of the Basque population expressed "total support" for ETA.
10. *Kyrn*, n° 22, juin 1972.
11. In the 1967 legislative elections, the leader of the ARC obtained only 2.3 %of the vote.
12. Two policemen were killed in the exchange of fire.
13. http://www.inhesj.fr/fichiers/ondrp/crimes_et_delits_2011/08_corse.pdf, date accessed 29 May 2012.
14. The independentist tendency imploded between 1989 and 1990. Three factions engaged in a deadly conflict between 1995 and 1996, which resulted in around 15 deaths.

15. This is paradoxical if we consider their electoral collapse, which resulted from the electoral system used in 2009. It raised the eligibility threshold from 5–7%, and the majority bonus from 6–18% of the seats.
16. The list was supported by the Socialist Party. However, that party is an insignificant political actor in Corsica, and contributed very little.
17. Note that recognition of the "Corsican people" (P3) and the power to experiment with legislation (P5) have been criticized by the Constitutional Council because they are constitutional issues subject to its review.
18. The very centralizing method adopted in P4 was an exception. The government wanted to reassert its authority in the face of the challenge brought by a clandestine organization.
19. *Corsica*, No. 4 and 10.
20. We are basing this on the study of the monthly publication entitled *Kyrn*.
21. The co-official status was adopted also by 36 votes to 47, on May 17, 2013, but it could be unconstitutional.
22. Namely, the question of regional legislative powers.
23. The 1998 Noumea Accord, which has been constitutionalized, deviates from several key features of the French Constitution (unitary citizenship, equality in employment and in elections, etc.).
24. See http://www.ifop.com/media/poll/situationcorse.pdf, date accessed 23 July 2012.

# References

Assemblée nationale. (2001). *Rapport au nom de la commission des lois constitutionnelles [...] sur le projet de loi (n° 2931) relatif à la Corse*, by B. Le Roux, n° 2995, enregistré le 18 avril.

Capoccia G. (2002). "Anti-System Parties: A Conceptual Reassessment", *Journal of Theoretical Politics* Vol. 14, No. 1, pp. 9–35.

Choudhry S. (ed.) (2008). *Constitutional Design for Divided Societies. Integration or Accommodation?* (Oxford: Oxford University Press).

Crettiez X. (1999). *La question corse* (Bruxelles: Éditions complexe).

Crettiez X. (2007). "Lire la violence politique en Corse", http://xaviercrettiez.typepad.fr/diffusion_du_savoir/violence_en_corse/, 23 July 2012.

Cserg&#337; Z. and S. Wolff. (2009). "Regions of Nationalism in Europe", *2009 Annual Meeting of the American Political Science Association* Toronto, 3–6 September.

De la Calle L. and A. Fazi. (2010). "Making Nationalists out of Frenchmen? Sub-State Nationalism in Corsica", *Nationalism and Ethnic Politics* Vol. 16, No. 3, pp. 397–419.

Delors J.-P. and S. Muracciole. (1978). *Corse. La poudrière* (Paris: Alain Moreau).

Dottelonde P. (1987). *Corse. La métamorphose* (Levie: Albiana).

Elias A. (2011). "Party Competition in Regional Elections. A Framework for Analysis", *Working Papers ICPS*, 295.

Ettori F. (1971). "La Révolution corse", in P. Arrighi (ed.), *Histoire de la Corse* (Toulouse: Privat), pp. 307–368.

Filhon A. (2005). "D'une langue régionale à l'autre", in C. Lefèvre and A. Filhon (eds), *Histoires de familles, histoires familiales. Les résultats de l'enquête Famille de 1999* (Paris: Les cahiers de l'INED), 155, pp. 521–528.

Harguindéguy J.-B. and A. Cole. (2009). "La politique linguistique de la France à l'épreuve des revendications ethnoterritoriales", *Revue Française de Science Politique* Vol. 59, No. 5, pp. 939–966.

Héran, F., A. Filhon and C. Deprez. (2002). "La dynamique des langues en France au fin du XX$^e$ siècle", *Population & Sociétés* Vol. 11, pp. 376.

Keating M. (2008). "Rival Nationalisms in a Plurinational State: Spain, Catalonia and the Basque Country", in S. Choudhry (ed.) *Constitutional Design for Divided Societies. Integration or Accommodation?* (Oxford: Oxford University Press), pp. 316–341.

Leca A. (1994). " 'A Muvra' ou le procès de la France par les autonomistes corses (1920–1939)", in M. Ganzin and A. Leca (eds), *L'Europe entre deux tempéraments politiques. Idéal d'unité et particularismes régionaux* (Aix-en-Provence: PUAM), pp. 525–544.

Lenclud G. (1986). "De bas en haut, de haut en bas. Le système des clans en Corse" *Études rurales* Vol. 23, No. 101–102, pp. 137–173.

Lijphart A. (1975). *The Politics of Accommodation: Pluralism and Democracy in the Netherlands* 2nd edn. (Berkeley/Los Angeles: University of California Press).

Lluch J. (2010). "How Nationalism Evolves: Explaining the Establishment of New Varieties of Nationalism within the National Movements of Quebec and Catalonia", *Nationalities Papers* Vol. 38, No. 3, pp. 337–359.

McGarry, J., B. O'Leary and R. Simeon. (2008). "Integration or Accommodation? The Enduring Debate in Conflict Regulation", in S. Choudhry (ed.), *Constitutional Design for Divided Societies. Integration or Accommodation?* (Oxford: Oxford University Press), pp. 41–88.

Meguid B.M. (2005). "Competition Between Unequals: the Role of Mainstream Party Strategy in Niche Party Success", *American Political Science Review* Vol. 99, No. 3, pp. 347–359.

Melson R. and H. Wolpe. (1970). "Modernization and the Politics of Communalism: A Theoretical Perspective", *American Political Science Review* Vol. 64, No. 4, pp. 1112–1130.

Michalon T. (1982). "La République française, une fédération qui s'ignore ?", *Revue du Droit Public* Vol. 3, pp. 623–688.

Pearlman W. and K. G. Cunningham. (2012). "Nonstate Actors, Fragmentation, and Conflict Processes", *Journal of Conflict Resolution* Vol. 56, No. 3, pp. 3–15.

Renucci J. (1974). *Corse traditionnelle et Corse nouvelle* (Audin: Lyon).

Rudolph J. R. Jr. and R. J. Thompson. (1985). "Ethnoterritorial Movements and the Policy Process: Accommodating Nationalist Demands in the Develop World", *Comparative Politics* Vol. 17, No. 3, pp. 291–311.

Silvani P. (1976). *Corse des années ardentes. 1939–1976* (Paris: Albatros).

Sorens J. (2012). *Secessionism. Identity, Interest, and Strategy* (McGill-Queen's University Press: Montreal).

Tilly C. (ed.) (1998). *Disturbances in France, 1830–1860 and 1930–1960: Intensive Sample* (ICPSR ed. Ann Arbor).

Watts R. (2000). "Islands in Comparative Constitutional Perspective", in G. Baldacchino and D. Milne (eds), *Lessons from the Political Economy of Islands. The Resourcefulness of Jurisdiction* (Basingstoke: Palgrave Macmillan), pp. 17–37.

# Part III
# Constitutionalism and the Practice of Autonomism, Federalism, and Devolution

# 7
# Flexible Accommodation: Another Case of British Exceptionalism?

*Stephen Tierney*

## Introduction

The period of territorial decentralization which began in the United Kingdom in 1998 has been dramatic. Since the election of a Labour government in 1997, the UK has experienced the greatest period of constitutional change since the 19th century and possibly since the Parliamentary union of Scotland and England itself in 1707. It is also notable that these changes have been, and continue to be, effected in an ad hoc manner, piece by piece without an overall grand plan for how they might fit within, or bring about the amendment of, the existing doctrines of the unitary constitution, most notably the legislative supremacy of the UK parliament, the constitutional dogma which offers a narrative of second-order power in the absence of a written constitution.

The fact that the process did not involve one overarching design for territorial decentralization or culminate in one foundational moment of constitutional renewal suggested to many in the late 1990s that the changes were likely to fail. But despite the fact that none of the designs for the ideal federal constitution developed within the academic literature over many decades were deployed to transform the unitary British constitution into a federal prototype, it is difficult to resist the conclusion after 15 years that the gradual devolution process, bringing about different models of government for each of Scotland, Wales, and Northern Ireland has been a remarkable success. The majority of citizens in these three territories, and even those of England who were not accorded devolved government, are content with devolution, albeit that many, particularly in Scotland, aspire to the decentralization of further powers. Furthermore, there has been a notable absence of serious disputes over the divisions of competences between the center and the devolved territories, with very few cases coming before the courts contesting vires limits of powers exercised by devolved organs of government.

In this chapter I will seek partly to endorse this positive conclusion. I will do so by exploring how the unique model of accommodation applied in the UK is in fact heavily contextualized by the specific history of these islands and how it was designed in a way that is highly sensitive to both the long-standing and the more recent political particularities of each of Scotland, Wales, and Northern Ireland; in other words, devolution in the UK might appear to be ad hoc but in fact from place to place it was carefully tailored to meet the United Kingdom's particular and very complex model of national pluralism. I will then explore the nature of the devolved settlement and in particular the asymmetry of "accommodation," and again, nodding to the historically tuned nature of each devolution settlement, I will again endorse the flexible approach which allowed the devolved models to emerge easily and which has also facilitated their further development over time.

The conclusion, however, cannot be one of simple self-satisfaction. I will also turn to the greatest challenge now facing the United Kingdom in the form of the Scottish government's planned referendum on independence which will be held in 2014. This promises the possible breakup of the state itself and as such it must logically raise the question: How can the Scotland Act 1998 be seen as a success story if less than two decades later Scots vote to leave the UK? But before all of this, I want to say something about the term "accommodation" as a tool of analysis in assessing the constitutional aspirations of substate nations within a plurinational state. This term is not entirely satisfactory in helping us to understand the dynamics of constitutionalism in the context of deep societal pluralism, and only by explaining this can we begin to comprehend the nature of the United Kingdom state's success as a union of national partners.

## Beyond accommodation: substate national societies and the quest for equality

I have elsewhere addressed the three main constitutional aspirations of substate national societies within plurinational states such as the UK, Canada and Spain as autonomy, representation, and recognition.[1] The term "accommodation" is frequently used to describe the demands of substate national societies for forms of constitutional reform short of secession. But the idea of "accommodation," when framed as "states managing minorities," does not adequately capture the constitutional challenge presented by substate national societies. This is because of the categorical distinction it implies between the entity doing the accommodating or managing (the "nation"-state) and that being accommodated or managed (the minority). It is precisely because it embodies *the* national society of the state that the dominant society is entitled, by the implicit assumption of standard liberal democratic accounts, to make decisions about how far to go in accommodating a cultural minority, while retaining the right, and indeed the duty, to maintain its own nation-building agenda in the name of societal stability.[2] But it is this very categorical distinction and this assumption of privilege that is questioned by substate nationalists. They contest the idea that "the State" represents a discrete category of nation which embraces the entire polity, an idea that is so embedded in political theory that the State is often presented as somehow neutral with regard to nationality.[3] Instead the State has been shown to be the institutional vehicle promoting the nation-building agenda of a dominant national society. In their radical claims, substate nationalists seek a conceptual reorientation of the nature of the State; only by dismissing the possibility of neutrality within existing arrangements can a new conception of the plurinational state be built, based upon mutual recognition that the different nations of the state form a partnership of equals. The powerful normative claims to be found in the narratives of substate national societies are rooted, therefore, not in the politics of difference but rather in the politics of similarity, pointing to the parallel processes of nation-building and consolidation which remain on-going within the state.[4]

Furthermore, many nationalists within substate national societies do not in fact seek secession from the state, or at least would prefer certain other forms of constitutional reform to secession as an option for change. A primary demand is autonomous self-government, or in many situations *more* autonomous self-government, given that the states I have mentioned are already significantly devolved. But it is also the case that self-government alone does not lead to a relationship of equals within a plurinational state. The substate national society's role is not complete and can be highly marginalized if it does not also play a significant and in some sense "co-sovereign" role in the making of decisions in relation to "reserved" or "federal" matters. This combination of demands for autonomy on the one hand, and better representation in central institutions and central decision making on the other, may seem to be self-contradictory:[5] the demand for greater autonomy seems to suggest a desire for greater detachment from the central state, whereas enhanced representation would inevitably bring with it a more integrated state involving enhanced, or at least more formalized, institutional arrangements for joint decision making. But this reality should not surprise us; it reflects the ambivalence of many modern nationalists who see value in attachments to both their substate national society and to the state, and who therefore accept the on-going importance of the central state and the decisions it makes for any substate national society belonging to it, in particular in those areas such as economic policy, defense, and foreign affairs which are invariably retained as central state matters. This ambivalence can mean that citizens of substate national societies want to assert their discrete national status while also believing in the benefits of the political and legal security offered by inclusion within a larger state; and it should not be overlooked that there are often high levels of citizen identification with and loyalty to the state within substate national societies even among those whose primary national identity is a substate one.

It is also the case that without enhanced representation accompanying autonomy, the position of a substate national society within a state can become one of heavy, and potentially centripetal, imbalance. If the substate nation has considerable autonomy but no role at the center, then the state can, over time, come to be seen as a threat to that autonomy, or simply as less and less relevant, strengthening arguments for full independence. It might well be asked if this has been the trajectory of the UK's relationship with Scotland since 1998, something which I will explore further below.

The third goal, recognition, is a curiously inchoate "accommodation" objective, and one which more than any other highlights the inadequacy of the language of accommodation in understanding the aspirations of substate national societies. The demand is that the constitution should, in its own description of the nature of the state, reflect, declare, and symbolize the reality of that state's national pluralism; in other words, a recognition that substate nations constitute distinctive, and crucially co-equal, demoi within their respective states.[6] This has often proven to be the goal which the central state has been most reluctant to concede, as we see in tortuous debates for example over the notion of "differential fact" in Spain, and the "nation"/"nationality" distinction in the Spanish constitution;[7] and in Quebec's "distinct society" debate and the protracted period before any formal recognition of Quebec as a nation came about.[8] In the UK, recognition has in fact been a far less problematic issue. It is a commonly held view even within England that Scotland and Wales are nations, not merely regions, a point readily conceded partly due to historical memory, partly because English people are conscious of their own national identity below the level of Britishness, and also partly because it was for a long time a concession which seemed to bear no prospect of constitutional cost since political nationalism in Scotland and Wales was until the 1970s very weak. But what can be concluded from the three main constitutional aspirations of substate nationalists, particularly in the recognition demand, is the implicit expectation that the constitution will reflect the principle of national equality within the state, rather than merely the "accommodation" of cultural difference by the dominant group.

## The plurinational United Kingdom in historical perspective

The unique way in which the UK constitution has dealt with the constitutional demands that have accompanied its national pluralism and the relatively high level of success this approach has had to date can only be understood from a historical perspective. The UK came together as a series of unions, and the notion of the UK as a "union state" has remained important in informing the self-description of their countries as "nations" by the peoples of England, Scotland, and Wales (the situation in Northern Ireland is of course more complicated). The symbols and motifs of the state such as its flag, the titles of the royal family etc., also denote this union nature, informing the political culture of the state.

A second feature of the historical reality of the UK as a union of nations has been the gradual acquisition of constitutional recognition of this status through the incremental devolution of powers beginning in the 19th century with moves toward "home rule," a process which focused mainly, but not exclusively, upon recognition of Ireland's national distinctiveness, and which led in due course to "administrative devolution" for Scotland and Wales in the 20th century. In some sense, 1998 is merely a recent chapter of a much longer story, dating back to the unions of the 16th century (Wales and England), 17th and 18th centuries (Scotland and England) and the beginning of the 19th (Great Britain and Ireland). And devolution is not such a new story either. We need to situate the process of decentralization at the end of the 20th century in the context of a period stretching over a century during which each of these unions was gradually restructured. Central to this process was Gladstone's commitment to some degree of self-government for Ireland embodied in the government of Ireland Bill

1886. Over time the distinctive national characters of Ireland, Scotland, and Wales were gradually recognized, and in very different ways this recognition was accorded constitutional embodiment. The Liberal commitment to Irish Home Rule led to the eventual independence of the Irish state after the First World War. But it was not until the latter half of the 20th century that we see a shift in the political culture of both Scotland and Wales as many citizens within these territories became increasingly nationalist in outlook and aspiration. All of this serves as an important backdrop to 1998, which in some sense was not such a radical break with the past but in fact the culmination of this period of recognition of substate national distinctiveness and the constitutional aspirations which come with such markers of difference.

A third feature is the organic way in which devolution developed in each of the three territories. Already by the start of the 20th century, the ways in which the respective constitutional aspirations of each territory came to be assessed, and power to be decentralized, were very different from place to place. To understand this we also need to note that the UK came together through historical contingencies rather than in dramatic founding moments, an observation which helps illuminate how, in the same way, its reorganization has also been led by such contingencies, including inter- and in some cases intra-party competition, again piece by piece and from place to place. In so far as we can talk of the "fissuring" of the UK, this has taken place in a contingent and gradual way, first with Ireland slowly breaking its bonds with Westminster, the Stormont Regime being established (temporarily) for the remaining six counties after the creation of the Irish Free State, and "administrative devolution" being extended in the inter-war establishment of a UK government department for Scotland and the creation of a minister of Welsh Affairs in 1951. In this light, 1998 was another step in the same direction, whereby these three territories gradually acquired more and more responsibility for their own domestic affairs, but in a way that built upon the powers and to some extent the institutional arrangements already in place, or, in Northern Ireland's case, previously tried.

In the Spring of 1997, the Labour Party came into government in the UK for the first time since 1979. During its time out of government it had overcome high levels of opposition within the party to decentralization and formed a firm commitment to devolution for Scotland and Wales. The new government moved quickly to give effect to its plans for decentralization, and since this period coincided with the climax of a peace deal in Northern Ireland, which itself centered around a new model of autonomy for the six counties, 1998 witnessed the passage of three pieces of legislation – the Scotland Act, the government of Wales Act, and the Northern Ireland Act.

Another important dimension to the devolution story, particularly when we consider the close relationship that now attends the further devolution of power in the United Kingdom and the proliferating use of the referendum,[9] is the influence of civil society in the process that led to the 1998 legislation. We see this if we take Scotland as a brief case study. The Scotland Act 1998 built upon an extra-Parliamentary campaign for devolution within Scotland which was orchestrated by the political opposition and certain important civic institutions (local government, trades unions etc.) through the 1980s and 1990s, largely as part of a broader campaign by the labor movement against successive Conservative governments. The extent to which the eventual Parliamentary process toward devolution, adopted by the Labour-led UK Parliament in 1997, reflects this movement is unsurprising given that this campaign was led in large measure by the Labour Party in Scotland. And in observing the significance of the Labour Party in shaping the 1998 Act, we must also look back to the failure of a devolution proposal put forward by the Callaghan government in the late 1970s. Although a detailed model of devolution was enacted by Parliament in 1978, and won a small majority in a referendum in 1979, it failed to meet the requisite threshold of support in that referendum.[10] This failure, and accusations that the threshold rule was designed to frustrate the devolution proposal, continued to haunt the Scottish Labour Party in opposition. With the election of a Conservative government in 1979 and its subsequent re-election in 1983, a push for devolution was set in train by Labour and by other opposition groups, including in due course the Liberal Democrats, who united in the view that the Conservative agenda was given to excessive centralization. This movement continued to offer constitutional proposals throughout the next two decades.

The campaign for constitutional change began with the Campaign for a Scottish Assembly launched in 1985. This resulted in a document, *A Claim of Right for Scotland*, issued in 1988. What is notable about this paper, and others which subsequently emerged through this process, is the extent to which they drew upon the notion of "union" as the fundamental constitutional principle of the UK. This had three implications. First, the *Claim of Right* asserted the distinctive national identity and cultural and institutional specificity of Scotland (each of which had to some extent been recognized in the Acts of Union 1707) and argued for the on-going constitutional relevance of this "multinational" conception of the United Kingdom. Second, the document aired the grievance that the "union state" pact stemming from 1707 had been undermined by subsequent UK constitutional practice.[11] Third, the *Claim of Right* declared an entitlement to Scottish self-government based upon the notion that a distinctive national identity carried with it a legitimate, indeed inherent, political right of self-determination.

It is also notable that important Scottish elites not only set the agenda for devolution during this period, they were also heavily influential in shaping the substantive model eventually enacted in the Scotland Act 1998. The *Claim of Right* 1988 recommended that a cross-party Scottish Constitutional Convention (SCC) be established which would have the task of drawing up a model of devolution that would generate popular support and hence "assert the right of the Scottish people to secure the implementation of that scheme." This SCC was inaugurated on 30 March 1989 and over the next seven years it enjoyed similar involvement to the *Claim* process, including not only the Labour and Liberal Democratic parties, but also local authorities, Churches and the Scottish Trades Union Congress. This resulted in a series of publications, the most important of which (*Scotland's Claim, Scotland's Right*, 1995) set out a detailed blueprint for devolution.

The level of detail in this document meant that the process by which legislation was passed after Labour came to power in 1997 was very swift. The political climate in 1997–1998 was highly conducive to devolution; a Labour Administration elected with a large majority in 1997 was committed to the principle, and so, heavily influenced by Scottish Labour MPs, the government steered the devolution settlement through in the first session of the new Parliament. Upon taking office, and relying heavily upon the detail in *Scotland's Claim, Scotland's Right*, the government issued a White Paper – *Scotland's Parliament* – which was, therefore, able quickly to set forth a comprehensive plan for devolution. Although some minor changes were made by Parliament to the devolution proposal after the referendum in 1997, the model finally enacted in the Scotland Act was in substantive terms the same as that voted for in the referendum, which in turn reflected heavily the pre-1997 deliberation.

In light of the influence of civil society in framing Scottish devolution, the three implications which I identify in the *Claim of Right* process need to be kept in mind as essential background to the Scotland Act 1998 and to the creation of the Scottish Parliament. The Scottish Parliament was created out of a sense of Scottish popular sovereignty. Another factor at play in making 1998 such a key focal-point of this "self-determination" argument is that while the extra-Parliamentary process was largely the preserve of elite actors and suffered from the lack of participation of both the Scottish Conservative Party, which, favoring the status quo, never took part, and indeed the Scottish National Party itself which withdrew after early involvement, citing a failure to address independence for Scotland as a serious constitutional option, the creation of the Scottish Parliament was in the end the direct result of a referendum in 1997, and one which saw a very high level of support for devolution.[12]

Scotland is certainly a particular case for the level of influence civil society and the local political class had in shaping the devolution model, but it is also the case that political actors in each of the territories played a very significant role in pushing for devolution and in shaping internally what it would look like. Wales had the most top-down process and the model for devolution was largely formulated on the hoof once Labour came to power in 1997.[13] But even here, devolution had become a firm commitment of the Labour Party during its period in opposition and during this time there was an ongoing debate within Wales about what a devolved system should look like. The Northern Irish model of devolution was certainly developed with a large degree of organic engagement;[14] and the Belfast Agreement, as were the devolution settlements for Scotland and Wales, was endorsed by a referendum, ascribing each with an important symbol of popular authorship and endorsement.

## The flexible constitution: the UK's unique approach to accommodation of national identity

It is notable that these different changes in 1998, although being legislated for in the same year, were effected not by an overarching constitutional settlement, or the introduction of a written constitution, but by separate pieces of legislation formulated in very distinctive processes and emerging from very different extra-Parliamentary processes of negotiation or consultation. In this sense the devolution process was not "joined up," nor were the three settlements particularly well coordinated *inter se*.

So how have elements of autonomy, representation, and recognition been embedded in the devolution process? It has become commonplace to talk about the UK system as one of asymmetry. But this perhaps serves to suggest that the different models of devolution were planned through a grand and totalizing vision designed to bring together distinctive constitutional settlements, each one carefully tailored to meet the aspirations of the particular nation it was designed to serve, and all resulting in a new constitutional settlement greater than the sum of its parts. This is arguably a valid description of the outcome of the 1998 settlements, but it does not explain how change came about, which as we have seen was by way of three largely contingent processes, each in varying ways combining civil society consultation and elite-level constitutional construction, without too much thought as to how the three devolution settlements would relate to each other.

For reasons I will discuss, it may be better to describe the UK model not so much as "asymmetrical accommodation" but more as "lop-sided accommodation." Nonetheless, since the language of asymmetry is well established, I will continue to use this term. The UK's devolution model is we might say doubly asymmetrical. Unlike many decentralized states, the three regions/substate national societies which have achieved self-government have models of autonomy very different one from one another. Scotland acquired a strong model of self-government – a Parliament with law-making powers and the devolution of all matters not expressly reserved to Westminster in the Scotland Act 1998. The Northern Ireland Act 1998 embodies a highly complex consociational model of decision making designed to cause the two national societies/national minorities within the one small territory, each with their attachments to a different kin state, to work together. And the result has been the devolution of a range of powers to the Northern Ireland Assembly that is not dissimilar in content to that of the Scottish system. By contrast, the government of Wales Act 1998 accorded far fewer powers to the new Welsh Assembly, which was denied the legislative discretion to make laws in devolved areas without Westminster's involvement; in short, a much weaker model of devolution than either of the other two.

But the differences within these models make sense in light of the very different histories of each territory and the particularities of their respective relationships to the central state; they also make sense given that the political systems within each territory highlighted highly variable constitutional aspirations and different levels of enthusiasm for devolution at all. We see this in Northern Ireland where devolution itself is a compromise between the prevalent aspirations in the late 1990s among nationalists for unification with Ireland and among unionists for a strong continuing relationship with the UK state. We should also note that in the referendum in Scotland an overwhelming majority – 74% – voted for devolution, while only the narrowest of majorities – 51% – did so in Wales.

Another aspect of this particular dimension of asymmetry is that the regions of England don't have self-government at all, and indeed nor does England as a whole which continues to be governed by the UK government and Parliament. And the one attempt by the Labour government to create regional government in England back-fired in a postal referendum in the North East in November 2004 which resulted in a high percentage vote (78%) against regional devolution among the 48% who responded. In light of this process, no further initiative to create regional government anywhere else in England has even been tried.

While the heavy asymmetry that attends the different models of autonomy among the four large territories of the UK (including England) now embedded in statute makes sense given the historical and political differences that attend them, the second aspect of asymmetry is the feature that makes the system lop-sided; it is also therefore more problematic, certainly if we are to compare the UK to some ideal model of federalism. The development of sophisticated autonomy models has not brought with it very much in the way of adjustment in how the central institutions of government of the state are either constituted or do their business, and in fact the institutional form and doctrinal presuppositions of Parliament have largely remained in place. Where we have seen constitutional reform at the center, it has been largely detached from, rather than informed by and bound up with, devolution (e.g. the Constitutional Reform Act 2005). In the same way, the Crown as embodiment of the legal and constitutional authority of the central executive power remains a unified and highly centralized entity in terms of composition, constitutional role, and powers, including a formally unified civil service structure. Some of the functions of the Crown have inevitably been passed over to the devolved administrations, but these were largely exercised at substate level in any case under the pre-devolution administrations.

What has not taken place is either the emergence of new institutions at the center specifically created for the making of joint decisions on reserved matters which actively engage the devolved institutions, or the serious engagement of devolved administrations or parliaments in existing institutions for the making of these decisions. To take Scotland once more as our example, the Scotland Act actually has little to say about what in federal systems is known as intra-state federalism, with a lack of detail on how institutions to coordinate policy for the UK as a whole would be set up, far less about how these should be designed or how they should operate. And the result is that there is not a formalized, and legally protected, set of mechanisms in place for occasions where serious competence disputes arise. Instead, institutions operate largely at the behest of the center and, therefore, depend upon the goodwill of the central government and parliament for their continuation.[15] We see this in the informal arrangements for inter-executive cooperation.[16]

At the executive level, inter-governmental aspects of the devolution settlement for Scotland are organized through informal or quasi-formal structures. The Joint Ministerial Committee (JMC) established a format for co-operation between ministers in Whitehall and their counterparts in Edinburgh and the other devolved administrations.[17] Generally it operates through meetings between officials or in direct relationships between one London department and its devolved equivalent. Its remit is to deal with reserved matters insofar as they might affect devolved territories, and devolved matters where they impact upon the rest of the UK. Flowing from this arrangement are a series of Memoranda of Understanding, and Supplementary Agreements known as "concordats."[18] But in such a semi-formal model there is no legal requirement to conduct relations with the Scottish government in a particular way (or indeed at all), the UK government can set the terms for such discussions, can table the agenda it wants, and can offer greater or lower levels of cooperation to the devolved administration, or individual departments within it, based upon political preference.[19] In this way, the devolved institutions can be induced into a position of political compliance in order to gain a role in these discussions. More importantly, just as there is no legal requirement to enter into negotiations, similarly there is no obligation on the UK government to reach agreement with the devolved institutions on any issue of policy, even where it affects the devolved territory. Inter-governmental cooperation can be, and often is, simply a process of passing on information concerning decisions already taken by the center. Furthermore, such quasi-formal mechanisms as have been established through the JMC have not been utilized systematically, with some departments at UK level operating in a significantly more structured way with their Scottish counterparts than others.[20]

The potential for tensions to be exacerbated is also evident at the level of inter-parliamentary relations between the Scottish Parliament and Westminster. One issue concerns a lack of clarity in the division of competences between legislatures, and the second is the lack of protection of the competences of the devolved legislature from the risk of central retrenchment; the latter in particular is specific to the UK's unitary model in contrast to a more formally demarcated federal system. The former issue has led to the infamous West Lothian Question.[21] In the absence of an English parliament, an argument persists that MPs from the devolved territories exert too great an influence within the House of Commons.[22] The contention is that since certain matters which are devolved to the competence of the devolved legislatures are dealt with for England by the Westminster parliament, it is unfair that MPs who are returned to the House of Commons from the devolved territories can vote on matters which affect only England. This has become particularly controversial in situations where the UK government has relied upon MPs from across the UK to pass legislation which will not have effect in the devolved territories. The consequence of this unhappy state of affairs, which is no more than a consequence of an inchoate process of decentralization, is that it has led to political difficulties that seem to have been entirely avoidable. In light of this it can be seen to have the potential to stoke up resentments across the Union. Voters in England might justifiably feel aggrieved that their preferences are not being met; whereas attempts to resolve the issue, for example, by establishing a Grand Committee within the House of Commons whereby only English MPs could vote on bills concerned only with England,[23] might suggest to citizens in other parts of the UK that the Westminster parliament is now increasingly an English parliament and that their interests might be better served by gaining more powers for their own devolved legislature. This has led to the formation of the McKay Commission to consider issues arising from devolution in the United Kingdom and their effect on the workings of the House of Commons (its remit is "To consider how the House of Commons might deal with legislation which affects only part of the United Kingdom, following the devolution of certain legislative powers to the Scottish Parliament, the Northern Ireland Assembly and the National Assembly for Wales").[24] If this suggests some model of amending the legislative procedure of Parliament in line with the principle of "English votes for English laws," this might require substantial changes to how Parliament operates and will create different categories of MPs. It would also have a knock-on effect at executive level as departments adjust to new models of law making.

The West Lothian Question displays how, in terms of its constitutional culture, the Westminster model does not, at the level of decision making, institutionalize in a meaningful way the symbolic recognition of the UK as a multinational, multilevel state. The UK Parliament has clearly not developed the persona of anything akin to a federal legislature, able and willing to act as a forum for negotiating different territorial interests. One opportunity for change seemed to lie in reform of the House of Lords. A major development occurred in 1999 (House of Lords

Act 1999) with the removal of most hereditary peers, but no attempt was made to transform the second chamber into a "territorial" house along federal lines. Nor in the various proposals for further change which have been put forward since has there been any serious plan to move reform in this direction.

## UK constitutional flexibility: advantages and disadvantages

The post-1998 arrangements, while very untidy, are perhaps an unavoidable consequence of the flexibility of the system which was able to bring to life so quickly such highly varied models of devolution. And it is undeniable that it was thanks to an unwritten constitution that devolution was effected in such an ad hoc way, by ordinary legislation and without the need for elaborate constitutional amendment. Another advantage of the UK system is that the devolution settlements have continued to develop case by case without the need for any large-scale exercise in constitutional reframing. In Wales' case, the asymmetry of the system led to some degree of neighbor envy as pro-devolutionists peered greedily at the extensive legislative powers enjoyed by the Scottish Parliament, and agitation for further change led to various modifications to the devolution model which were effected by the government of Wales Act 2006. This Act effectively establishes a clear distinction between the National Assembly and the Welsh Assembly government, putting it on a standard Parliament-Executive footing whereby the government is drawn from the Parliament and in turn is accountable to it. Furthermore, under the Act, a provision was made for the National Assembly to have competence to make a new category of legislation to be called "Measures" which is, in essence, primary legislation. A referendum, as provided for by the 2006 Act, on extending the law-making powers of the National Assembly for Wales, was held on 3 March 2011 and the new powers were supported by a majority of those voting.[25]

Flexibility has also allowed for crisis-management. The devolution system in Northern Ireland seemed to go into reverse from time to time in the early period with the suspension of the devolved institutions by the central government, but these suspensions were only temporary in nature, creating breathing-space until political agreement as to the way forward could be secured. We have also seen gradual moves on issues such as disarmament and the further devolution of issues such as justice and policing.

This growth of powers for Scotland is already having knock-on consequences for the stability of the devolution model as a whole. One inevitable consequence is that the new tax powers will stimulate further debate in Wales. Already the Commission on Devolution in Wales ("the Silk Commission"[26]) has been reviewing existing financial and constitutional arrangements, investigating the possibility of devolving additional fiscal powers to the National Assembly for Wales. And even the mode of ratification of further change can differ; whereas a referendum was held in Wales in 2011 on the powers in the 2006 Act, the 2012 Act for Scotland was passed simply by the UK Parliament with the consent of the Scottish Parliament, with no serious political calls for a referendum.

The remarkable feature of the system since 1998 is that it has continued to evolve so rapidly without any major constitutional upheavals. The present landscape may well continue into the future with gradual developments, or we may see two other and more dramatic changes. One of these might be a move towards federalism in a state that in 1998 self-consciously avoided any turn towards the formality of a federal system. The second is of course the possibility of the very break-up of the state itself as we look toward the referendum in Scotland on independence in 2014.

## The constitutionalization of devolution?

The lack of representation at the center is a real issue, and one we are seeing now in Scotland which through the 2012 Act is accruing further powers with almost no regard to the reform of London-based institutions. But the dominance of the center continues to be supported by the doctrine of parliamentary sovereignty, and any move to federalism would inevitably mean the formal modification of this doctrine. It has long been questioned how long this centralization of the sovereign power could survive devolution. And it does seem that the notion of Parliament's supremacy is beginning to creak in light of the recognition by English courts of the supremacy of EC law while the UK is a member.

There is evidence, too, that devolution is leading to some questions about whether the Scotland Act 1998 and Northern Ireland Act 1998 are just statutes like any other or whether they have reached a particular level of constitutional status which defies one feature of the Parliamentary sovereignty doctrine, namely that all statutes are of the same constitutional value. The highest courts have been hinting at this. In the *Robinson* case, the Northern Ireland Act 1998 was described by the House of Lords Appellate Committee (at that time the highest court of appeal in the UK until replaced in 2010 by the Supreme Court of the

UK) as "a constitution for Northern Ireland" by Lord Hoffman, whereby the Belfast Agreement upon which the Act was based should be used as aid to interpretation of the statute.[27] The role of the referendum in endorsing this Agreement (or "constitution for Northern Ireland") was taken to be a significant factor by the High Court in Northern Ireland[28] in an earlier hearing of this case, and this led McEvoy and Morison to argue that the 1998 Act has such a constitutional status in part because "it is a manifestation of the wishes of the Northern Ireland people."[29] Indeed, for them: "The judiciary has begun to address, however tentatively, the idea that the Northern Ireland Act represents something more than simply one more Act of Parliament ... It represents, in our view, a fundamental 'constitutional moment' wherein the Agreement and the Act that implemented it, are *constituent* acts in the establishment of a new polity."[30]

The courts have not so far offered such an explicit connection between the popular endorsement of devolution in Scotland and the constitutional status of the Scotland Act 1998; judges have generally been cautious in defining the constitutional status of the Scottish Parliament.[31] But implicit recognition of this can be found. In the case of *Jackson*, Lord Steyn argued that the nature of the Act might even call into question the supremacy of Westminster: "The settlement contained in the Scotland Act 1998 ... point[s] to a divided sovereignty."[32] Two other judges made similar interventions. In the more recent *AXA* case we saw the Scotland Act being described as of "real constitutional importance"[33] and recognition of *"sui generis"* constitutional status of Acts of the Scottish Parliament. In light of this, Lord Hope stated that the courts should "intervene, if at all, only in the most exceptional circumstances" (para 49) in reviewing the legality of legislation of the Scottish Parliament. This does not directly challenge the powers of Westminster to amend the Scotland Act without the consent of the Scottish Parliament but it does consolidate the status of the Scottish Parliament as a legislature.

And so there are tentative steps being taken by the courts that seem to suggest that a vision of sovereignty that takes no account of the radical division of governmental and legislative authority since 1998 no longer makes sense. But this judicial move to quasi-federalism, if that is what it is, is not as we have seen backed up by similar moves in the other two branches of the central UK state, and in particular the UK Parliament itself operates much as before.

Nonetheless, the method of passage of the Scotland Act 2012 was in itself constitutionally significant and does show that a strong constitutional convention has already developed whereby the Westminster Parliament will respect the devolved powers of the Scottish Parliament. In addition to the substantive changes which the 2012 Act will bring, the long and convoluted process by which it was passed has also helped to consolidate the constitutional status of the Scottish Parliament. Under the Scotland Act 1998 there is a residual power for the UK Parliament to legislate in devolved areas (Scotland Act, Section 28(7)),[34] but as the Scotland Bill 1997–98 was being passed it was suggested that a constitutional convention would develop to the effect that the UK Parliament would not do so without the consent of the Scottish Parliament through a Legislative Consent Motion. Such a convention has indeed developed, known as the Sewel Convention.[35] Notably, the later Scotland Bill (which became the 2012 Act) was contested. It had originally been proposed by the Labour government before it lost the General Election of 2010 and was then picked up by the new Conservative–Liberal Coalition. Accordingly, the Bill changed under the latter government. Both manifestations of the Bill were challenged by the SNP government in Scotland which, while attracted by the grant of more powers, was suspicious of some of the content of the Bill. Since the Bill was introduced twice to Westminster, this meant that it required to be presented twice to the Scottish Parliament in the quest for successive Legislative Consent Motions in line with the Sewel Convention. In the end, each of these was granted by the Scottish Parliament. This process seems to have hardened the Sewel Convention still further when we consider that each of the two UK governments was keen to see this Bill passed and had to put up with delays while the Scottish Parliament satisfied itself as to the Bill's terms. Despite this protracted process, at no point was there any effort to invoke s28(7) of the Scotland Act to drive the Bill through the UK Parliament without an LCM in order to overcome the opposition of the Scottish government. This suggests that it is scarcely conceivable today for the UK Parliament to legislate for Scotland in devolved areas without the consent of the Scottish Parliament, a fact which seems to have diminished the sovereignty of the UK Parliament.

## Conclusion: Scotland and the 2014 referendum

With devolution has come the opportunity for substate administrations to hold their own referendums. In January 2012, the Scottish government announced its intention to hold a popular poll on independence in the Autumn of 2014. A draft Referendum Bill to this effect was published which asserted the authority of the Scottish Parliament to hold such a referendum, while a public consultation exercise was embarked upon.[36] Although the United Kingdom government immediately challenged the legislative competence of the Scottish Parliament to pass this Bill, and in doing so launched its own consultation process,[37] to the surprise of many, on 15 October, an agreement ("The Edinburgh Agreement"[38]) was reached between the two governments. The result of this agreement is that the UK Parliament has approved an Order[39] which for the avoidance of doubt confirms the power of the Scottish Parliament to legislate for a referendum to be held before the end of 2014 on whether Scotland should become independent of the rest of the United Kingdom.

The future is therefore uncertain, although the polls early in 2013 suggest that the pro-independence campaign is firmly behind in the race. One interesting feature is that we don't yet know exactly what the SNP government means by "independence." Its detailed proposal will be published in a white paper toward the end of 2013, but already we see signs that the proposal will offer some forms of on-going union. We need to trace the clues for this conclusion back a little way. On 30 November 2009, the Scottish Executive published the White Paper, *Your Scotland, Your Voice*, which set out an examination of various constitutional options for Scotland's future – the status quo, further devolution, and independence.[40] The model of independence presented by the consultation paper is somewhat attenuated. The Queen would remain as Head of State: "The current Parliamentary and political Union of Great Britain and Northern Ireland would become a monarchical and social Union – united kingdoms rather than a United Kingdom – maintaining a relationship forged in 1603 by the Union of the Crowns." Furthermore, "within this relationship, a broad range of cultural, social and policy links would continue and it is likely that both an independent Scotland and the remainder of the UK would seek to maintain and build on a series of cross-border partnerships and services." And finally, "Scotland would continue to operate within the Sterling system until any decision to join the Euro by the people of Scotland in a referendum." We wait to see if these areas of "union" are once again put forward in 2013.[41] There are of course uncertainties; even if there is a Yes vote, the rest of the UK might well not agree to a form of continuing union with an "independent" Scotland.

What is clear is that the UK is heavily integrated and the desire within Scotland even among many of those favoring independent statehood to maintain some ties of union is strong. Furthermore, the referendum campaign is likely to be run with the No side offering alternative models of change not only for Scotland but possibly for other devolved areas of the UK as an alternative to independence. And indeed this is not surprising. For over 120 years the decentralization of the UK has been an ongoing process and the relationships and unions across the islands, particularly when set against the backdrop of that other Union across Europe, look set to continue. When looked at in the context of a century of constitutional change, we can say that the constitutional story of the UK's evolution has not been one of "accommodation" of substate nationalism but rather a growing realization that the UK is inherently a compound state, deriving its very self-understanding from the national pluralism of which it is composed. Since 1998, this has been a rapidly evolving story and for the foreseeable future it looks like to remain so.

## Notes

1. Stephen Tierney, *Constitutional Law and National Pluralism* (Oxford: OUP, 2004).
2. John McGarry, "Federal Political Systems and the Accommodation of National Minorities" in Ann L. Griffiths (ed.), *The Handbook of Federal Countries* (Montreal: McGill-Queen's University Press, 2002), pp. 416–447.
3. Michael Billig, *Banal Nationalism* (London: Sage Publications, 1995).
4. Stephen Tierney, "Giving with one Hand: Scottish Devolution within a Unitary State" *International Journal of Constitutional Law* (2007), 22, pp. 572–597.
5. Philip Resnick, *Thinking English Canada* (Toronto: Stoddart, 1994), p. 18.
6. As Fossas puts it: "national minorities often conceive the structure of the system more as a confederation than a federation. Their basic claim does not consist in defending the political community as culturally diverse, but in sustaining that more than one political community exists, each of which has the right to govern itself." Enric Fossas, "Asymmetry and Plurinationality in Spain", working paper 167, *Institut de Ciències Politiques i Socials* (Barcelona: Universitat Autònoma de Barcelona, 1999).
7. Ferran Requejo, "Political Liberalism in Multinational States: The Legitimacy of Plural and Asymmetrical Federalism", in A. Gagnon, C. Taylor and J. Tully (eds), *Multinational Democracies* (Cambridge: Cambridge University Press, 2001), pp. 122, n. 19.
8. In 2006 the House of Commons passed a resolution recognizing that Quebec forms a nation "within a united Canada": "Resolution Respecting the Recognition of Quebec as a Nation", Canadian Hansard; 39th Parliament, 1st Session; No. 087; 27 November 2006. Quebec nationalists observe that this recognition is not in any sense "constitutional".
9. Most recently in the devolution context, a referendum was held in Wales in 2011 on extending the law-making powers of the National Assembly, as provided for under Part IV of the government of Wales Act 2006.

10. 52% voted for devolution on a 64% turnout, failing to meet the requirement in the Scotland Act 1978 that at least 40% of the entire electorate should vote in favour.
11. Owen Dudley Edwards, *A Claim of Right for Scotland* (1989), p. 19.
12. On the first question, I agree that there should be a Scottish Parliament, 74% voted Yes; and on the second, I agree that a Scottish Parliament should have tax-varying powers, 63.5% voted Yes.
13. Richard Wyn Jones and Roger Scully, *Wales Says Yes: Devolution and the 2011 Welsh Referendum (Cardiff: University of Wales Press, 2012)*.
14. Colin Irwin, *The People's Peace Process in Northern Ireland* (Palgrave Macmillan, 2002).
15. "Memos show how Blair and Brown 'ignored' McConnell", *Sunday Times* (Scottish edn.) 16 September 2007, at 7.
16. Richard Rawlings, "Concordats of the Constitution", *Law Quarterly Review*, 116, p. 257.
17. The JMC was established under the Memorandum of Understanding, Cm 4806, July 2000.
18. Rawlings op cit.
19. Alan Trench, *Central Government's Responses to Devolution*, Economic and Social Research Council Devolution Briefing No. 15, (London: Economic and Social Research Council, 2005).
20. Charlie Jeffery, *Devolution: What Difference Has it Made?*, Interim Findings of the ESRC Devolution and Constitutional Change Programme (London: Economic and Social Research Council, 2004).
21. The anomaly was raised in the late 1970s by Tam Dalyell, MP for West Lothian.
22. Despite reduced representation by way of the Scottish Parliament (Constituencies) Act 2004.
23. "Tories Will Hand Crucial Powers to English MPs", *Observer* 28 October 2007.
24. http://www.parliament.uk/documents/commons-vote-office/5-DPM-Devolution.pdf
25. Richard Wyn Jones and Roger Scully, *Wales says Yes: Devolution and the 2011 Welsh Referendum* (University of Wales Press, 2012).
26. For details, see http://commissionondevolutioninwales.independent.gov.uk/
27. "The 1998 Act is a constitution for Northern Ireland, framed to create a continuing form of government against the background of the history of the territory and the principles agreed in Belfast." Robinson v Secretary of State for Northern Ireland and Others (Northern Ireland), [2002] UKHL 32 per Lord Hoffman, para 25. See also Lord Bingham, para 11. And Kieran McEvoy and John Morison, "Beyond the 'Constitutional Moment': Law, Transition, and Peacemaking in Northern Ireland", *Fordham Int'l L.J.* 26 (2002), pp. 961–995, 967.
28. IN THE MATTER OF AN APPLICATION BY MARK PARSONS FOR JUDICIAL REVIEW (2002) NIQB 46, para 34. 2002.
29. Kieran McEvoy and John Morison, "Beyond the 'Constitutional Moment' Law, Transition, and Peace-making in Northern Ireland", *Fordham Int'l L.J.* 26 (2002) pp. 961–995, 968.
30. Kieran McEvoy and John Morison, "Beyond the 'Constitutional Moment': Law, Transition, and Peacemaking in Northern Ireland", *Fordham Int'l L.J.*

26(961) (2002), pp. 961–995, 969. Notably the constituency is itself a wide one, embracing multiple constituents – unionists and nationalists within Northern Ireland but also the two kin states of the UK and Republic of Ireland.
31. Whaley v Lord Watson 2000 SC 340 the Lord President (Rodger) at p 348; Lord Prosser at pp 357–358.
32. Jackson and others (Appellants) v. Her Majesty's Attorney General (Respondent) [2005] UKHL 56 para 102.
33. *AXA General Insurance Ltd. v. The Lord Advocate* 2011 SC 31 (IH), para 87 per Lord Hope.
34. Note also the White Paper preceding devolution Scotland's Parliament, Cm 3648 para 42: "The United Kingdom is and will remain sovereign in all matters."
35. Named after Lord Sewel who, speaking for the government, suggested this process in Parliamentary debate on the Scotland Bill. Hansard, H.L. Vol. 592, col. 791 (21 July 1998).
36. http://www.scotland.gov.uk/Publications/2012/01/1006
37. http://www.scotlandoffice.gov.uk/scotlandoffice/files/17779-Cm-8203.pdf
38. *Agreement between the United Kingdom Government and the Scottish Government on a referendum on independence for Scotland*, available at: http://www.scotland.gov.uk/About/Government/concordats/Referendum-on-independence
39. A draft Order in Council under s 30 of the Scotland Act 1998 was attached to the Agreement.
40. The Draft Referendum (Scotland) Bill was an annex to the Consultation paper: Scotland's Future: Draft Referendum (Scotland) Bill Consultation Paper.
41. Although this has been hinted at in a recent document: "Scotland's Future: From the Referendum to Independence and a Written Constitution", Scottish government 5 February 2013, http://www.scotland.gov.uk/Resource/0041/00413757.pdf. See Stephen Tierney, "After the referendum – the Scottish Government's proposal for a written Constitution", UK Constitutional Law Group Blog, 12 March 2013, http://ukconstitutionallaw.org/2013/03/12/stephen-tierney-after-the-referendum-the-scottish-governments-proposal-for-a-written-constitution/

# 8
# Italy: Autonomism, Decentralization, Federalism, or What Else?

*Francesco Palermo and Alice Valdesalici*

## Introduction

More than a decade ago, Italy was championing the movement toward federalization, having just introduced the most significant "federalizing" constitutional reform of the western world in decades. Twelve years later, despite slow but remarkable implementation of the reform, the economic crisis that severely hit the country seems to be strangling regional autonomy and the whole federalizing process, bringing about a counter-wave of centralization.

This raises serious questions as to the requirements and preconditions for federalization, far beyond the Italian case. Italy is extraordinarily diverse in terms of economic development, culture, ethnic composition of the population, and administrative capacity: nevertheless, the main driver of the most recent wave of the federalizing process has been the economy. While other factors, including the country's diversity, prompted the first stages of regionalization, after the introduction of a major constitutional reform in 2001 the federalism debate has been captured by economic constraints and financial intergovernmental relations. Federalism has thus been equated with "fiscal federalism" and the political discourse has considered federalism nothing else than a different system of financial relations among the levels of government. As a consequence, in recent times, many have claimed that "federalism is dead" just because of budget constraints. To what extent is federalism an institutional construct that is primarily driven by financial/fiscal prerogatives? What are some of the other conditions necessary for federalism to flourish as a constitutional and political system? If not federalism, what is the process Italy has been undergoing in the last 10–15 years as its territorial model has evolved and been restructured?

As the Introduction to this volume notes, "the notion of accommodation in plurinational polities ... needs to be unpacked and disaggregated and all of its multiple dimensions need to be analyzed." To examine the multiple dimensions of the politics of accommodation, not just constitutionalism needs to be examined but also other dimensions such as political culture. Thus, this chapter takes a close look at constitutionalism and federalization in Italy, but also considers the political culture of federalization in Italy.

The chapter will first illustrate the institutional and political developments of Italian regionalism from its inception, focusing on the main changes introduced by the constitutional reform in 2001 and its implementing norms. Subsequently, what became the main element of the reform, the new intergovernmental financial relations, introduced in 2009 and further implemented in the following years, will be illustrated. A close look will hence be given to the measures introduced by the "emergency Government" led by Mr Monti in 2011–2012 and the subsequent constitutional adjudication will be closely examined. Finally, critical variables, hampering a transformation of the country into a federation, will be emphasized. To conclude, some general considerations will be drawn from the Italian case regarding the essential elements of a federal reform, especially if imposed from the top down.

## The long and twisting road of regionalism in Italy

Since the achievement of national unity, completed in the 1860s, the Italian state has been modeled according to the French blueprint of a centralized and bureaucratic administration. It was only with the republican constitution of 1948 that an innovative but at the same time feeble experiment with regionalization was made.

From the very beginning, Italian regionalism has been characterized by its asymmetrical design, both as a matter of constitutional law and in terms of effective use of powers transferred to the Regions. At first, only five "special" or "autonomous" Regions were established, all situated on the periphery: three in the Alpine arch in the North, with consistent minority groups (Aosta Valley, Trentino-South Tyrol, Friuli-Venezia Giulia), and the two main islands (Sicily and Sardinia).[1] Each of them is guaranteed autonomy by a "special statute," a basic law with constitutional rank (Palermo 2008: 33–49).

As an innovative experiment, the regionalization of the whole country, a "third way" between a federal and a unitary system, aimed at avoiding too strong an asymmetry between these areas and the rest of the territory, and even their possible secession. Regionalization, however, although laid down in the constitution of 1948, was fully developed only in the 1970s, when the "ordinary" Regions were established and legislative powers eventually devolved to them. Since then, a permanent increase in the regional powers gradually narrowed the gap between "ordinary" and "special" Regions. The path has been far from straightforward and coherent, influenced by shifting political priorities and very much determined by constitutional adjudication: as there is still no effective institutional representation of regional interests at central level, progress could often be achieved only through litigation by challenging state legislation before the Constitutional Court (Bin 1996: 61–78). These conflicts and a jurisdiction underlining the necessity of cooperation and consultation led to the gradual emancipation of the regional level and to the establishment of instruments aimed at improving cooperation among the levels.

A series of important reforms of the public administration and of the system of local self-government were adopted between the late 1980s and the late 1990s, thus encouraging the more active Regions to really start developing their potential for self-government. Reflecting the socio-economic cleavage between the North and the South, the political demand for more self-government became an absolute priority for the rich and industrialized northern Regions and at the same time also for the government in Rome. Also due to pressures by a "federalist," and on occasions "secessionist," political party, the Northern League, the issue of "federal reform" could no longer be left to experts only, but had to be dealt with politically and in more comprehensive and symbolic terms, thus requiring a constitutional reform.

## The constitutional reform and its difficult implementation

In 1999 and 2001, two constitutional amendments were approved, considerably increasing the powers and the political profile of the (ordinary) Regions. The first reform introduced the direct election of the regional president (the only case in Europe) in order to enhance political stability in the ordinary Regions. It also strengthened their constitutional autonomy, as the regional basic laws are now adopted by the ordinary Regions themselves in a special procedure, which resembles that for amending the national constitution (double approval, qualified majority, and possible referendum).[2] The reform of 2001 completely reshaped the constitutional provisions on the relations between state and Regions, often according to previous jurisprudence of the Constitutional Court. Although the autonomous Regions were not directly affected by the reform, due to their "special" constitutional status, a preferential clause guarantees them all benefits, i.e. "more favorable" features compared to their current powers and status.

The reform states the equality of all component units of the "Republic" (State, Regions, provinces, municipalities):[3] sounding unfamiliar for a federal system, this is intended to express the concept of (functional) "spheres" rather than (hierarchical) levels of government (Pizzetti 2001: 1153–96). The "two track asymmetry" – ordinary and autonomous Regions – is confirmed, but single ordinary Regions may request additional powers to be transferred to them by the state (Article 116.3; Palermo 2003: 55–62). Most importantly, the reform drastically changes the distribution of legislative and administrative powers between state and Regions: the constitution (Article 117) now lists all legislative powers of the state as well as the fields of concurrent legislation (i.e. those in which Regions can legislate only within the framework of general guidelines determined by a national law). By contrast with the situation before, the residual powers lie with the Regions, according to classic federal schemes. Administrative powers are no longer connected with the legislative ones, but distributed in a flexible manner according to the criteria of "subsidiarity, differentiation and proportionality" (Article 118). The new provision on fiscal federalism grants partial financial autonomy to subnational entities (Article 119, see below) and all Regions have to establish a consultative body for the representation of local authorities within their territory (Article 123). The elimination of preventive state control (before the reform, all regional laws had to be approved by the government before entering into force) marks the equal rank of Regional and state legislation.

Despite these and other typical federal elements, the implementation of the reform proved to be extremely difficult. Although some amendments had immediate effect, in particular the new distribution of legislative powers, the new lists proved to be incomplete and to contain many overlaps giving rise to an enormous increase of controversies (Bin 2006: 889–902; Groppi 2007, 421–432; Onida 2007: 11–26). In consequence, the Constitutional Court had to face the fundamental task of redefining the competences, and frequently this led to the justification of an expanding role of the state: through the assumption of "cross-cutting issues" instead of narrow competence-matters, and the interpretation of the state as guardian of a "national interest," the Court on several occasions supported a rather centralistic interpretation of the new distribution of competences (inter alia, Judgments 303/2003, 14/2004).[4] This is even more paradoxical as before the reform the Court had been the strongest ally of the Regions in developing their competences.

A second group of reform provisions required further legislation on details, e.g. the new financial relations between the layers of government, but the center-right coalition government under Mr Berlusconi elected immediately after the reform entered into force (2001) did not show any interest in completing the reform inherited from its predecessor: thus, only in 2003 and 2005, respectively, were two by-laws finally adopted on the implementation of some amended provisions of the constitution (Law 131/2003 and law 11/2005, as replaced by Law 234/2012; Cavaleri & Lamarque 2004). However, the issue of financial relations remained unresolved as will be better explained later ("Trajectories of fiscal federalism"). This delay caused additional confusion and gave rise to more controversy and judicial litigation.

In addition, the then government (including the Northern League which sought to gain more radical results) presented its own, more far-reaching constitutional "counter-reform." This reform proposal concerning 53 articles of the whole constitution was finally adopted by the center-right coalition's majority in Parliament on November 2005. However, its entry into force was prevented by a popular vote (61% against) in a referendum held in June 2006, just after Mr Berlusconi's government lost the general elections; the successor, Mr Prodi, started to complete implementation of the reform of 2001, but was forced to resign after less than two years in power. Finally, another government under Mr Berlusconi was elected in April 2008, with a strong majority in Parliament and decisive support from the Northern League, which immediately announced the intention to bring forward another comprehensive constitutional reform making Italy a "fully fledged" federal country. Such a reform never materialized and the government collapsed as a result of not being able to face the economic crisis.

Under the transitional government led by Mr Monti (2011–2012), a new, comprehensive constitutional reform was drafted, aiming at transferring several important powers back under the full control of the state, by introducing a general supremacy clause and strengthening the role of the state in the area of concurrent legislation. Furthermore, the state power to coordinate public finances was to be strengthened to the extent that hardly any margin would remain for regional discretion. The reform, however, was not adopted due to early dissolution of Parliament in December 2012. Despite the various attempts to revise the constitutional reform of 2001, therefore, it remains in force.

However, even the Regions themselves did not make much use of the new opportunities provided by the reform of 2001: in particular, the process of passing new basic laws has been very slow[5] and the new opening-clause for more differentiation among the ordinary Regions has been left disregarded (Palermo 2012a: 9–26).

## Trajectories of "fiscal federalism" in Italy

The design of the intergovernmental relations in the area of fiscal and financial matters is pivotal for the very existence of every compound state, but in Italy the issue has recently monopolized every aspect of the federalizing process. From a comparative perspective, the Italian case is unique in this regard. In a multilevel system the modification of the financial settings usually comes together with a comprehensive reorganization of the intergovernmental relations, but in Italy such a logical pattern has been turned upside-down. While the 2001 constitutional reform intended to comprehensively address the institutional design of a (quasi) federal state, after that political attention was paid predominantly (and lately exclusively) to the financial dimension.

### The new financial relations and their controversial implementation

Since 2001, more financial autonomy has been vested in territorial entities. According to the constitution (Article 119), territorial entities shall enjoy autonomy both on the revenue and expenditure side; at the same time, equality among all territories by means of solidarity, cohesion, and coordination of public finance has to be ensured.

A better link between political and financial accountability has been the main driver for reform. A new financial setting had to be envisaged, where the spheres of those who benefit, who decide, and who vote are overlapping, in order to ensure democratic control and foster efficiency. The previous system, mostly based on state grants, had to be reshaped, as the recognition of autonomy on the revenue side is perceived to be conducive to more accountability for the Regions.

Contrary to all expectations, the constitutional provision remained completely unimplemented for more than eight years. Only in 2009 did the Parliament finally adopted Law no. 42/2009 with the declared purpose of ensuring the accountable and efficient management of public functions and finances.

However, the law has not proven able to foster financial and political responsibility. This is due partly to the law itself and partly to the settings of the new system. On the one hand, Article 119 of the constitution and Law no 42/2009 set only the general principles without giving any concrete content to the new financial regime. On the other hand, the new system has proven to be much more a new model of subnational financing and of rationalizing the decentralized spending than a comprehensive reallocation of powers in fiscal and financial matters.

Indeed, the law is nothing else than a delegation from Parliament to the Executive of the power to adopt several by-laws (nine enactment decrees) in two years' time, in order to allow the concrete functioning of fiscal federalism (the literature refers to it as a "mega-delegation": Scuto 2010). At present, all decrees have been adopted, but the new regime is still a work in progress as the decrees themselves provide for a gradual move from the old to the new system. A transitional phase toward the new system began in 2013, and is supposed to be complete and fully operative from 2016.

As a consequence, Regions and municipalities are still predominantly financed by central state transfers and the fiscal gap between the state and all other territorial entities has been widened rather than reduced. While subnational entities are in charge of about 50% of public spending (excluding pensions and interest rates), they are responsible for raising less than 18% of the tax revenue. The vertical fiscal gap of 32% shows the system's lack of political accountability which has for years been fostering an uncontrolled increase in decentralized spending (Antonini 2009: 7).

The lack of political and financial accountability is the consequence of a reform that took the first step (the decentralization of relevant and costly administrative functions) but not the second (the corresponding reshaping of financial and institutional relations).

Besides, doubts can be expressed about the prescriptive force of the enactment decrees. Most of these by-laws are not self-executing: either they need further integration by means of administrative rules, or they postpone the definition of essential aspects. With regard to the first point, other decrees are expected to correct possible malfunctioning or to integrate deficiencies, while the second problem can be traced back to the existing normative gaps. The government failed to coordinate well the adopted measures and they turned out to be rather inadequate and ineffective in reorganizing the system in a comprehensive and rational way. This is, for instance, the case of the new equalization concept based on standard criteria. The government provided only a fragmented regulative scheme and did not tackle core elements: it failed to calculate the new financing criteria, and did not define the methodology to be applied.

In addition, the choice of entrusting the implementation of a very generally framed law to the Executive means in practice that the Executive and not Parliament determines the real contents of the financial relations. From a comparative perspective, this is quite unusual. In all European compound states, the financial settings are either designed in detail in the constitution (i.e. Germany and Swiss Confederation) or in a normative act vested with constitutional (or quasi-constitutional) binding force. Besides, they rely on a law of the Parliament and not on a governmental decree (for instance, Austria, Spain, or Belgium). In Italy, by contrast, the political majority will decide upon it without the need to reach such a broader consensus, which would have been expected for a matter of constitutional relevance (Parolari & Valdesalici 2011: 344–53). During Mr Monti's government, for instance, some key elements of the new system have been changed by decree, such as the municipal estate-tax (IMU). The tax should have become operational in 2014 but was anticipated to 2012 and 50% of its revenue, originally foreseen as exclusively for the municipalities, was transferred to the state in order to counter the financial crisis.

Actually, both the Parliament and the territorial entities have been conferred a marginal and ineffective role in the decision-making process (Lupo 2009). The approval of the governmental decrees has to follow a complex process, requiring the involvement of both a Parliamentary commission and a prior agreement with the territorial entities through ad hoc bodies (Articles 3–5, Law no 42/2009), although these agreements are not binding (Bifulco 2009; Cabras 2009). This is highly critical considering that the choices will interfere with divergent individual and territorial interests.

### Where lies accountability? The new regional financing system

Having regard to regional financial autonomy, the most significant change concerns the abolition of all central transfers, with the sole exception of equalization transfers and specific-purpose grants for extraordinary circumstances (Article 119.5 constitution). The current "state-transfer-based" system has been disabled in favor of a "tax-revenue-based" model. As a consequence, territorial entities have to fully finance their functions by means of own-tax sources, shared taxes, or equalization transfers.

Despite linking regional financing to tax revenue, no other dramatic change has taken place. The tax system still remains mostly centralized. The state holds the power to set and levy the most significant taxes, while own-taxes of the Regions are the exception (Decree no. 68/2011; Buglione & Jorio 2011).

Further, the established doctrine of the Constitutional Court additionally limited the scope of regional autonomy. For the Court, regional taxes are only those set and regulated by a regional law, i.e. very few, as the fiscal legislation is almost entirely preempted by the state (Judgments 296/2003, 297/2003; 216/2009. Nicolini 2010: 911–938).[6]

All in all, regional financial autonomy still remains a declared principle, far from being properly translated into practice. Fiscal matters are perceived as the stronghold of sovereignty and the constitutional adjudications have stretched the state interference on subnational autonomy further on.

Moreover, Law no 42/2009 stipulates the gradual overcoming of the current criterion, which grounds the transfers on the resources spent by a specific administration in the previous financial exercise (so-called historical spending). Such a parameter for determining the funding of subnational governments has to be progressively replaced by a set of objective criteria linked to predefined benchmarks, to generally applied and neutral indicators as well as to a unified methodology (so-called standard costs and needs). These should be applied to the equalization system, allowing a standardization of territorial financing (Ferrara and Salerno 2009; Jorio et al. 2009). The new concept should foster efficiency and accountability, while the old approach enhanced inefficient and irresponsible spending, as the more a Region spent and accumulated debt, the more the state allocated to its funding the following year.

### Recent developments: Crisis vs federalism?

All in all, the implementation of fiscal federalism failed to provide a coordinated and comprehensive regulation, and turned out to be rather inadequate and ineffective in reorganizing financial relations.

The situation even worsened due to the grinding economic crisis. The stringent EU obligations imposed on national finances as well as the rocketing rise in interest rates (that made state debts more expensive than in the past) and pressures on the financial markets indirectly impacted both subnational budgets and autonomy. As a matter of fact, between 2011 and 2012, the governments led by both Mr Berlusconi and Mr Monti have approved several executive decrees aiming to rationalize public finance. The main driver was the emergency and their efforts predominantly targeted the balancing of the budget. Evidence of this can be seen in the recently adopted constitutional revision (Constitutional Law no 1/2012), where the principle of a balanced budget has been stated with a strong impact on financial autonomy, especially on the spending side (Bifulco 2012; Salerno 2012).

At a very early stage, the call for stability has been translated into a mere redistribution of spending and revenue capabilities among all constituent units of the Italian Republic. The measures have largely affected the revenue side through an increase in the tax effort, while on the spending side the state has unilaterally introduced drastic shortcuts to the decentralized spending capacity.

Even more importantly, the state has further expanded its scope of interference as the economic conditions have worsened. Since 2011, the government has introduced austerity measures, which have institutional relevance and somehow reshape the intergovernmental relations. In particular, the last decree approved by Mr Berlusconi's government (Decree no 138/2011) and the ones adopted by Mr Monti's government (Decree nos 201/2011 and 95/2012) contain provisions which directly address the territorial structure of the Italian Republic and impact the long-stagnating federalizing process.

All the numerous measures adopted are unsystematic and based on the emergency. They are aimed at resolving contingent rather than structural problems. This way, the necessary and comprehensive reorganization of intergovernmental relations – even beyond the financial ones – has not taken place. On the contrary, most provisions severely interfere with regional autonomy.

Firstly, they unilaterally reduce the state transfers, severely affecting the subnational degree of autonomy on the spending side.

Secondly, they set limitations to the regional governing bodies with a view to reducing the number of seats within the legislative chamber as well as the remuneration of both the executive and legislative members by formally considering these aspects as "benefits," although these issues would indeed belong to the regional competence. Furthermore, the "financial blackmail" has been camouflaged in the promised reduction of the regional contribution to the National Stability Pact (Sterpa 2011: 4). In addition, the Constitutional Court has adjudicated that the margin of autonomy has been preserved, since the state has only set overall criteria in order to control spending and by these means to guarantee equal rights to all citizens within the Italian territory (Judgment 198/2012).

Thirdly, the government imposes compulsory forms of intermunicipal cooperation in the provision of public services for all small municipalities. The parameter is the population: when municipalities have less than 5.000 inhabitants, they are obliged to deliver certain services in cooperation with other neighboring municipalities through a "municipal Union." Besides, the measures encourage municipalities to cooperate and find an adequate territorial dimension as a general rule for providing local public services.

Finally, by the same token, the overall reorganization of local self-government – by abolishing the provinces and saving costs by optimizing the functions – has also failed. The initial proposal was to abolish all provinces (there are more than 100),[7] but a compromise option has finally prevailed. A governmental decree has prescribed the merger of provinces on the basis of a twofold parameter: population (min. 350,000) and territorial extension (min. 2,500 km$^2$). However, the process was subsequently stalled due to the early dissolution of the Parliament and later to the constitutional decision of illegitimacy adopted over the decree (Judgment 220/2013).

Overall, measures adopted urgently and under pressure are often messy and uncoordinated. They fail to tackle the problems effectively and – in one succeeding the other – create a stratification of legal dispositions that jeopardizes their legal certainty. On the other hand, both the structural reorganization and the cost-effective benefits require plenty of time to be realized and, paradoxically, all institutional reforms more easily cause an increase than a decrease in administrative costs over the short term.

Additionally, it has to be underlined that the modifications have been imposed unilaterally by the central state without any involvement of the subnational authorities. They do not participate in the decision-making process at national level and in general terms the intergovernmental system has been revealed as rather ineffective in protecting territorial interests and their constitutional guarantees, as if the provisions regarding the intergovernmental relations were less binding than other constitutional rules.

By and large, the emergency decrees can be perceived as a counter-wave of recentralization. In challenging the constitutional guarantees of autonomy, they dismantle the progress made so far in the federalizing process.

Firstly, instead of starting with the reform of the financial relations, the logical pattern would have called for a preliminary implementation of the institutional and functional settings set forth by the constitution and related to the intergovernmental relations. This would have fostered the coherence of the system, avoiding today's perception of territorial entities as mere administrative branches of the state. The status quo allows for the governmental irruption in subnational competences and powers, while territorial entities are considered in the constitution as constituent units of the Republic formally vested with political autonomy and significant powers (Article 114 constitution).

Secondly, while financial relations have been the cutting edge of the federalizing process, later on this feature has turned out to be an element of instability. As economic resources have become scarce, fiscal federalism has been perceived as an optional component of the intergovernmental structure.

Thirdly, territorial entities as a whole did not demonstrate an ability to cope with new and increased responsibilities. They did not show the expected administrative and political ability nor the capacity to foster institutional innovation. Waste of resources and administrative inefficiencies still reflect the regional scenario, even if to very different extents from one entity to another. Furthermore, uniformity still characterizes the territorial pattern. Despite the deep cleavage that divides the territorial panorama (in particular, the North from the South), autonomy has not been translated into a significant differentiation either of policies or of legislation (Palermo 2012b).

The overall picture has further deteriorated due to the embitterment of the crisis. At present it seems that territorial entities alone are responsible for the whole budget deficit as well as for the entire public debt. As a consequence, the austerity measures are very popular when they cut the decentralized spending or even challenge the very existence of the entities. The paradox is that they seriously (even if indirectly) affect the civil and social rights of the population, as subnational entities are the terminal of the welfare state.

Even in this case, the future of the federalizing process is in the hands of the Constitutional Court. This feature boosts the ongoing trend whereby the jurisprudence contributes more to the strangling than to the development of the federalizing process. If the state legislation has forced the boundaries of the decentralized competences, the Court has gone along with this trend, legitimating such interference in the light of contingent requirements (Di Marco 2011).

Indeed, a faint light could come from those constitutional adjudications, which deem the constitutionality of the austerity decrees only if they pursue the rationalization of public finances by means of mere transitional and time-limited measures and set the overall objectives alone, leaving to subnational entities the decisions on both the instruments and the way of proceeding (Judgments 193/2012; 232/2011; 326/2010). As a consequence, great expectations are placed on the future Judgments on the austerity measures addressing the intergovernmental system.

## Critical variables: party system and the civil service

On top of the mentioned institutional and financial[1] elements, other factors are hampering a complete and smooth transformation of the country into a fully-fledged federal system (for criteria see Watts 2008). Among these, the party system (and political culture) and the organization of the civil service need to be mentioned.

### The party system

Federalism has to some extent always been part of the agenda of political parties in Italy. However, the attitude toward it has been far from straightforward, ultimately making the Italian party system a rather centralized one.

In some parts of the territory, notably in the special Regions, there have always been territorial parties with a clear federalist (and occasionally also secessionist) political agenda. Among those with the longest tradition, it is worth mention the Südtiroler Volkspartei (the ethnic party of German-speaking South Tyroleans), the Union Valdôtaine (a territorial rather than ethnic political movement from the Aosta Valley) and the Partito Sardo d'Azione (a party arguing for more autonomy and linguistic rights in Sardinia). While all three have suffered some schism from other (and mostly more radical) movements, they have always been present and have dominated or at least strongly influenced the political landscape in their respective Regions, while their impact at national level has always been limited. In addition, several "territorial" parties are being created both in the North and in the South and on the left and the right side of the political spectrum (Pallaver 2007: 130–43).

As to the main political parties, the attitude toward federalism has changed in the course of history. It is worth noticing, in particular, that the two main parties in the constitutional assembly which drafted the constitution in 1946–1947 (the Christian-Democrats and the Communists) had opposite views on the topic: the Christian-Democrats, inspired by the social doctrine of the Catholic Church, advocated the principle of subsidiarity and promoted moderate decentralization in the text of the constitution; the Communists, for their part, firmly opposed decentralization as a principle at odds with democratic centralism. The compromise between these two main political forces (combined with some influence of the moderately federalist liberals and socialists) produced a very modest regionalization in the constitution of 1948. However, just after the elections in 1948 (when the Christian-Democrats won the majority and formed a government with the Liberals, pushing the Communists into opposition), the attitude toward decentralization radically changed out of political opportunism: the Christian-Democrats, ruling in Rome, opposed any form of decentralization in order to preserve their power, and the Communists supported it for exactly the same reasons, as they were in opposition in Rome but very strong in some parts of the country (especially in central Italy). It is not by chance that the ordinary Regions were set up only in the 1970s, when a center-left Coalition was built (Christian-Democrats and Socialists) and some form of political cooperation with the Communist Party was started.

The turning point was in the early 1990s, when the old party landscape was trumped by corruption scandals. In the North, a new political movement, the Northern League, was able to intercept many votes previously cast for the Christian-Democrats. Its presence in Parliament increased suddenly.[8] This party had federalism at the top of its agenda (and for a while, between 1996 and 1998 even the secession of the North) and its influence since then has made federalism an unavoidable reference for all political parties.

Nowadays, the political landscape is quite confused with regard to federalism. All parties nominally advocate federalism, although to very different degrees and clearly with different perceptions. However, this has suddenly stopped as the economic crisis began to bite: federalism disappeared from the agendas of the main parties and in the Press the Regions were presented as mere money wasters. This shows that, in practice, lip service has always been paid to federalism rather than it being a real goal. It is not by chance that at both ends of the political arena, the main parties are accused by influential members from the periphery (regional presidents, majors, etc.) of not taking federalism seriously.

### Federalization in the civil service?

So far, the decentralization of powers and responsibilities initiated by the constitutional reform of 2001 has had limited consequences on the structure of the public service. While most of the legislative powers now lie with the Regions, and most of the administrative functions belong to the municipalities, the vast majority of civil servants are still state employees (66.9%). Only 32.5% work for the regional or local governments (Ministero pubblica amministrazione e innovazione 2008: 46).[9]

However, these figures do not paint the entire picture. The largest portion of civil servants (about one third of the total) is employed in the school system. In most of the Regions, the teachers and other school personnel are state employees (although the Regions themselves enjoy concurrent legislative power in the field of education),[10] while in a few others they are employed by the regional administration. This means that in those Regions, the ratio is the opposite as it is nationwide: for instance, in South Tyrol, state employees are less than 10% of the total number of civil servants. In general, the biggest number of regional employees work in the field of healthcare, which is almost entirely within the competence of the Regions and makes up the most significant part of the regional budgets. At present, the Regions control (and spend) 43% of the overall resources (UIL 2007) and are responsible for, inter alia, the entire health-care system (Balduzzi 2005: 717–42), which has produced debts so far of €45b, which need to be covered by the state budget.[11]

The law on "fiscal federalism" also opens up the possibility of coming to different contractual arrangements for civil servants in different parts of the country, with a view to "ensuring a correspondence between the power to determine the Regions' own revenue and the autonomy in managing the related personal resources" (Article 2.2, lit ii). The national level will support differentiated contractual schemes with some additional resources, with a view to stimulating the most virtuous administrations (lit. n): this means in other words that the Regions should in future be allowed to obtain additional resources from the center in order to increase the salaries of their civil servants, and these resources will be made conditional upon the overall performance of the regional administration. This new provision, while using careful language and leaving several issues open for further clarification, for the first time breaks the taboo of equal payment in the civil service for the same job profiles in different parts of the territory.

The political opportunity and the legal feasibility of different salary schemes for the same types of public employees in different Regions has been debated for a long time: given the significant differences in cost of living in different parts of the country, the same salary has very different buying power in different areas. While the door is formally open for differentiated salary schemes and this opportunity will long remain on paper, in practice public salaries have been frozen over recent years.

## Concluding remarks

The Italian federalizing process has always gone in waves. To simplify, one can identify five main stages: (a) asymmetric regionalism (1948–1970); (b) equalizing regionalism (more symmetry); (c) administrative federalism (1990s); (d) constitutional federalism (2001–2006); (e) fiscal federalism (2006 to the present day). Each stage was marked by different political priorities, doing away with the previous ones, and by diverging interpretations as to the role of subnational authorities in the constitutional system.

The only unifying common element has been the absence of a shared culture of federalism, and this is even more paradoxical if one considers the extreme cultural diversity existing among Italian Regions. Put differently, the most significant unifying element has been the absence of any real understanding of the theory and practice of federalism.

On a closer look, however, the paradox is only apparent. In a federal system everything can be (and possibly is) different, except a minimum of shared political culture aimed at pooling some powers for common goals. In Italy, federalism is either (more or less firmly) opposed, or is used as a slogan for challenging the very existence of a common nation. Too much diversity without unity brings about unstable unity aimed at controlling diversity: a vicious circle. Common to both the advocates and opponents of federalism is the absence of a political and institutional culture of federalism, although the essence of federalism is not exhausted either in the constitutional design or in the institutional settings, but needs to set its roots in a sound federal political culture as well as in the civil society itself (Elazar 1994: 162–168; Caminal 2002: 171–72; Watts, 2008; Kincaid and Cole 2010). Moreover, while political culture and other variables may change based on political priorities, and never amount to a minimum federal standard, litigation is increasing and the decisive role is played by the Constitutional Court. The Court is, therefore, the main actor of Italian federalism and its role is proportional to the federal immaturity of the political parties, at both the national and regional levels. Such a role has been played by the Court for at least three decades and this situation is likely to continue for the decades to come.

Furthermore, intergovernmental relations have become all the more unstable since the economic crisis has loomed. First, the reform of financial relations alone without a coherent restructuring of the intergovernmental system has weakened subnational autonomy. Second, as economic resources have become insufficient, the pattern has turned out to be definitely not functional. Since fiscal federalism is still a work in progress, the state alone has de facto power to decide on financial and fiscal issues and has severely targeted territorial entities. Third, the negative performance of several regions as well as the scandalous behavior of certain local politicians has even worsened the situation, so that the need to cope with the markets' pressures and to reach a balanced budget has finally prevailed over the fundamental principle of autonomy.

Against the background of a highly diverse country, with significant federal traits but lacking a political and institutional culture of federalism, where intergovernmental relations are almost entirely adjudicated by the Constitutional Court (and lately determined predominantly by the financial crisis), one can conclude that Italy is much less a federal country now than it was about a decade ago. In spite of the efforts to focus on the development of "federal" financial relations, the intergovernmental relations are overall less "federal" than they used to be. Thus, the Italian case demonstrates that financial issues are just a small part of the broader picture of federalism. To place excessive attention on fiscal federalism – especially if this is in the end not adequately implemented – might be detrimental to the cause of federalism, if not combined with adequate institutional structures and committed political support.

It is safe to conclude that Italy is not a federation, but it is impossible to say what it is instead. For sure, the Italian case shows that a federal system cannot be the result of institutional planning, especially if such planning is chaotic and changing in its priorities. Not even a (declared) political commitment to federalism, nor an extraordinary cultural diversity, are enough to fuel a federal system. Federalism – expressed in its different varieties including regionalism – rather requires the combination of institutional, cultural, political, social, and economic factors. It can neither be imposed from the top down, nor just from the bottom up.

## Notes

Sections 2, 3, 6 by Francesco Palermo, Secions 4, 5 by Alice Valdesalici, Introduction and Conclusions by both.

1. Their differentiated treatment was mainly a reaction to complex problems of regional diversity: international obligations imposed by the 1946 Peace Treaty and fears regarding the secession of these peripheral areas.
2. See Article 138 const. for the amendment procedure of the national constitution, and Article 123 const. for the amendments to the regional basic laws.
3. Article 114 const., as amended in 2001, reads: "The Republic is composed of the municipalities, the provinces, the metropolitan cities, the Regions and the State.."
4. See on these Judgments the special issue of the journal *Le Regioni* 4-5/2005, 771-896, papers by V. Onida, A. Anzon Demmig, R. Bifulco, R. Bin, P. Caretti, A. D'Atena, G. Falcon, S. Mangiameli, E. Rossi, A. Ruggeri, I. Ruggiu, R. Tosi, L. Vandelli.

5. The process of adoption of new statutes took an entire decade for the ordinary Regions, with Veneto being the last one to pass the new Statute in 2012. While all ordinary Regions have thus now adopted their new regional constitutions, none of the five special Regions has done so to date. This clearly proves the existence of a serious and unresolved issue regarding the constitutional (and political) position of special Regions in the current Italian territorial setting.
6. All Judgments of the Italian Constitutional Court are available at: http://www.giurcost.org/decisioni/index.html.
7. With the exception of the Autonomous Provinces of Trento and Bolzano, which enjoy a special status.
8. This party was not represented in Parliament before 1992, while in the elections that year it won 80 seats (55 MPs and 25 senators), with about 8.6% of votes nationwide.
9. The overall picture is quite different than, for instance, a country like Spain, where the regionalization of the civil service has taken place much more rapidly: at present, the majority of Spanish civil servants are employed by the Comunidades Autónomas (OECD, 2011).
10. More precisely, Article 117.2 lit. n const. provides that the state has exclusive legislative power with regard to "general provisions on education," and Article 117.3 establishes a shared legislative competence (concurrent legislation) in the field of education.
11. Several studies on the health-care system show that the pro capita expenses in the South are twice as much as in the North, while the quality of the service is much lower. See the report published by the Catholic University of Rome, available at www.rm.unicatt.it, and the Health Report by the NGO Cittadinanza Attiva (www.cittadinanzattiva.it).

# Bibliography

Alber E. (2011) ."Einer für alle, alle für einen? Eine finanzföderalistische Zwischenbilanz rund um das Jubiläum 150 Jahre italienische Staatseinheit", Europäisches Zentrum für Föderalismus-Forschung Tübingen (ed.), *Jahrbuch des Föderalismus 2011* (Baden Baden: Nomos), pp. 242–254.
Antonini L. (2009). *La rivincita della responsabilità. A proposito della nuova legge sul federalismo fiscale* (Milano: Fondazione per la sussidiarietà)
Antonini L. and A. Pin. (2009). "The Italian Road to Fiscal Federalism", *Italian Journal of Public Law* Vol. 1, pp. 1–16.
Anzon Demmig A. (2002). *I poteri delle regioni dopo la riforma costituzionale* (Torino: Giappichelli)
Balduzzi R. (2005). "Cinque anni di legislazione sanitaria decentrata: varietà e coesione di un sistema nazional-regionale", *Le Regioni* Vol. 5, pp. 717–742
Bifulco R. (2009). "Il parlamento nella tenaglia degli esecutivi: il federalismo fiscale e la riforma del Senato", Nel Merito, http://www.nelmerito.com, 30 October 2012
Bifulco R. (2012). "Jefferson, Madison e il momento costituzionale dell'Unione. A proposito della riforma costituzinale sull'equilibrio di bilancio", AIC, 2, 14 December 2012

Bilancia, P. (2012). "L'associazionismo obbligatorio dei comuni nelle più recenti evoluzioni legislative", Federalismi, 16, 2012, http://www.federalismi.it/, 14 December 2012.

Bin R. (2006). "I criteri di individuazione delle materie", Le Regioni, Vol. 5, pp. 889–902.

Bin R. (1996). "Veri e falsi problemi del federalismo in Italia", L. Mariucci et al. (eds), *Il federalismo preso sul serio* (Bologna: Il Mulino), pp. 61–78

Buglione, E. and E. Jorio. (2011). "Schema di decreto legislativo in materia di autonomia di entrata delle regioni a statuto ordinario e delle province, nonché di determinazione dei costi e dei fabbisogni standard nel settore sanitario", A. Ferrara and G.M. Salerno (eds), *Il federalismo fiscale. Commento alla legge n. 42 del 2009* 2nd ed. (Napoli: Jovene)

Cabras D. (2009). "Il processo di attuazione della legge delega in materia di federalismo fiscale: il ruolo del Parlamento", Federalismi, 12, http://www.federalismi.it/, 31 October 2012

Caminal M. (2002). *El Federalismo Pluralista: Del Federalismo Nacional al Federalismo Plurinacional* (Madrid: Editorial Paidos)

Cavaleri P. and E. Lamarque. (eds) (2004). *L'attuazione del nuovo titolo V, parte seconda, della Costituzione. Commento alla legge "La Loggia"* (Torino: Giappichelli)

Court of Auditors (2005, 2006). *Report on Financial Management of Ordinary Regions*, http://www.corteconti.it

Di Marco C. "La stabilizzazione finanziaria 2011 alle prese con il sistema delle autonomie territoriali", Amministrazione in Cammino, 2011, http://www.amministrazioneincammino.luiss.it, 10 December 2012

Elazar, Daniel J., (ed.) (1994). *Federal Systems of the World: A Handbook of Federal, Confederal, and Autonomy Arrangements* 2nd ed. (Harlow, Essex: Longman).

Falcon G. (2012). "La crisi e l'ordinamento costituzionale", *Le Regioni* pp. 1–2, pp. 9–19.

Ferrara G. and G.M. Salerno (eds) *Il federalismo fiscale. Commento alla legge n.42 del 2009* (Napoli: Jovene).

Italian Government (2010) *Report on Fiscal Federalism,* http://www.riformeistituzionali.it/documentazione/riforme-istituzionali/il-federalismo-fiscale/relazione-tecnica-del-governo-sul-federalismo-fiscale.aspx, 4 October 2012

Groppi T. (2007). "Il Titolo V cinque anni dopo, ovvero la Costituzione di carta", *Le Regioni* pp. 3–4, pp. 421–432

Jorio E., S. Gambino and G. D'Ignazio. (2009). *Il federalismo fiscale. Commento articolo per articolo alla legge 5 maggio 2009, n. 42* (Santarcangelo di Romagna: Maggioli)

Kincaid J. and R. Cole. (2010). "Citizen Attitudes toward Issues of Federalism in Canada, Mexico and the United States" *Publius: the Journal of Federalism* Vol. 14, No. 1 , pp. 53–75

Lupo N. (2009). "Il procedimento di attuazione della delega sul federalismo fiscale e le nuovi sedi della collaborazione tra i livelli territoriali: commissione bicamerale, commissione tecnica paritetica e conferenza permanente", Federalismi, 23, http://www.federalismi.it/, 3 October 2012

Ministero per la pubblica amministrazione e l'innovazione (2008) Relazione al Parlamento sullo stato della Pubblica Amministrazione, Year 2007, Vol. 1, Roma, http://www.innovazione.gov.it/ministro/pdf/RelazioneAnnuale_2007_VolumePrimo.pdf

Morrone A. (2007). "Il federalismo differenziato", *Federalismo fiscale* Vol. 1, pp. 139–390

Napoli C. (2012). "Il livello provinciale nella legislazione anticrisi del Governo Monti", Federalismi, 21/2012, http://www.federalismi.it/, 15 December 2012

Nicolini M. (2010). "La disciplina transitoria statale sui tributi propri delle Regioni e la potestà legislativa regionale in materia tributaria. Il caso della regionalizzazione dell'IRAP", *Giurisprudenza Costituzionale* Vol. 1, pp. 911–938

Nicotra I. (2012). "La Provincia e il fondamento costituzionale del diritto all'integrità territoriale delle popolazioni locali", Federalismi, 23, http://www.federalismi.it/, 15 December 2012.

OECD. (2011). "Government at a Glance 2011", OECD Publishing, available also online at: http://www.oecd-ilibrary.org/

Onida V. (2007). "Il giudice costituzionale e i conflitti tra legislatori centrali e locali", *Le Regioni* Vol. 1, pp. 11–26.

Palermo F. (2012a). "Federalismo fiscale e Regioni a statuto speciale. Vecchi nodi vengono al pettine", *Le istituzioni del federalismo* Vol. 1, pp. 9–26.

Palermo F. (2012b). "Salviamo il federalismo procedurale", Osservatorio federalismo, 2, http://www.osservatoriofederalismo.eu/default.asp, 15 December 2012

Palermo F. (2011). "Per un quadro normativo del federalismo fiscale", F. Palermo, E. Alber and S. Parolari (eds), *Federalismo fiscale: una sfida comparata* (Padova: CEDAM), pp. 407–424.

Palermo F. (2008). "South Tyrol's Special Status within the Italian constitution", J. Woelk, F. Palermo and J. Marko (eds), *Tolerance Through Law. Self Governance and Group Rights in South Tyrol* (Leiden/Boston, Nijhoff), pp. 33–49.

Palermo F. (2003). "Il regionalismo differenziato", T. Groppi and M. Olivetti (eds), *La Repubblica delle autonomie. Regioni ed enti locali nel nuovo titolo V* (Torino: Giappichelli), pp. 55–62.

Pallaver G. (2007). "Die Territorialisierung der Parteien – Auswirkungen des (asymmetrischen) Föderalismus auf die Parteinlandschaft. Das Fallbeispiel Italien", F. Palermo, R. Hrbek, C. Zwilling and E. Alber (eds), *Auf dem Weg zu asymmetrischem Föderalismus?* (Baden-Baden:Nomos), pp. 130–143.

Parolari S. and A. Valdesalici. (2011). "Le fonti dell'ordinamento finanziario e le tendenze riformiste: spunti per una comparazione", F. Palermo, E. Alber and S. Parolari (eds), *Federalismo fiscale: una sfida comparata* (Padova: CEDAM), pp. 339–370.

Pizzetti F. (2001). "Le nuove esigenze di 'governance' in un sistema policentrico 'esploso'", *Le Regioni* Vol. 6, pp. 1153–1196

Salerno G.M. (2012). "Dopo la norma costituzionale sul pareggio di bilancio: vincoli e limiti all'autonomia finanziaria delle Regioni", *Quaderni costituzionali* Vol. 3, pp. 563–1185.

Saporito L. (2008). *Regionalismo, federalismo e interesse nazionale* (Napoli: Jovene)

Scuto F. (2010). "The Italian Parliament paves the way to fiscal federalism", Perspectives on Federalism, 1, http://www.on-federalism.eu, 31 October 2012

Sterpa A. (2012). "Il decreto legge n. 138 del 2011: riuscirà la Costituzione a garantire l'autonomia di Regioni e Comuni?", Federalismi, 16, 2011, http://www.federalismi.it/, 15 December 2012.

Tucciarelli C. (2010). "Federalismo fiscale, ma non solo: la legge n. 42 del 2009", A. Ferrara and G.M. Salerno (eds), *Il federalismo fiscale. Commento alla legge n. 42 del 2009* (Napoli: Jovene).

UIL. (2007). Studio sui bilanci di previsione delle regioni, http://www.uil.it/regioni-sint-loystampa.pdf

Watts R. (2008). *Comparing Federal Systems* 3rd edition. (Montreal: McGill-Queens University Press).

# 9
# Autonomous Areas as a Constitutional Feature in the People's Republic of China and Finland

*Markku Suksi*

## Introduction

Unitary states such as the People's Republic of China (hereinafter given as China) and Finland are much less monolithic in terms of institutional design than the reference to the unitary nature of the state indicates.[1] Although this may be a surprise to the outside observer, the flexibility in the internal state structure signals an implementation of the wish in both countries to recognize the existence of different minorities and population groups inside their national territories.

In China, the recognized minority ethnic groups are together number 55. Under the Constitution of China, two different forms of local people' congresses (LPCs) are recognized for the purposes of the minority ethnic groups. The first form of LPC is created under Article 116 of the Constitution of China, as specified in Article 66 of the Legislation Law and Article 19 of the Law on Regional Ethnic Autonomy. This form of local autonomy is characterized by the possibility to exercise so-called law-varying powers, which means that national law can be modified through a decision of an LPC of this kind provided that the national authorities confirm the local variant of the law. The second form of LPC is created under Article 100 of the Constitution of China, as specified in Article 66 of the Legislation Law and Articles 7 and 43 of the Organic Law on the Local People's Congresses and Local People's Governments. This form of local autonomy is empowered to pass by-laws that implement national law. The Finnish Constitution, in addition to identifying Finnish and Swedish as national languages and establishing linguistic and cultural autonomy for the Sami, opens up a recognition in Article 17(3) of the Constitution of other minorities, too, with the Roma and those who use sign language explicitly mentioned.

While the truly autonomous nature of the two forms of the LPCs may be doubted, Article 31 of the Chinese Constitution opens up for so-called Special Administrative Regions as established by law. This possibility has been used in two cases, Hong Kong and Macau, after China concluded an international treaty with the United Kingdom, on the one hand, and Portugal, on the other, about granting a high degree of autonomy to each of the areas. The international treaties are entitled Joint Declarations, and they make provision for the distribution of legislative powers between mainland China and the two areas that used to be governed by the two colonial powers. In several respects, the status of the Åland Islands in Finland was and is similar, in particular during from 1920–1994, when the formal constitutional acts of Finland did not contain any provision about the autonomy or self-government of the Åland Islands. There was constitutional silence in spite of the fact that there had been an international commitment on behalf of the Åland Islands by Finland through the 1921 Åland Islands Settlement under the auspices of the League of Nations. The current Constitution of Finland establishes an autonomy arrangement for the Åland Islands, with powers that are not quite as extensive as those of Hong Kong and Macau but with an entrenchment that is more elaborate.

Because the Chinese commitment with respect to Hong Kong and Macau is temporary, extending over 50 years until 2047 and 2049, the future challenge lies in the constitutional regulation of the position of the two autonomous areas after the international commitment expires. Finland has some experience with the potential of expiry of an international commitment: the international organization that undertook the supervision of the commitment concerning the Åland Islands, the League of Nations, disappeared in the wake of the Second World War. How can the disappearance of an international autonomy commitment be dealt with by a state? In which ways can open constitutional regulation of autonomous areas be positivized in the constitution of a country and how has this been done in a comparative perspective? Could the method of incorporating provisions concerning the Åland Islands in the Constitution of Finland be relevant for regulating the future position of Hong Kong and Macau in the Chinese state structure?

In addition to these similarities in law, some similarities in fact can also be referred to. The autonomous areas are of a similar size in the national context, around or less than 0.5% of the population, which means that the national governments are probably not viewing these areas as primary governmental matters in their everyday politics. As a consequence, the areas run the risk of being forgotten about in the grand scheme of political events that the national governments have to deal with on a continuous basis. These autonomous areas are also relatively wealthy in comparison to the rest of the national territory: the GDP per capita of Hong Kong a few years ago was US$44,000, while that of mainland China was US$3,000 (and probably increasing while this chapter is being written). In the Åland Islands, the same figure is in excess of US$50,000 in comparison to US$28,000 for the whole of Finland.

## Incorporation of the international autonomy commitment into national law

A common feature in the international commitments of the two countries is the fact that the international commitment identified the national act by which the commitment would be implemented in the national legal order. In the case of the Åland Islands, the Settlement of 1921,[2] although not a formal treaty under public international law, identified the Autonomy Act (that is, the 1920 Self-Government Act) as the vehicle of implementation of the guarantees for the autonomy of Åland, while the Joint Declarations identify a so-called Basic Law as the vehicle of implementation for the high degree of autonomy accorded to Hong Kong[3] and Macau.[4]

A striking similarity between China and Finland is that the international commitments concerning autonomous areas have been incorporated into the national legal order in more or less the same way, namely transcription or almost exact transformation. In principle, the emergence of the international commitment was different with respect to the two states: the details of the Finnish commitment were developed by Finland and Sweden under the auspices of the Council of the League of Nations, while the details of the Chinese commitments were actually developed and proposed by the Chinese Government and appended to the general part of the two Joint Declarations. The Chinese definition of the details of the two autonomy arrangements was done in a manner that made the appendices about the contents of the two autonomy arrangements parts of the binding treaty commitments.

As established in Paragraph 1 of the Åland Islands Settlement, "Finland, resolved to assure and to guarantee to the population of the Åland Islands the preservation of their language, of their culture, and of their local Swedish traditions, undertakes to introduce shortly into the Law of Autonomy of the Aaland Islands of 7 May 1920, the following guarantees: [...]." These guarantees and special rights for the inhabitants of the Åland Islands were registered in 1922 in a separate Act containing Special Provisions concerning the Population of the Åland Islands, or the so-called Guaranty Act. The Parliament of Finland did not formally speaking amend the 1920 Self-Government Act, but enacted instead a separate piece of law as a complement to the Act of 1920. The Guaranty Act was enacted in the same order as the Self-Government Act, that is, in the constitutional order involving a qualified majority of two-thirds. The Guaranty Act was hence enacted with the same special and regional entrenchment stipulations as the Act of 1920. From that perspective, it is possible to say that the Guaranty Act was vested with the same elevated constitutional status as the first Self-Government Act. However, the particular legislation concerning the sale of real property in the Åland Islands, mentioned in Sub-section 2 of Paragraph 2 of the Settlement, was enacted by the Parliament of Finland only in 1938 as the Act on the Exercise of the Right of Redemption at Sale of Real Property in the Åland Islands (currently based on an act from 1975), which means that the particular protection mechanism regarding real property was inoperative during the first 15 years of the autonomy of Åland. It is possible to say against this background that immediately after the entering into force of the 1919 Form of Government (Constitution) Act, the formula of "one state" and the newly gained sovereignty of Finland were challenged and that Finland had to agree to and implement special measures in order to protect its territorial integrity.

In terms of the legislative strategy chosen to incorporate the Åland Islands Settlement in the legal order of Finland, it is possible to say that it was *not* incorporated in the normal way as a treaty under international law. The reason for this is that the Åland Islands Settlement is not a treaty under international law and thus there was no treaty to be incorporated under those constitutional provisions that existed from 1921–1922. Instead, the Settlement was brought into force domestically through another procedure, namely transcription (or, in other words, reception). In this context of the Åland Islands Settlement, this method of incorporation means that the text of the Settlement, which was originally drafted in French and English, was translated in Finland *expressis verbis* into Swedish and Finnish (with the exception that the order of the sections of the Guaranty Act is different from the order of the paragraphs in the Settlement). After the translation was completed, the Government of Finland submitted the text to the Parliament of Finland in the form of a Bill, which was enacted in the Parliament pursuant to the requirements of a qualified majority and in the fast track order of constitutional amendments. The 1951 Self-Government Act incorporated the provisions of the Guaranty Act with some modifications, which means that the method of incorporation actually shifted over from transcription to transformation, and this latter method is also the one that applies to the incorporation of the Settlement through the 1991 Self-Government Act (Suksi 2008: 277–79). In principle, the Self-Government Act introduces a series of exceptions to the Constitution of Finland that apply in the territory of the Åland Islands.

While regional autonomy and other forms of minority protection are regular features of the Chinese Constitution in relation to the 55 recognized minority ethnic groups of China, the situation with respect to Taiwan may have been the main reason for amending the Constitution in 1984 so as to allow the creation of special administrative regions. It is likely that Hong Kong and Macau were also in the picture early on (Ghai 1999: 56; Xiao Weiyun 2001: 9–11; Leung 2006: 19; Chen 2009: 755ff.). The existence of a constitutional provision concerning special administrative regions was found to be a suitable normative framework for the re-incorporation of Hong Kong and for assigning the autonomy arrangement a legal basis in the constitutional fabric of the country. Article 31 of the Constitution of the People's Republic of China (PRC) grants the state the power to establish special administrative regions when necessary. In addition, the social, economic, and legal systems to be instituted in special administrative regions shall be prescribed by law enacted by the National People's Congress in light of the specific conditions. The constitutional provision is open and does not say much about the powers granted to a special administrative region (SAR), but the reference to "administrative" indicates that the powers to be exercised could be at least regulatory in nature.

It was evidently deemed necessary to establish such SARs as a means to facilitate the transfer of sovereignty over Hong Kong and Macau from the UK and Portugal to China, as recorded in the Joint Declarations between the Governments of the three countries. For Hong Kong, the requirement of regulation through law was fulfilled by the National People's Congress (NPC) on 4 April 1990, when it adopted the Basic Law of the Hong Kong Special Administrative Region of the People's Republic of China. A similar Basic Law for Macau was enacted on 31 March 1993. The specific condition that was taken into account was the need to return Hong Kong and Macau to China, both places with a different economic and legal system. Through the Basic Law, the capitalist system of Hong Kong with the British styled common law tradition was fitted into the overall Socialist system of China both in the area of economics and law by creating an exception to what the Chinese Constitution required. A similar strategy was followed concerning Macau, which follows the Portuguese civil law tradition of a continental European kind.

An explicit reference to Article 31 of the Constitution of China was included in Section 3(1) of the Joint Declaration concerning Hong Kong (and in Section 2(12) of that of Macau), which creates an international commitment for the internal solution. The legal basis for the domestic solutions is established in the two Basic Laws which spell out in detail the contents of the arrangement under Article 31 of the Constitution, but which in spite of their names seem to be regarded as more or less ordinary pieces of law. Article 3(1) of the treaty concerning Hong Kong provides that the PRC, while upholding national unity and territorial integrity and taking account of the history of Hong Kong and its realities, has decided to establish, in accordance with the provisions of Article 31 of the PRC Constitution, a Hong Kong Special Administrative Region upon resuming the exercise of sovereignty over Hong Kong. A provision which is to some extent similar is included in Article 2(1) of the treaty concerning Macau. Similarly to the regional autonomies, the Joint Declarations establish that the Governments of the two entities will be composed of local inhabitants. Finally, the two Joint Declarations provide that the basic policies established in the Declarations – and elaborated in Annex I to the treaties as declarations made by China – are to be stipulated in a Basic Law for each of the two entities, enacted by the National People's Congress, which will remain unchanged for 50 years from 1 July 1997 in the case of Hong Kong and 19 December 1999 in the case of Macau.

Pursuant to the Joint Declarations, reinforced by the two Annexes I, the NPC was obligated, after ratification, to enact and promulgate a Basic Law of the Hong Kong Special Administrative Region of the People's Republic of China (hereinafter given as the HK Basic Law) and a similar one for Macau (the Macau Basic Law) in accordance with the Constitution of the PRC. The obligation stipulates that after the establishment of the two SARs, the Socialist system and Socialist policies shall not be practiced in the SARs and that the previous capitalist systems and lifestyle shall remain unchanged for 50 years. Because the two social orders would normally be understood as antagonistic, the "NPC adopted a formal decision on the same day it passed the Basic Law, declaring that the Basic Law is consistent with the PRC Constitution" (Hualing Fu et al. 2007: 3). Also, the two Annexes I declare that apart from displaying the national flag and national emblem of the PRC, the two SARs may use a regional flag and emblem of their own and are in charge of the maintenance of public order in the SARs. Although military forces may be sent by the central government of China to be stationed in the two SARs for the purpose of defense, they shall not interfere in the internal affairs of the SARs. The two Annexes I also contains a section on basic rights and freedoms according to which the Governments of the SARs shall protect the rights and freedoms of their inhabitants and other persons according to law and maintain the rights and freedoms as provided for by the laws previously in force in Hong Kong and Macau. Hence, in both entities, a number of rights not available to the inhabitants of mainland China are guaranteed to the inhabitants of the two SARs.

The fact that the two Joint Declarations are relatively faithfully reproduced in the two Basic Laws would almost indicate that a transcription of the international commitment has taken place in the national implementation. However, transformation may be the better characterization of the form of national implementation, a method toward which Finland had already moved in 1951 after the transcription in the 1922 Guaranty Act. It is important to point out in this context that the texts of the international commitments concerning the Åland Islands, on the one hand, and Hong Kong and Macau, on the other, have not become parts of the national legal order through ratification. They are thus not self-executing in the event the national implementation measures would produce results that deviate from the international commitments.

## Entrenchment of autonomy arrangements

The Joint Declarations (including their Annexes), as formal treaties under international law which have been ratified by China, entrench the two autonomy arrangements in international law and provide an international legal guarantee for upholding the obligation. The guarantee is, formally speaking, bilateral and not multilateral for each of the entities, since the UK is the only other party to the international commitment concerning Hong Kong and Portugal concerning Macau. The Joint Declarations do not stipulate any supervisory mechanism, which means that China is expected to implement its obligations in good faith on the basis of the treaties by means of national law explicitly mentioned in the treaty itself (Ghai 1999: 72; Leung 2006: 417). Article 3(12) of the Joint Declaration stipulates that implementation will take place by means of a Basic Law of the HKSAR enacted by the National People's

Congress, and a similar provision exists concerning Macau. In this way, China committed itself in the Joint Declarations to implementing an unusually detailed set of treaty provisions in its domestic legislation by means of a legislative decision of the highest law-making body in a piece of law which is specifically named in the treaty (see also Xiao Weiyun 2001: 13, 76, 200, 213).

However, the Joint Declarations provided nothing specific about the normative level at which each of the Basic Laws should be enacted, nor were they understood by the Chinese Government so that the Declarations should be turned into national law *expressis verbis*: although the main bulk of the provisions in the Basic Laws, including their name, come from the Joint Declarations, they contain provisions which are not prescribed by the Joint Declarations at the same time as some provisions of the Joint Declarations are not explicitly featured in the Basic Law, although one can always find an implicit connection. While the title of the Acts, the Basic Law, could imply that they have an elevated normative status which falls between the Constitution and ordinary legislation or as an organic law of some sort, it seems that the Basic Laws were enacted under the Constitution of China as ordinary pieces of legislation. From that perspective, the Basic Laws are, in the Chinese legal order, pieces of ordinary legislation, sometimes attributed with the characteristics of a "special law" in the hierarchy of norms because the general legal principles of China imply that special laws prevail over ordinary laws: "At the national law level, laws which have the status of a special law prevail over ordinary pieces of law," and the Basic Laws are considered to be such law (Leung 2006: 42). Hence, the Basic Laws might have some sort of elevated status (Ghai 1999: 101; Xiao Weiyun 2001: 177; Morris 2007: 105). A more tangible entrenchment effect can be accorded to the fact that the autonomy arrangements concerning Hong Kong and Macau are based on international treaties (Suksi 1998). The entrenchments are of an international nature and imply that China cannot legally rid itself of the arrangements during the established period of time without the consent of the other state party to each of the two treaties. Therefore, from a holistic perspective, the two entities are entrenched on a semi-constitutional level of some sort, the exact nature of which may be difficult to determine.

The total entrenchment effect is more multifarious concerning the Åland Islands. Although not a specific treaty-based entrenchment, there is nonetheless an entrenchment under international law through the unilateral commitment of Finland to the Åland Islands Settlement even after the Second World War. Here there is an approximate correspondence between China and Finland, but the picture is different in terms of the other entrenchment forms that apply to the Åland Islands. From the very beginning, the Self-Government Act has been enacted in the order prescribed for constitutional amendments, involving a qualified majority of two-thirds when the final decision concerning the adoption or the amendment of the Self-Government Act is being made in the Parliament of Finland. Therefore, there is a special entrenchment involved, but in a manner that does not actually elevate the Self-Government Act to the rank of a formal constitutional act. Instead, the special entrenchment indicates that the Self-Government Act, which does not identify itself as a constitutional act, is a so-called Act of Exception. There also exists a so-called regional entrenchment for the autonomy arrangement of Åland by the requirement in the Self-Government Act which requires that any amendment to it, including the enactment of a new Self-Government Act, has to be approved by the Legislative Assembly of the Åland Islands by a two-thirds qualified majority. What this means is that the Parliament of Finland cannot by means of a unilateral decision cause negative amendments to, or rid itself of, the autonomy arrangement. Instead, a high level of consensus is required, a consensus that is protective of the Åland Islands. Finally, through amendments in the 1990s, the Constitution of Finland was supplemented with provisions that created a so-called general entrenchment, now established in Sections 75[5] and 120[6] of the Constitution that entered into force in the year 2000.

Admittedly, and in comparison with autonomies in other countries, the autonomy arrangement of the Åland Islands is extremely well entrenched in the constitutional fabric of Finland and in the legal order. In comparison with Hong Kong, where the entrenchment is in many ways weaker, the Åland Islands seem solidly entrenched so as to give the impression of the arrangement as a permanent feature of the Finnish as well as of the European and international legal order. The one significant entrenchment type that is not present in any of the entities reviewed here is entrenchment under the principle of the self-determination of peoples. This is due to the fact that the populations of the three areas are not peoples in the meaning of Article 1 of the CCPR and cannot therefore enjoy the protection of the argument that an autonomy arrangement accorded to a collectivity that is designated as a people should not be weakened or abolished. It can even be doubted whether any of the populations of the entities reviewed here are minorities. This is not the case with the inhabitants of Hong Kong and Macau, and also in respect of the inhabitants of the Åland Islands, this could be the case, because they might also be understood as members of the Swedish-speaking minority in Finland.

## Distribution of powers by enumeration

The essence of autonomy is constituted by the powers accorded to the substate entity. Section 31 of the Constitution of China makes reference to special administrative regions, which indicates that such entities could be in the possession of at least regulatory powers of an administrative nature. Section 75(2) of the Constitution of Finland is clearer in this respect, because it goes on to hold that the enactment of Acts of Åland is determined in the Self-Government Act. Hence, the Constitution of Finland makes a distinction between two different sets of acts in Finland, one set produced by the Parliament of Finland and the other set produced for the Åland Islands by another legislator. The constitutional norms (understood in the broad sense) of both countries thus delegate the determination of powers of the substate entities to particular legislation. In Finland, the 1991 Self-Government Act of Åland establishes the Legislative Assembly of the Åland Islands as the legislature in charge of law-making powers in Åland concerning a certain part of the legal order, while in China, the two Basic Laws identify legislative powers for the Legislative Councils of Hong Kong and Macau in a more comprehensive manner.

In China, the two Joint Declarations state that the Special Administrative Regions will each be directly under the authority of the Central People's Government of the People's Republic of China, but at the same time, they will enjoy a high degree of autonomy, except in foreign affairs and defense which are the responsibilities of the Central People's Government. This creates the impression that the two autonomous entities may exercise the residual powers, while the national government holds a minimum of enumerated powers, those central to preserving national unity and territorial integrity. However, it is clear already on the basis of the Joint Declarations that the powers of the autonomous entities are enumerated in a manner that creates exclusive law-making powers for the legislatures of Hong Kong and Macau. The debate in China is perhaps more about whether the National People's Government has enumerated powers or perhaps residual powers: the central government of China and Chinese doctrine seem to be strongly opposed to the characterization of the distribution of powers by reference to the fact that the central government would hold a few enumerated powers, while the residual powers, that is, the vast bulk of the legislative powers, would be vested in the SARs.

The argument put forward by the mainland Chinese authorities and academics is that China is not a federal state in which the federation would hold enumerated powers and the states the residual powers on the basis of a distribution of powers. Instead, so the argument goes, China is a unitary state, and because the Basic Laws are pieces of ordinary legislation in the legal order of China, the residual powers are actually held by the central government, not by the SARs. Because the NPC has the plenary powers of the sovereign lawmaker, the NPC could revoke the Basic Laws. Consequently, so the argument continues, there is no distribution of powers as in a federal system, but a delegation of powers on the basis of the Basic Laws from the central government to the SARs. Moreover, the ultimate residual powers are held by the NPC (Ghai 1999: 148–53; Xiao Weiyun 2001: 60, 92–95, 98–101, 134; Leung 2006: 34–36). In this respect, the position of the mainland Chinese doctrine concerning the congressional sovereignty of the NPC is akin to the concept of parliamentary sovereignty in, for example, the United Kingdom or the concept of plenary powers of the US Congress.

From the point of view of the SARs, things can be understood differently, supported by the stipulations in the Joint Declaration and its Annex I: the international commitment signals an intention on the part of China to distribute powers between the central government and the SARs, not only to devolve powers in a manner which allows a withdrawal of those powers at the will of the central government. Therefore, while the theory of the devolution of power of the Chinese Government seems entirely plausible after the period of 50 years has lapsed, at which point the legislature of China is free to amend the autonomy arrangement as it pleases or to continue or discontinue the arrangement, China's international obligations based on the Joint Declarations to uphold the high degree of autonomy of Hong Kong and Macau with the distribution of powers established in the Joint Declarations and their Annex I points in the other direction. It seems that the autonomy arrangements of Hong Kong and Macau have been created in a manner that is by and large in line with our theoretical models that juxtapose autonomy with federalism: China is not a federal state, and at the same time as the central government holds the ultimate residual competences and some of the competences of the central government are enumerated, the competences of the two autonomies remain enumerated.

Hong Kong and Macau have been granted, under the Basic Laws, complete legal powers by means of enumeration in almost all areas of the law. They have also been granted powers in the area of foreign affairs. In the area of defense, however, the central government holds the entire measure of powers as laid down in Article 14 of the Basic Laws.

As indicated above, the Joint Declarations and their Annexes I as well as the Basic Laws contain several confirmations or enumerations of the powers of Hong Kong and Macau. Much of the same substance appears in the enumerations of the two Basic Laws, as faithfully established by the Chinese lawmaker against the background of the Joint Declarations and their Annexes I, but there are also a number of specifications of competences in the Basic Laws (Ghai 1997: 68, 144–47). These legislative powers cover a wide range of areas and encompass most of the legal order. They are supported by appropriate criminal provisions in Hong Kong and Macau law. The Basic Law is generally silent on criminal provisions passed within the legislative powers of Hong Kong and Macau (except in Article 23 of the Basic Law), which may be interpreted as evidence of the inapplicability even in the most serious cases of mainland Chinese criminal law in the two autonomies. According to Article 23 of the Basic Law, the SARs shall enact laws on their own to prohibit any act of treason, secession, sedition, and subversion against the Central People's Government, or theft of state secrets, to prohibit foreign political organizations or bodies from conducting political activities in the Region, and to prohibit political organizations or bodies of the Region from establishing ties with foreign political organizations or bodies. This demonstrates that the mainland Chinese lawmakers do not have lawmaking powers with regard to the jurisdiction of the HKSAR or Macau even in this core area of provisions connected to the sovereignty of the state.

Clearly, these enumerated powers cannot be withdrawn or repealed by the Chinese central government before 2047 or 2049 without breaching the international obligations of China, in particular when considering the direct link established in the preambles of the Basic Laws to the Joint Declarations. It is difficult to understand how the enumerated competences of the central government, on the one hand, and the competences of the two autonomies, on the other, would not constitute a distribution of powers on a more permanent basis than is the case with a mere administrative devolution. Certainly, in some rare instances, the competences mentioned in the Basic Laws are of a devolved nature. Provisions which grant powers to the two autonomies as authorized by the central government indicate the existence of an administrative devolution, perhaps also of a shared competence. However, for the most part, it would seem that exclusive legislative powers are established for the two autonomies by way of enumeration on the basis of Annexes I of the Joint Declarations.

In addition, the reference in the Joint Declarations to a high degree of autonomy may be contrasted with the concept of autonomy in Articles 112–22 of the PRC Constitution. *Prima facie*, it seems that the high degree of autonomy granted to Hong Kong and Macau amounts to much more autonomy than the autonomy which has been granted to the autonomous regions elsewhere in China because the two SARs are vested with executive, legislative, and independent judicial power, including that of final adjudication, and because the laws in force in the two entities at the time of the transition remained basically unchanged after the transition, as provided by the two Basic Laws. However, when considering the issue from the vantage point of the Chinese constitution, the picture may become somewhat blurred because Article 31 of the Constitution of China does not offer any substantive protection for any arrangement created on that constitutional basis and does not even mention the concept of autonomy. The fact that Article 31 excludes a special administrative region from the regular structures of regional autonomy, which certainly do not have any exclusive legislative powers independent of the powers of the central government, sustains the argument that the special arrangements created under Article 31 could also be different with respect to the allocation of powers. On the face of it, Article 31 could be so broad as to contain not only administrative devolution of the sort regulated in Articles 112–22 of the Constitution but also a number of other possible arrangements. In fact, the reference to "special" in Article 31 should probably mean something besides administrative devolution, which as a maximum contains law-varying powers subject to approval by the central government.

In comparison, other autonomous areas created in Mainland China, such as Tibet, based on Articles 4 and 116 of the PRC Constitution, seem to enjoy a form of autonomy which is mainly of a regulatory nature, although such autonomous entities may also have the power to modify national legislation, a power which appears to be, in practice, seldom exercised. In cases where an autonomous area in mainland China wishes to modify national law, the modification can be approved by the authorities of the autonomous area, but there is the additional requirement that such modifications must be approved by the central government in order to take effect. Hence, the effect of Article 31 of the Constitution is to place the system of special administrative regions outside of the framework of the regular regional autonomies and to distinguish the SARs from the regular regional autonomies.

Section 75(2) of the Constitution of Finland contains an implicit recognition of the fact that two legislatures exist in Finland (the Parliament of Finland, on the one hand, and the Legislative Assembly of the Åland Islands, on the other), because the section lays down that the enactment of acts passed by the Legislative Assembly of the Åland Islands is governed by the provisions of the Self-Government Act. Under the 1991 Self-Government Act, this distribution of legislative competence is established by means of an enumeration of two spheres of legislative competence, one for the Legislative Assembly of the Åland Islands and another for the Parliament of Finland. Neither the constitutional recognition nor the double enumeration formed a part of the original arrangement from 1920–22. This means that the legal rules concerning the position of the Åland Islands have undergone a significant evolution during the past 90 years.

Originally, the distribution of powers was fashioned in a more "federal" manner in the 1920 Self-Government Act so that the legislative powers of the Parliament of Finland for the purposes of producing legal norms for the jurisdiction of Åland were enumerated, while the legislative powers of the Legislative Assembly of the Åland Islands were of a residual nature (Suksi 2005: 172). This attribution changed in the 1951 Self-Government Act so that the law-making powers of both legislatures were enumerated, and this is also the point of departure in the 1991 Self-Government Act. From a practical point of view, the shift in the strategy concerning the distribution of legislative powers was probably not very dramatic, but from the point of view of principle, the issue is of some importance, because the arrangement indicates that a preemption of some sort was built into the 1920 Self-Government Act. Generally speaking, therefore, it is not always beneficial to operate under the assumption that a residual competence for the substate entity is a better option, because such a "residual" point of departure may open up the need to recognize or accept a smaller or a greater window for national preemption through a supremacy doctrine.

The 1991 Self-Government Act followed the principle of enumeration of both spheres of competence. According to Section 17, the Legislative Assembly of the Åland Islands shall enact legislation for Åland, and the actual legislative powers of the Legislative Assembly are listed in Section 18 of the Self-Government Act. The conclusion that the legislative powers of the Åland Islands are exclusive in relation to the powers of the Parliament of Finland means that the Parliament of Finland cannot, by its own enactments, fill a normative void within the competence sphere of the Legislative Assembly. Conversely, authorities of the Åland Islands cannot use legislation from the competence sphere of the Parliament of Finland to fill a void in the competence of the Åland Islands (Palmgren 1997: 88).

This is also established in a number of cases by the Supreme Administrative Court (hereinafter: the SAC). For instance, in SAC 2003:1, the Court concluded that in the absence of a provision concerning the self-rectification of an administrative decision in legislation of the Åland Islands, the Government of the Åland Islands could not, by means of a decision of its own, carry out such a self-rectification, and the provision in the Administration Act applicable in mainland Finland could not be applied. In SAC 1982-A-II-1, the Court stated that provisions which in mainland Finland were included in an Act concerning the steering of agricultural production had not been enacted in the Åland Islands within the legislative competence of the Legislative Assembly. As a consequence, corresponding steering measures could not be undertaken in the Åland Islands. Therefore, in concrete instances, the parallel existence of the two legal orders is based on mutual exclusivity, which does not permit the use in one jurisdiction of such norms that belong to the other jurisdiction. The incapacity of the Parliament of Finland to enact legislation for the Åland Islands within the legislative competence of the Legislative Assembly means in effect that the national parliament cannot act on the basis of any principle of preemption in relation to the Åland Islands when enacting ordinary legislation.

Against this background, it can be concluded that the Åland Islands and the two SARs are similar in the distribution of powers because they are based on enumerations of the exclusive legislative competences for the autonomous entities. However, the rules at the level of the central state are somewhat differently fashioned in that the Chinese legislator can probably be understood as one that has kept the residual powers (and at the same time identified some enumerated powers for itself), while the Parliament of Finland functions on the basis of enumerated powers in relation to the Åland Islands. Hong Kong and Macau are therefore more typical territorial autonomies, while the Åland Islands can be termed a modified territorial autonomy.

## Peculiarities of competence control

The asymmetries introduced by the autonomous entities are underlined by the asymmetries of the mechanisms that are created for the purposes of competence control. Although the Court of Final Appeal has the final powers of adjudication of concrete cases in the jurisdiction of Hong Kong and a similar court exists in Macau, interpretations of the Basic Laws are issued by the Standing Committee of the NPC. This means that the final word about how provisions of the Basic Law should be interpreted is outside of Hong Kong and Macau. In addition, the power of interpretation is placed with a political organ. However, the Standing Committee of the NPC is assisted in its task by Basic Law Committees, one for each SAR, which contain representatives of Hong Kong and Macau and which give opinions to the Standing Committee on how the Basic Laws should be interpreted. So far, the Standing Committee of the NPC has issued three interpretations concerning Hong Kong,[7] while it seems it has not issued any concerning Macau.

In Finland, competence control is curious in that the actual legal interpretation of the compliance of the Ålandic enactments with the enumerated legislative competences of the Åland Islands in Section 18 of the Self-Government Act is carried out by the Supreme Court of Finland in a particular procedure *ante legem* in a manner that is similar to that of the *Conseil Constitutionnel* of France. If the Åland Delegation, a joint committee of experts from Finland and the Åland Islands, finds that there may be a competence problem with an Ålandic enactment, the Ministry of Justice passes the Ålandic enactment to the Supreme Court that gives an opinion to the President of Finland for the purposes of using the veto (which normally is exercised in a partial manner in 2–4% of the enactments). This is the regular competence control system created by the Self-Government Act for the Ålandic competences.

However, at the same time, the Constitutional Committee of the Parliament of Finland is, under Section 74 of the Constitution of Finland, the authoritative interpreter of the constitutionality of those proposals for legislative enactments that the Parliament of Finland is empowered to enact, that is, all draft laws concerning mainland Finland and a portion of the legislation that is intended to take effect in the Åland Islands. This latter portion is defined in Section 27 of the Self-Government Act, that is, in the enumeration of the exclusive legislative powers of the Parliament of Finland within the territory of the Åland Islands. Hence, the confusing situation exists whereby two provisions contained in the same Act are interpreted at the highest instance by two different bodies, one of which is a court and the other a political body (Suksi 2005: 537).

So far, the system has functioned surprisingly well, with only a few problematic situations. A major confrontation between the

Constitutional Committee and the Supreme Court over the issue of who is the highest interpreter of the constitutional issues arose over the enactment of the Lotteries Act by the Parliament of Finland in 2001. Legislation of lotteries is, for the jurisdiction of the Åland Islands, within the competence of the Legislative Assembly of the Åland Islands. Therefore, an attempt by the Parliament of Finland to prevent Ålandic lotteries from being offered via the Internet for customers in mainland Finland on the basis of legislation which had been approved by the Constitutional Committee and which would have established administrative procedures, led the President of Finland to request, on the basis of Section 77 of the Constitution, an Opinion from the Supreme Court. In its Opinion, the Supreme Court concluded that the provisions in the enactment of the Parliament, as formulated by the Constitutional Committee, were in breach of the distribution of competence in the Self-Government Act. As a consequence, the President exercised her right to return the enactment to the Parliament of Finland, which enacted the law with the problematic provision, but which at the same time enacted a corrective amendment to the Lotteries Act that entered into force at the same time as the Act itself (Suksi 2005: 185–89). In the context, the question arose: Which body, in fact, is the highest interpreter of the Finnish Constitution or at least of the Self-Government Act, the Constitutional Committee or the Supreme Court? Another situation, although not as accentuated, arose when the Parliament of Finland in 1992 enacted the Act on Travel Tax, in which situation the Constitutional Committee concluded that because the travel tax was not such a tax on business income that the Legislative Assembly could decide about, the legislative competence was on the Parliament of Finland, which could enact the tax law with reference to the tax being a tax on consumption (Suksi 2005: 216). It is possible to conclude that this was a unilateral interpretation of the competence line.

The Chinese and Finnish forms of competence control are thus comparable from an institutional point of view: in both cases, the competences of territorial autonomies are determined by committees of the national legislatures, but obviously to different degrees. In the case of China, the Standing Committee of the NPC has the authority to issue interpretations regarding the entire scope of the two Basic Laws, while the Constitutional Committee of the Finnish Parliament is in principle empowered to express itself for the jurisdiction of the Åland Islands only with regard to those law-making powers that are exercised by the Parliament of Finland. In the Finnish case, however, there is the possibility that the Constitutional Committee will move the boundaries of the law-making competences of the Parliament of Finland into the competences of the Legislative Assembly of the Åland Islands, where the Supreme Court is the body issuing the judicial interpretations. At that point, two spheres of competence stand in conflict with each other, which is not a good situation in a legal order that strives for a situation where there is no conflict between different parts of the legal order. It is also notable that for the purposes of competence control, both constitutional systems have created expert bodies: the Basic Law Committees and the Åland Delegation (although the Åland Delegation also has other tasks than those attached to interpretation of Section 18 of the Self-Government Act and to competence control).

## From comparison to constitutional rules: Formulating the normative challenge

The recognition of legislative autonomy in the constitution of a country for a territorial jurisdiction within that state is not a simple issue. The above account has indicated two dimensions along which the two countries, China and Finland, could be compared with a view to the entities that have been created as territorial autonomies.

On the one hand, there is the dimension of the normative level, which in broad terms varies between the level of the ordinary law and the level of the constitution. Autonomy arrangements that are only based on an ordinary piece of national law face the risk of being changed or even revoked by the national law maker in a simple legislative order. If, however, the autonomy arrangement is established in the constitution of the country by means of explicit provisions, it would normally be more difficult to undertake unilateral action on the part of the central-state institutions in a manner that affects the stability and continuity of the autonomy arrangement and the commitment to upholding the autonomous jurisdiction. Between the two principal extremes of the dimension (ordinary law and the constitution), it is possible to place some other normative instruments, such as organic laws of some kind and international treaty arrangements.

Evidently, the autonomy of the Åland Islands is established at the level of the Constitution of Finland, a position that is strengthened by the particular nature of the Self-Government Act and by the unilateral international commitment that Finland recognizes in relation to the Åland Islands. The situation is somewhat similar in China concerning the Local People's Congresses, for which there is an explicit constitutional recognition and an infrastructure in institutional legislation.

However, the situation is different in China with respect to Hong Kong and Macau, where the Constitution does not contain any explicit recognition of the autonomous status of the two SARs, but leaves the two jurisdictions to be regulated, under the treaty commitments, on the basis of Basic Laws that are to be understood as pieces of ordinary legislation, potentially with a slightly elevated normative status. The two SARs pose a normative problem with a view to legal certainty and legal continuity, because the arrangements may at least in theory be facing termination at the end of the 2040s, when the international commitments expire. However, it should be noted that the two Basic Laws are not enacted for a limited period of application, so they could remain in force also after the expiry of the treaty commitments.

On the other hand, there is the dimension of the powers accorded to the substate entities. It is possible to grant exclusive law-making powers to autonomous jurisdictions, but it is also possible to grant powers of a lesser nature to substate entities; for instance, administrative powers of a regulatory kind. The powers of Hong Kong and Macau are vast and contain almost every conceivable area of the legal order, while the powers of the Åland Islands are not as extensive and deal mainly with the area of public law, leaving the area of private law to the Parliament of Finland. These three substate entities (Hong Kong, Macau and the Åland Islands) can be termed territorial autonomies proper. They stand in marked contrast to the two categories of Local People's Congresses in China, one category of which has, under Chinese constitutional provisions, normative powers of some sort, subject to confirmation by central authorities (LPC1 in Figure 9.1, below). The other category has even lesser normative powers than the power to vary national law: mainly powers to adopt secondary norms (LPC2 in Figure 9.1, below).

The two dimensions – that is, the normative level of the autonomy arrangement and the nature of the powers assigned to the autonomy arrangement – can be combined in a manner that illustrates the position of the different sub-state entities in relation to each other (see Figure 9.1).

When the treaty commitments of China concerning Hong Kong and Macau expire in the 2040s, the normative position of the two entities becomes in principle weaker, provided that the two Basic Laws remain in effect. At that point, it could be possible to say that the two autonomous jurisdictions are based on pieces of ordinary legislation, which may or may not be brought to expire. However, the point has been made by significant political authorities, such as Mr Deng Xiaoping (Deng Xiaoping 2004), that there is no reason to discontinue the

Autonomous Areas as a Constitutional Feature 219

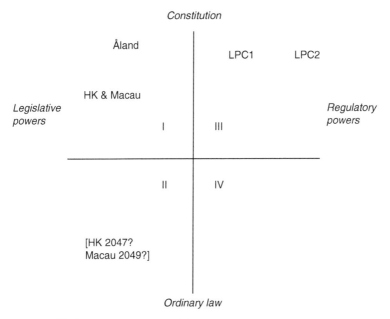

Figure 9.1 Various autonomy positions

autonomy arrangements after the expiry of the treaty commitments. Such a continuance of the two arrangements would, after mid-century, place Hong Kong and Macau in Section 2 of Figure 9.1, instead of in Section 1 as at present. Arguably, it should be important at that point to avoid a situation in which Hong Kong and Macau are placed under one of the two LPC regimes, such as the one with law-varying powers in Section 3 of the figure, or to degrade the two entities into a more provincial existence in Section 4.

In case there is a wish to ensure the continuance *de lege ferenda* of the two autonomy arrangements on a stable basis in a manner that would facilitate legal continuity and, in particular, legal certainty within Section 1 of the figure, it would not be far-fetched to seek normative solutions through amendments to the Constitution of China in a manner that identifies the autonomy arrangements of Hong Kong and Macau and describes the legislative powers of the two entities in general terms. The Constitution of Finland provides an interesting example of such constitutional regulation through Sections 75 and 120 concerning the Åland Islands, but there are obviously also other alternatives for the recognition of autonomy arrangements than the one that has been used in Finland.

Another possibility could be to develop the constitutional status of the two Basic Laws by elevating their individual normative position by means of building in some qualified decision-making formulas into the amending clauses of the two laws at the level of the NPC in a manner that would strengthen the embryonic doctrinal idea that basic laws may have a particular position in relation to ordinary legislation. Such a development took place in Finland in 1920 and immediately thereafter. At that point, the Parliament of Finland enacted the first Self-Government Act of the Åland Islands in the order prescribed for constitutional enactments without, however, prescribing explicitly that the Act would be a constitutional act. In addition, the 1921 Åland Islands Settlement required that this Autonomy Act be amended according to the material prescriptions of the Settlement in the order established in the Autonomy Act, that is, in the order of constitutional amendments. Perhaps a similar internal development would be possible in China, too, in spite of the fact that the international commitments do not make reference to any such procedure that would result in an elevation of the norm-hierarchical position of the two Basic Laws.

## Notes

This chapter was first presented at the second Sino-Finnish Seminar of Comparative Law in 2011, and a more extensive version of it is projected for a subsequent conference publication by the Chinese Academy of Social Sciences.

1. This chapter was first presented at the second Sino-Finnish Seminar of Comparative Law in 2011, and a more extensive version of it is projected for a subsequent conference publication by the Chinese Academy of Social Sciences.
2. For the text of the Åland Islands Settlement, see The Åland Islands Agreement before the Council of the League of Nations, V. Minutes of the Seventeenth Meeting of the Council, 27 June 1921. League of Nations Official Journal, September 1921, at 701.
3. Joint Declaration of the Government of the United Kingdom of Great Britain and Northern Ireland and the Government of the People's Republic of China on the Question of Hong Kong, 19 December 1984, 1399 UNTS 33.
4. Joint Declaration of the Government of the Portuguese Republic and the Government of the People's Republic of China on the Question of Macao, 13 April 1987, 1498 UNTS 195.
5. "The legislative procedure for the Act on the Autonomy of the Åland Islands and the Act on the Right to Acquire Real Estate in the Åland Islands is governed by the specific provisions in those Acts. The right of the Legislative Assembly of the Åland Islands to submit proposals and the enactment of Acts

passed by the Legislative Assembly of Åland are governed by the provisions in the Act on the Autonomy of the Åland Islands."
6. "The Åland Islands have self-government in accordance with what is specifically stipulated in the Act on the Autonomy of the Åland Islands."
7. *Interpretation of 26 June 1999* by the Standing Committee of the National People's Congress of Articles 22(4) and 24(2)(3) of the Basic Law of the Hong Kong Special Administrative Region of the People's Republic of China, *Interpretation of 6 April 2004* of the NPC Standing Committee of Article 7 of Annex I and Article III of Annex II to the Basic Law concerning amendments to the method of selection of the Chief Executive, *Interpretation of 27 April 2005* of the NPC Standing Committee of Paragraph 2, Article 53 of the Basic Law of the Hong Kong Special Administrative Region of the People's Republic of China by the Standing Committee of the National People's Congress.

# References

Chen, Albert H.Y. (2009). "The Theory, Constitution and Practice of Autonomy: The Case of Hong Kong", in J. Costa Oliveira and P. Cardinal (eds), *One Country, Two Systems, Three Legal Orders – Perspectives of Evolution. Essays on Macau's Autonomy after the Resumption of Sovereignty by China*. (Springer Verlag: Berlin & Heidelberg), pp. 23–50.
Fu, Hualing, Lison Harris and Simon Young. (2007). "Introduction", in Hualing Fu, L. Harris and SNM Young (eds), *Interpreting Hong Kong's Basic Law – The Struggle for Coherence*. (New York: Palgrave Macmillan), pp. 78–91.
Ghai, Yash. (1997). *Hong Kong's New Constitutional Order – The Resumption of Chinese Sovereignty and the Basic Law* 1st ed. (Hong Kong: Hong Kong University Press).
Ghai,Yash. (1999). *Hong Kong's New Constitutional Order – The Resumption of Chinese Sovereignty and the Basic Law* 2nd ed. (Hong Kong: Hong Kong University Press).
Leung, Mei-fun P. (2006) *The Hong Kong Basic Law: Hybrid of Common Law and Chinese Law*.(Hong Kong, Singapore, Malaysia. LexisNexis).
Morris, Robert J. (2007). "Forcing the Dance – Interpreting the Hong Kong Basic Law Dialectically", in Hualing Fu, L. Harris and SNM Young (eds), *Interpreting Hong Kong's Basic Law – The Struggle for Coherence*. (New York: Palgrave Macmillan), pp. 67–89.
Palmgren, Sten. (1997). "The Autonomy of the Åland Islands in the Constitutional Law of Finland", in L. Hannikainen and F. Horn (eds), *Autonomy and Demilitarisation in International Law: The Åland Islands in a Changing Europe*. (The Hague, London & Boston: Kluwer Law International), pp. 98–103.
Suksi, Markku. (1998). "On the Entrenchment of Autonomy", in Suksi M (ed.), *Autonomy: Applications and Implications*. (Dordrecht: Kluwer Law International).
Suksi, Markku. (2005). Ålands konstitution (Åbo: Åbo Akademis förlag).
Suksi, Markku. (2008). "Stegvisa förändringar i Ålandsöverenskommelsens innehåll?", in M. Aarto and M. Vartiainen (eds), *Oikeus kansainvälisessä maailmassa – Ilkka Saraviidan juhlakirja*. (Edita: Helsinki).

Suksi, Markku. (2011). *Sub-state Governance through Territorial Autonomy* (Berlin & Heidelberg: Springer-Verlag)(forthcoming).

Weiyun, Xiao. (2001). *One Country, Two Systems – An Account of the Drafting of the Hong Kong Basic Law* (Beijing: Peking University Press).

Xiaoping, Deng. (2004). *On "One Country, Two Systems"* (Hong Kong: Joint Publishing).

# Index

accommodation, 1–3, 6
　constitutional policy, 151
　defined, 2–3
　disaggregating, 6–16
　flexible, 14, 159–79
　island regions, 87–107
　research needed, 70
　strategies, 135–6
accountability, 186, 187–8
Act for Scotland 2012, 173
Act on the Autonomy of Åland, 91–2, 103, 202, 220
Act on the Exercise of the Right of Redemption at Sale of Real Property in the Åland Islands, 203
Act on the Right to Acquire Real Estate in the Åland Islands, 220n.5
Act on Travel Tax, 216
Action Régionaliste Corse (ARC), 139
Acts of Åland, 209
Acts of Union 1707, 165–6
agency, role of, 9
Åland Islands, 12, 15–16, 87–8, 90–4, 201, 202, 213–17*passim*, 220, 220n.5, 221n.6
　constitution, 91–2
　entrenchment, 207–8
　nationalism, 92–3
　state accommodation strategies, 93–4
Åland Islands Settlement, 202–3, 203–4, 207–8, 220n.2
Åland Social Democrats, 92
Ålands Framtid, 93
Alfonsi, Nicolas, 142
Anglo-Saxonism, 35
Aosta Valley, 3, 15, 181, 192
Argelaguet, Jordi, 12–13, 108–31
Arizona borderlands, 24
Association of Municipalities for Independence (AMI), 117, 129n.13
Ateneo Puertorriqueño, 23
audience, 49–50, 66

autonomy/autonomism, 1, 10, 12, 15, 25, 26–7, 38, 40n.17, 103, 139, 148, 152
　Åland Islands, 202, 219
　asymmetrical, 90–4
　China, 212–13
　devolved, 87
　distribution of powers, 209–17
　entrenched arrangements, 206–9
　islands, 88–9
　Italy, 181, 197n.7
　Sardinia, 100
　self-government, 161
　territories, 15–16, 27
Autonomous Community, 52, 72, 73, 77, 111
　*see also* Catalonia
Autonomous Provinces of Trento and Bolzano, 197n.7

Baglole, Harry, 97
Basic Law(s), 202–12*passim*, 215, 218, 220, 221n.7
Basque Country, 56, 71–9*passim*, 117, 127, 132, 133, 134, 137, 153n.9
Belfast Agreement, 167, 174
"A Bill to Provide a Process Leading to Full Self Government for Puerto Rico," 23
Bloc Québécois, 59
Bolzano, 197n7
British North America, 59, 67n.4
British North America Act, 95
The Brothers and Sisters of Cornelius Howatt, 96–7

Cameron, David, 81
Campaign for a Scottish Assembly, 165
Canada, 11, 12, 59–67
　constitutive diversity, 62–3
　federation, 62
　*see also* Prince Edward Island; Quebec

Candidatura d'Unitat Popular (CUP), 109, 115, 119, 128n.2
Casañas Adam, Elisenda, 11, 46–69
Catalan Statute Decision, 65–6
Catalan Statute of Autonomy of 2006, 11, 46, 51–9, 67n.1
Catalonia, 11–12, 12–13, 51–9, 65–7, 112
  free Catalan land, 118, 129n.16
  independentism, 108–31
  nation, defined as, 52–4
  national identity, 112–14
  options about independence, 120–6
  politics, 109, 114–20, 128n.4
  public opinion, 82n.1, 110–11, 112
  secessionism (2006–2013), 70–83
  Spanish concessions, possible, 127
  tax administration, 73
centralist nation-state model, Spain, 118
centralization, US, 31, 32
Central People's Government, 209
centripetalism, 3, 26
challenge, normative, 217–20
China, People's Republic of, 209, 215, 218
  Autonomous Areas, 200–22
  devolution of power, 210
  *see also* Hong Kong; Macau
Choudhry, Sujit, 4
Christian-Democrats, 192–3
citizenship, 29, 34
CiU. *See* Convergència i Unió
Ciudadanos – Partido de la Ciudadanía (Cs), 57, 109, 128n.2
civil service
  Italy, 192, 193–4
  Spain, 197n.9
*A Claim of Right for Scotland*, 165–6
clan system, Corsica, 133, 139
Clarity Act of 2000, 64–5
*classe dirigente*, 101–2
commonwealth, enhanced, 27–30, 38
Compact Clause, 29
competence control, 170–1, 204–6, 214–17
concordats, 170
confederation vs federation, 177n.6
conflict. *See* violence

Conservatives, 96
consociationalism, 3, 26
Constitution, 4, 6–7, 48–9
  Canada, 60–1, 95–6
  China, 200, 201, 204–5, 209, 212–13, 219
  crisis, 66
  Finland, 91–2, 200, 209, 213, 216–20*passim*
  flexible, 167–73
  France, 132–3, 147
  islands, 103
  Italy, 180, 196nn.2,3
  national identity and, 167–72
  New Caledonia, 153n.4
  Sardinia, 99–100
  Spain, 55–7, 71, 76–82*passim*, 82n.6, 110, 117
  UK, 159, 167–73
  US, 28–9, 32
  *see also* Statutes of Autonomy
Constitution Act of 1867, 59, 67n.4
Constitution Act of 1982, 95
Constitutional Act of 26 February 1948, 99
constitutional amendment
  Canada, 59, 64
  Finland, 204, 208, 220
  France, 132
  Italy, 182
  Spain, 74, 76–7
  UK, 172
  US, 24–5, 28–9
Constitutional Convention of 1787, 31
constitutionalism, 1–3, 217–20
  Catalonia, 81, 88
  defined, 5
  devolution, 173–5
  limits of, 70–83
  plurinational, 5
  Puerto Rico, 3–12*passim*, 27–33
  Spain, 56
  UK, 14
constitutional law
  politics and, 11
  US, 29
constitutional moment
  Catalonia, 114–20
  Corsica, 13–14, 132–56, 154n.17

defined, 7
non-constitutional moment, 132–56
Puerto Rico, 9–10
UK, 174, 178n.27
constitutional reform, Italy, 15, 182–5
Constitutional Reform Act 2005, 169
consultation, popular
   Basque, 76–9*passim*
   Catalonia, 78, 79, 80, 116
   Corsica, 145, 148
   islands, 104–5
   Italy, 104, 182
   Sardinia, 101
   UK, 167, 168, 176
containment, 64
Convergència i Unió (CiU), 58, 72, 73, 78, 80, 81, 109, 119, 128n.2
Cook Islands, 89–90
Corsica, 13–14, 132–56
   accommodation policies, 134–5, 137
   geography, 153n.5
   officials, 147, 154n.18
   people, 154n.17
Corsists, 138
courts, sensitivity, 48, 50
crisis-management, flexibility and, 172
Cs. *See* Ciudadanos – Partido de la Ciudadanía
culture/cultural policy, 8, 15, 22–3, 37, 75–6, 76–9
CUP. *See* Candidatura d'Unitat Popular

decentralization, process, 163
Declaration of sovereignty and right to decide of the people of Catalonia 58–9, 67, 109
demos, 4, 6–7
   "monistic demos," 21
   Puerto Rico, 22–4
   unified, 21
Deng Xiaoping, 218–19
devolution, 10, 14
   administrative, 163
   constitutionalization of, 173–5
   development, 164
   process, 159
   UK, 167–72

discrimination, 35
diversity, 3, 26
   identity and, 37
   regional, 196n.1
   US, 1787, 32–3
   *see also* ethnicity; national identity

economics
   Åland Islands, 94
   austerity measures, 191
   Canada, 94–5, 96
   Catalonia, 72–5, 116, 117–19, 128n.9
   China, 202
   Cook Islands, 89–90
   Corsica, 137, 138
   Finland, 94, 202
   fiscal federalism, 188–91, 194, 196
   Italy, 185–91, 195–6, 197n.11
   New Zealand, 89–90
   Nieu, 89–90
   Prince Edward Island, 94–5, 96
   Sardinia, 99, 100–1
   Spain, 12
ELA. *See* Estado Libre Asociado
Elazar, Daniel, 8
"equal footing" doctrine, 32
equality, quest for, 160–3
Esquerra Republicana de Catalunya (ERC), 52, 78, 80, 81, 109, 115, 119, 120, 128n.2
Estado Libre Asociado (ELA), 25, 28
ethnicity, 33, 36, 37, 40n.45, 200
   *see also* diversity; national identity
European Union (EU), Åland, 93–4

Falklands, 90
Fazi, André, 13–14, 132–56
federacy, 12, 87, 90–4
federalism/federalists, 1, 8, 10, 15, 26–7, 33, 196
   asymmetrical, 27, 31
   fiscal, 15, 185–8
   Italy, 15, 185–8
   parties and, 192–3
   political culture, 35–6, 39
   political systems, 25, 26
   Puerto Rico and, 30–3
   society, 35
   symmetrical, 30

## 226   Index

federalism/federalists – *continued*
   US, 30–1
federalization, 14–15
   Italy, 180, 195
   process, 191
   waves, 194–5
federation, 12, 25, 35–6
   confederation vs, 177n.6
   constituent unit of, 87
   national, 30, 39
   Prince Edward Island, 95
finance. *See* economics
Finland, 12, 215, 216
   Autonomous Areas, 200–22
   *see also* Åland Islands
fiscal federalism, 188–91, 194, 196
   *see also* economics
fragmentation, 140–2, 154nn.14
France, 13–14, 132–3
   Corsica policy, 143–9
   Italy and, 181
   *see also* Corsica
Friedrich, Carl J., 8

geopolitics, 90
Gewirtz, Paul, 31–2, 33
Giacobbi, Paul, 142, 153
Glazer, Nathan, 33
Government of Ireland Bill of 1886, 164
Government of Wales Act, 165, 168
Guaranty Act, 203

Hawaii, 90
health-care system, Italy, 197n.11
Hepburn, Eve, 12, 87–107
heterogeneity, 152
Higham, John, 34–5
home rule, 163
Hong Kong, 15–16, 201–15*passim*,
   218–20, 220n.3
Hong Kong Special Administrative
   Region, 205
House of Lords Act 1999, 171–2
Howatt, Cornelius, 96–7
Huntington, Samuel, 37

Ibarretxe, Juan José, 76, 78
ICV-EUiA. *See* Iniciativa per Catalunya
   Verds – Esquerra Unida i Alternativa

identity. *See* national identity
immigration, 33, 138
independence, 25–6
   declaration of, 79–80, 82n.9
   rejected, 89
   Scotland, 176
independentism
   Catalonia, 108–31
   Corsica, 139, 149, 153n.14
Iniciativa per Catalunya Verds –
   Esquerra Unida i Alternativa
   (ICV-EUiA), 109, 115, 119, 128n.2
institutions, 103
   emergence of, 169–70
   policy coordination, 169
   Spain, 115, 118, 129n.15
*Insular Cases*, 25
integration, 2, 89, 103–4
interaction among nations, 8–9
intermunicipal cooperation, 189–90
international treaties, 201
intra-state federalism, 169
Ireland, devolution, 163
Irish Free State, 164
Irish Home Rule, 164
islands, 12
   accommodation and, 88–90
   autonomy, 85–107
   defined, 87
   Italy, 12, 14–15, 180–99
   *see also* Sardinia

Johnston, Bennett, 23
Joint Declarations, 201, 205–12*passim*,
   220n.3
Joint Ministerial Committee (JMC), 170
judicial containment, 46–69
judicial decisions, interpretative
   framework, 49
judicialization, 47–50
Judicial Power, 72
judiciary, autonomy of, 49

Karst, Kenneth, 35
Kosovo, declaration of independence,
   79–80

Labour Party, 164–5, 167
language

## Index

Åland, 91, 92, 93
Catalonia, 72, 75–9*passim*, 112, 117–21*passim*, 127
Corsica, 133, 137, 139, 147–8, 149
Finland, 200
immersion, 13, 75–6
Puerto Rico, 22–3, 31–2, 33, 36–8, 41n.52
law
  comparative, 3–4, 5–6
  politics and, 11
Law on Regional Ethnic Autonomy, 200
legal scholarship, 5–6
legislature, 77, 197n.10
  devolved, 170–1
legitimacy
  court, 50, 67
  declaration of independence, 79–80, 82n.7
  secession, 61–2
*Ley Orgánica de Financiación de las Comunidades Autónomas* (LOFCA), 73, 74
liberalism, 30
Liberals
  Åland Islands, 92
  Prince Edward Island, 96
Lijphart, Arend, 2
Llorente, Rubio, 77
Lluch, Jaime, 1–18, 21–45
Local People's Congresses (LPCs), 218, 200, 201
López Bofill, Héctor, 11–12, 70–83
Lotteries Act, 216
Loughlin, Martin, 5

Macau, 15–16, 90, 201–15*passim*, 218–20
majority, 9, 63–4
  evolution of the power, 65–6
  nationalism, 36–7
Mas, Artur, 72, 73, 74, 116
McKay Commission, 171
mediation, 49
Mena, José, 128n.6
Moderates, 92
modification, 12
Monge, Trías, 33

Montserrat, 90
Moreno-Linz question, 112
multiculturalism. *See* diversity
multinational states, 1–3, 12, 136
  *see also* Corsica
myth, functional, 4

nations, 56, 66
  Catalonia and, 52–4, 71
nation-state, 1
  centralist nation-state model, Spain, 118
National Assembly of Catalonia (ANC), 117
National Day of Catalonia, 117, 119
national identity
  Catalonia, 112–14
  Corsica, 138–9, 154n.17
  Puerto Rico, 22–3, 24, 36–8, 39
  subjective, 108
  UK, 165, 167–72
  *see also* diversity; ethnicity
National Party, 100
National People's Congress (NPC), 204
nationalism/nationalists, 1, 4, 8–13*passim*
  Åland, 92–3
  Catalonia, 56, 110
  Corsica, 133, 134, 137–40*passim*, 143
  evolution, 148–9
  islands, 88, 89, 103–4
  parties, 142, 154nn.13,15
  pluralism, 34–36
  Prince Edward Island, 96–7
  Puerto Rico, 35, 36–8
  rights, 33
  Sardinia, 100–1
  secessionist, 13
  UK, 161, 162
nationality, 22–3
  *see also* national identity
nations
  mutual interaction, 8–9
  quasi-, 32
  stateless, 1, 22, 39, 39n.1
  substate, 2
nativism, American, 34–5

Navarra, 71, 73, 74, 127
*neo-sardismo*, 101
New Caledonia, 153n.4
New Commonwealth, 28, 29
New Zealand, 89–90
Niue, 89–90
Non-Aligned Coalition, 92
normative challenge, 217–20
Northern Ireland, 14, 167, 172
  constituency, 178n.30
  devolution, 174
Northern Ireland Act, 165, 168, 173–4, 178n.27
Northern League, 184
Noumea Accord, 153n.4, 154n.23
nuclear testing, USA, 102

Official English movement, 37
Organic Act (*Ley Orgánica*), 52, 77
organic laws, 55

Palermo, Francesco, 14, 180–99
Parti libéral du Québec, 59
Parti Québécois (PQ), 59
Parti radical de gauche (PRG), 142, 153
Partido Popular (PP), 52, 53, 57, 58, 81, 109, 115, 117
Partido Popular Democrático, 40n.18
Partido Socialista Obrero Español (PSOE), 74, 117
parties, non-nationalist, 142, 154n.15
Partit dels Socialistes de Catalunya (PSC), 109, 115, 128n.2
Partito Sardo d'Azione (Psd'Az), 98, 101
Party of the Communists of Catalonia (PCC), 128n.2
party system, 103–4
  federalization and, Italy, 192–3
patriotism, US, 37
Peace Treaty 1946, 196n.1
People of Freedom Party, 100
People of Liberty Party, 101
People's Party, 74
People's Republic of China. *See* China, People's Republic of
political culture, 8, 14, 34–36, 39
  defined, 8

politics, 90, 137, 141, 142
  accommodation, 133–5, 143–51, 151–3
  Catalonia, 112
  comparative, 3–4, 6
  Corsica, 133–4
  difference, vs politics of similarity, 14
  economy, 24
  judicialization, 47–8
  law and, 11
  priorities, 8
  Spain, 81
  stability and continuity, 50–1
  state and substate, 144
  traditions, 34
  *see also* nationalism
Popular Legislative Initiative (PLI), 116, 129n.12
powers, distribution by enumeration, 209–17
PP. *See* Partido Popular
President's Task Force on Puerto Rico's Status (2005, 2011), 27–30
presidentialism, 31
PRG. *See* Parti radical de gauche
Prince Edward Island, 12, 87, 88, 94–8, 103
  constitution, 95–6
  nationalism, 96–7
  State accommodation, 97–8
PSC. *See* Partit dels Socialistes de Catalunya
PSOE. *See* Partido Socialista Obrero Español
Public Law 600, 25
public opinion
  Catalonia, 82n.1, 114
  Scotland, 176–7, 178n.12
public schools, language, 75
Puerto Rico, 10–11, 21–45
  culture, 22–3
  substate demos, 22–4

quasi-nations, 32
Quebec, 11, 59–67, 67nn.2,3, 177n.8
Quebec Secession Reference, 11, 46, 60, 65–6

# Index

racism, 35
radicalization, 139
Rajoy, Mariano, 74, 81
recognition, 162–3
referendum, unofficial, 116
referendum day, 129n.11
reform, initiating, 190–1
regions/regionalism, 10, 56
   Corsica, 137, 139, 140, 142, 150
   Italy, 181–2, 187–8, 189
representation, 173
Resolution 5/X, 109
revision, 12
Rocher, François, 11, 46–69

Salmond, Alex, 81
Sami, 200
Sardinia, 12, 87, 90, 98–102
   Constitution, 99–100
   nationalism, 100–1
   State accommodation, 101–2
SAR. *See* special administrative region
Scotland, 14, 164, 165–6, 172–3
   devolution, 163, 169–70, 174
   referendum 2014, 175–7
   secession, 80, 81
Scotland Act
   1978, 178n.10
   1998, 160, 165, 168, 173, 174, 175
   2012, 169–70, 174–5
*Scotland's Claim, Scotland's Right*, 166–7
Scottish Conservative Party, 167
Scottish Constitutional Convention (SCC), 166
Scottish Labour Party, 165
Scottish National Party, 167
secessionism
   Catalonia, 70, 108, 109, 120–6
   growth of, 127
   nationalism, 13
   options, 120
   socio-political variables, 121–6
self-determination, 2
   Catalonia, 77–2*passim*, 88–9, 114–18*passim*, 124, 127
   Greenland, 124
   islands, 91, 93, 99
   Italy, 190
   Puerto Rico, 25

Quebec, 63
Sardinia, 98
Scotland, 166, 167, 168
UK, 161, 163, 169
Self-Government Act 1920, 200–4 *passim*, 208, 212–17*passim*, 220
Senate Bill 710, 38
Settlement of 1921, 202
Sewel Convention, 175, 178n.35
social bases, options about Catalan independence, 120–6
social diversity thesis, 38
Socialist Party, 51, 58, 154n.16
Socialist system and policies, 205
Solidaritat per la Independència (SI), 128n.2
solidarity, 9–10
Soru, Renato, 101, 102
South Tyrol, 3, 15, 21, 181, 192, 194
sovereignty, shared, 88
Spain, 11–12, 12–13, 51–9, 65–7, 129n.15
   constitutional framework, 76–9
   GDP, 74
   *see also* Catalonia
Spanish Constitutional Court, 51–9
   Decision of 2010, 13, 59
Spanish Socialist Workers Party, 74
special administrative region (SAR), 201, 204–5, 205–6, 210, 211, 214, 218
Special Statute in 1948, Sardinia, 101, 102, 103
*Staatsvolk*, 39, 40n.41
State accommodations, 12
   Åland, 93–4
   islands, 88, 104
   Corsica, 143–4
   Prince Edward Island, 97–8
   Sardinia, 101–2
statehood, Puerto Rico, 38–9
stateless nations, 1, 22, 39, 39n.1
state nationalism. *See* majority nationalism
state-wide parties (SWPs), 13, 140, 142, 143, 151, 153, 154n.16
Statute of Autonomy of Catalonia, 52–8, 70, 71–5, 78, 114–15, 116, 128nn.6,7,8, 129n.18
statutes, adoption, 197n.5

Sterling system, 176, 179n.41
Stormont Regime, 164
substates (regional)
  politics of accommodation, 149–51
  national societies, 39n.1, 160–3
  nationalist mobilization, 70
  nations, 2
Suksi, Markku, 15–16, 200–22
Sweden, Åland Island and, 90, 95
SWPs. *See* state-wide parties

Taiwan, 204
taxation, 73
  municipal estate-tax (IMU), 187
  Italy, 187
Taxation Agency of Catalonia, 118
territories
  autonomy, 26–7
  decentralization, 159
  entities, 191
  parties, 142
  pluralism, 2, 3, 10–11, 21–45, 38, 108, 136
  unincorporated, 24, 38
*territoires d'outre-mer* (TOM), 132
territorialization, 140–2, 154n.14
Tierney, Stephen, 14, 159–79
Trentino–South Tyrol, 15
Trento, 197n.7

UK, 14, 159–79, 220n.3
*Union pour un Mouvement Populaire* (UMP), 142, 148, 152, 153

union, state, 14, 163, 165, 190
unitary state, 11, 13, 15, 90, 132, 200, 210
unity, 9–10
USA, 10, 13, 21–45
  original colonies, 31
  *see also* Puerto Rico

Valdesalici, Alice, 14–15, 180–99
Verba, Sidney, 8, 34
violence, 2, 16n.1
  Basque Country, 137, 153n.9
  Catalonia, 66–7
  Corsica, 13, 133, 139, 140, 147, 149–50, 153nn.9,12,14
voting rights, 24

Wales, 164, 167, 172–3
  devolution, 163
  referendum, 177n.9
Wales Act 2006, 172, 173
Weale, David, 97
West Lothian Question, 170, 171–2, 178n.21
Wyden, Ron, 24

xenophobia, 35

*Your Scotland, Your Voice*, 176

Zapatero, Jose, 51
Zuccarelli, Émile, 142

CPSIA information can be obtained
at www.ICGtesting.com
Printed in the USA
LVHW082115090620
657726LV00009B/2036